**TAKE
THIS
BOOK
TO THE
HOSPITAL
WITH YOU**

OTHER BOOKS FROM THE PEOPLE'S MEDICAL SOCIETY

How to Evaluate and Select a Nursing Home by R. Parker Bausell, Ph.D.; Michael A. Rooney, M.P.A.; and Charles B. Inlander, President, People's Medical Society

Medicine on Trial by Charles B. Inlander, President, People's Medical Society; Lowell S. Levin, Ed.D.; and Ed Weiner

Medicare Made Easy by Charles B. Inlander, President, People's Medical Society; and Eugene I. Pavalon, Esquire

Getting the Most for Your Medical Dollar by Charles B. Inlander, President, People's Medical Society; and Karla Morales, Director of Communications, People's Medical Society

PANTHEON BOOKS   NEW YORK

TAKE THIS BOOK TO THE HOSPITAL WITH YOU

A Consumer Guide to Surviving Your Hospital Stay

CHARLES B. INLANDER,
PRESIDENT, PEOPLE'S MEDICAL SOCIETY

ED WEINER

REVISED AND UPDATED EDITION

The People's Medical Society is a nonprofit consumer
health organization dedicated to the principles of better,
more responsive, and less expensive medical care.
Organized in 1983, the People's Medical Society puts
previously unavailable medical information into the hands
of consumers, so that they can make informed decisions
about their own health care. Knowing that consumers, as
individuals or in groups, can make a difference, the society
is involved in the debate over the future of the medical
care system.

Membership in the People's Medical Society is $15 a
year and includes a subscription to the *People's Medical Society
Newsletter.* For information, write to the People's Medical
Society, 462 Walnut Street, Allentown, PA 18102, or call
(215) 770-1670.

Copyright © 1985, 1991 by People's Medical Society

All rights reserved under International and Pan-American
Copyright Conventions. Published in the United States
by Pantheon Books, a division of Random House, Inc.,
New York and simultaneously in Canada by Random
House of Canada Limited, Toronto. Originally published in
different form, in paperback, by Rodale Press, Emmaus,
Pennsylvania, in 1985.

Library of Congress Cataloging-in-Publication Data

Inlander, Charles B.
    Take this book to the hospital with you : how to
survive your hospital stay / by Charles B. Inlander and
Ed Weiner.—[Rev. ed.]
        p.   cm.
    "A People's Medical Society book."
    Includes bibliographical references and index.
    1. Hospital patients. 2. Hospital care. 3. Hospital—
Psychological aspects. 4. Hospital patients—Legal
status, laws, etc. 5. Consumer education. I. Weiner,
Ed. II. Title.
    RA965.6.I55   1991   362.1'1—dc20   90-42188
    ISBN 0-679-72841-4

Book Design by Maura Fadden Rosenthal

Manufactured in the United States of America
Pantheon 1991 Revised Edition

For Dale and Ginger, Betty and Herb, Hilda and Sam, Amy and Jay

Contents

FOREWORD

Hospitals are not hotels. Despite all the public relations hype advertising their caring, competent staff, latest technology, and gourmet meals, the hospital remains a foreign country to most of us. To enter we don't need a passport, but an insurance card will substitute nicely. Once admitted, it won't take long to discover that hospital personnel speak a special language and work and live by rules and customs that differ from those in the outside world. You are a patient, not a guest. That means you are expected to adhere to hospital codes of conduct for patients. This is essential, you will be taught, in order to help the hospital help you. Sounds reasonable? Beware! Nothing could be more hazardous to your health than being a passively compliant patient. A passive role increases your vulnerability to medical mistakes and negligence in the care you receive.

The hospital environment can strip you of your adult status and make you feel and behave like a child. I have seen powerful and influential people enter the hospital and revert to childlike acceptance of authority of hospital personnel and the regimens they impose. These otherwise strong personalities seemed to offer no resistance and made few and only timid inquiries regarding details of their medical status, possible treatment options, and prognosis. It's no mystery why even such ordinarily self-confident and assertive people are so easily intimidated by the hospital experience. In cases of serious illness we put our trust and faith in experts and are thankful for their assistance. Under such circumstances we may believe that asking "too many" questions about our treatment could be misinterpreted by our caregivers as not having confidence in them. Or we may fear that our questioning can be seen as an indication that we are unappreciative of the care being offered and that this could lead to humiliating rebuke or even worse, indifferent care.

While such fears are understandable, there is little to support the retribution theory. On the contrary, a strong case can be made for the reality that a patient who actively participates in decisions affecting his or her medical care can substantially reduce the hazards associated with hospitalization. And these hazards, we are now beginning to realize, are far more serious and far more common than we had earlier believed. Medical and public health research shows these hazards to include virtually all aspects of care, including misdiagnosis, hospital-caused infections, errors of medication, unnecessary surgery, surgical error, excessive X-ray and laboratory testing, and a variety of technical-mechanical malfunctions. A comprehensive documentation of the hazards of medical care was recently published by the People's Medical Society (*Medicine on Trial* [Englewood Cliffs, N.J.: Prentice Hall, 1988; New York: Pantheon, 1989]).

Hospitals know about these problems. But they don't like to talk openly about them for fear of losing the public's trust and, ultimately, financial support. This is not to say that hospitals have not tried to correct some of the problems. Despite those efforts, however, there has been relatively little improvement. Hospitals have tried administrative strategies and they have tried to motivate hospital personnel to change their ways. The only approach they *haven't* tried is to bring the patient into the process as an active resource in quality control. The patient—you—is the critical force to protect from hospital hazards. It is the patient who must seek information about his or her condition, the relative benefits and safety of treatment options, and what they can do to help avoid predictable problems in care.

Becoming a self-protecting patient requires substantial knowledge of how a hospital runs. Hospitals are complex organizations, often with the multiple missions of research and teaching in addition to patient care. Lack of clear accountability for services is often cause for problems, and breakdowns in communication among disciplines is commonplace. Hospitals are even confusing to those who work in them. They are frustratingly bureaucratic and are often staffed (or understaffed) by overworked, burned-out caregivers. Knowing how the system works is the first step in learning how to work the system.

Opportunities for patient self-protection are numerous and have been proven effective. The purpose of this book is to show you where these opportunities are and how to take advantage of them. The author's suggestions do not require heroic confrontations with the system, but commonsense actions you can take to get the information you need and to gain and retain control of your health care.

No one can guarantee a totally safe journey through the course of a hospital stay, but most assuredly the odds are vastly improved when you can anticipate where the most serious hazards are and apply what experience has taught are effective ways to avoid them. In a very real way this book is your safe-conduct map through the minefield of hospital care.

Lowell S. Levin
Chairperson, Board of Directors
People's Medical Society

PREFACE

Take This Book to the Hospital with You was originally published in 1985. It was an idea that germinated in 1983, the year the People's Medical Society was formed.

Our motivation came from two sources. The most compelling was the mail the People's Medical Society received from consumers. At the time, we were getting three-to-five hundred letters a week. (Since then we have been known to get two-to-three thousand pieces of mail in a week.) While the subjects of the letters were many, the most universal problem people expressed was with hospitals. Their complaints ranged from not understanding the bill to poor quality of care, with everything else that could go wrong thrown in for good measure. No matter where they turned for help, the writers felt, they were not getting answers to their questions or satisfactory responses to their inquires. Furthermore, they noted there was not a single published resource that helped guide them through their hospital stay.

At a People's Medical Society staff meeting in October of that year, I suggested that we write a book about surviving a hospital stay. My concept was of a book that could be taken to the hospital, to guide, alert, and inform the patient of the medical minefield a hospital could be. We all agreed it was a good idea, but none of us had written a book and, besides, we were too busy getting the People's Medical Society off the ground.

About six months later, however, our second source of motivation emerged. It came in the person of Charles Gerras, an editor at Rodale Press. One day he called and asked me to lunch. He said he wanted to talk about some book ideas. We had never met, but I was quite interested. We agreed to meet for lunch the next day.

At the time of our luncheon the People's Medical Society had just passed its first anniversary. Not only had our nonprofit organization been a success in attracting members, but the national media had demonstrated its interest in the consumer viewpoint of health care. Stories had been written about us in newspapers all across the country. We had appeared on numerous radio and television programs. In fact, in April 1984, Phil Donahue devoted an entire program to the People's Medical Society. That program generated fifteen thousand phone calls to our office! Over twelve thousand of those persons subsequently become People's Medical Society members.

When Charlie Gerras and I met, he immediately got to the point. He said the People's Medical Society is truly a success. The Donahue response alone, he noted, demonstrated the public's deep desire for straightforward, unbiased medical and health information.

"Do you have any ideas for a book," he asked?

The magic words: Do we have an idea for a book?

For the next hour I described a book called *Take This Book to the Hospital with You.* He liked it. He asked me to go back and write a proposal and he would see what he could do.

The next day I delivered a proposal to him. Within two weeks we had made a publishing agreement. Seven months later Ed Weiner and I delivered the complete manuscript. Four months after that the book was on store shelves.

Take This Book to the Hospital with You was an immediate success. It received terrific reviews in magazines and newspapers. We appeared on radio and television programs in over twenty-eight cities to talk about it. Everyone in the media was shocked with what we disclosed in the book about nosocomial infections (those you get at the hospital) and iatrogenic disease (illnesses you get as a result of something a doctor does to you). They were also surprised at how blunt we were in telling people what they should do to avoid becoming a negative medical statistic. No one had ever done that before.

But more importantly, the book was a smash with consumers. Since the original publication, we have received thousands of letters from readers who credited the book with getting them out of the hospital quicker and well. Even a United States congressman contacted us about his experience with the book. Many people reported taking the book to the hospital with them and just laying it on their bedside table. One woman told of how she waited a day or two before bringing the book out into view at the hospital. She wrote to tell us that the way she was treated improved dramatically once she displayed the book.

Not everyone was pleased with the book. Many physicians and hospital administrators did not like the book at all. They claimed the statistics in the book were not true. When we showed them the medical studies from which they came, they still denied their validity. Anytime we were challenged, we offered to make a correction or public apology if the individual claiming our statistics or facts were wrong could provide us with one valid study that contradicted ours. Five years and 100,000 books later, not once has a study been provided.

Medical providers were also angry about something I had written in the original preface to the book. In it I said:

> This book is written for the consumer by consumers. It is a very biased book in that all we care about is the patient. We couldn't care less about the doctor and his bank account. We are not concerned if after reading this book, you or those who comprise the whole community stop using a particular hospital.
>
> More important, we couldn't care less if hospital administrators or medical personnel are offended by what we say or how we say it. This book is written for the user of hospital services, not the providers. . . .

We had challenged the high priests of medicine and they did not like it. In their view medical consumers were like children: they should be seen (for a hefty fee, of course) but not heard.

So here it is 1990. And thanks to Susan Rabiner, Fred Jordan, and Frances Jalet-Miller at Pantheon Books, this is a revised and updated edition of *Take This Book to the Hospital with You.* Why a revision? Why an update?

For one thing, a lot has happened since 1984 when we wrote the book. Back then hospitals were close to full. Today, on average, four out of every ten hospital beds are empty. While that may mean fewer people are exposed to the risks of hospitalization, it also means that hospitals are "marketing" themselves to attract new patients into their clutches. The consumer who is not familiar with their techniques may succumb to the hype rather than the facts. We talk about that in this edition.

We also have added two new sections to the book. One is on dying at the hospital, something which is getting harder and harder to do with the new life-sustaining technologies. In the original book we touched on the subject, but since then even the definition of death has changed.

The second new section is about Medicare. Since 1984 Medicare has made numerous changes in terms of benefits, hospital payments, and much more. For persons sixty-five and over, Medicare is the primary source of payment for hospital care. With all the changes and all the new wrinkles that have been added, we felt it absolutely essential to devote a section of the book to helping the consumer understand and get the most out of Medicare.

Other additions include insurance information not covered in the original text and more pointers on better hospital care that we have learned in the last six years.

Little from the original book has been removed. However, many of the statistics and facts have been updated.

Syndicated columnist and television commentator George Will recently began a response to a question from David Brinkley by saying, "There's bad news and bad news. . . ."

Sadly, the same can be said about hospitals. The bad news is that hospitals have not gotten much better since *Take This Book to the Hospital with You* was originally published. Infection rates have gone up, iatrogenic incidents have not gone down, drug errors continue to abound, cesarean-section rates have increased, unnecessary testing and procedures are rampant, and medical inflation is running two to three times the overall rate of inflation. That's the bad news.

Now for the bad news. The future does not hold out much sign of improvement.

Today's medical consumer, more than ever before, needs to be alert, informed, and vigilant. This is especially so for persons who are hospitalized and their families. Despite all the rhetoric, all the advertising, all the money spent, a hospital stay in the 1990s is no safer than it was in the 1980s. And, from reading the medical literature, it may be riskier.

So take this book to the hospital with you. It is designed to keep you whole and healthy. It is written with consumer empowerment in mind. You are your own best advocate. Nobody can represent your interests better than you can. The more you know, the better your chances of leaving the hospital healthier than when you entered.

Charles B. Inlander
President
People's Medical Society

Acknowledgments

Many people deserve heartfelt and eternal thanks for making this book possible. Without those whose names follow, *Take This Book to the Hospital with You* would still be merely an idea.

Special thanks to Susan Rabiner, our original editor at Pantheon Books. Her guidance, wisdom, and enthusiasm are the reasons this new edition is a reality. Thanks, too, to Fred Jordan, and Frances Jalet-Miller who upon arrival at Pantheon immediately confirmed Pantheon's commitment to medical consumerism and our projects in particular.

Thanks to the fine production staff at Pantheon who put it all together so that words get printed, copies get made, and books are distributed. These unsung folks are what make the difference between a publication and a book.

Thanks once again to Charles Gerras, the man responsible for having us create *Take This Book to the Hospital with You* in the first place. He has been an inspiration and a mentor ever since.

Anthony J. DeLuca and Ed Bartlett provided many insightful comments to help us fine-tune the original manuscript. Thanks, too, to the late Robert Mendelsohn, M.D., who encouraged us to keep fighting when many big cannons were turned in our direction.

The People's Medical Society is blessed with an enlightened and determined board of directors. Led by Lowell S. Levin, our board, which includes Robert Rodale, Lori Andrews, Thomas Belford, Harrison Wellford, Bonnie Prudden, John McKnight, Gail Ross, Pamela Maraldo, Irving Zola, and Alma Rose, are committed to the concept of consumer empowerment. It is a pleasure to be associated with them.

The quiet heroes of this book are the staff of the People's Medical Society. Grateful appreciation is extended to Mike Donio, Karla Morales, Bill Bauman, Paula Brisco, Linda Swank, Gayle Ebert, Miriam Flexer, and Karen Kemmerer.

Every author thanks his agent. But our agent, Gail Ross, is more than an agent and deserves more than just thanks. Since Gail and the People's Medical Society came together, our organization has authored six books and have five more in the works. That's because of Gail. She is an inspiration; a person whose commitment is to issues, not glitz and hype. She is a friend, a best friend, who not only has our respect for her work, but our admiration for her personal qualities. What a gem of a human being.

Finally, a special word about coauthor Ed Weiner. When we first wrote this book, Ed was the People's Medical Society senior editor. We wrote another book together, *Medicine on Trial,* while he was still on staff. After that book Ed left our staff to "go Hollywood." He has sold a movie script to a major studio and undoubtably will make a big name for himself on the silver screen. But Ed was the primary wordsmith of the original edition of this book. Despite the revisions, the updates, and the changes that have been made, Ed deserves the equal billing you see on the cover. He is a wonderful writer, a person dedicated to the rights of the consumer, and a friend to his coauthor and the People's Medical Society.

And of course, thanks to the members of the People's Medical Society. Since 1983 over 180,000 people have joined PMS. When all is said and done, this book is really theirs.

**TAKE
THIS
BOOK
TO THE
HOSPITAL
WITH YOU**

INTRODUCTION

The words "hospital" and "hospitality" come from the same root.

And with that their relationship ends.

Hospital patients don't find much hospitality nowadays. Tolerance is more like it. And confusion. And neglect. And unbelievable expense.

Sometimes checking into a hospital is like being a vacationing traveler who blithely and unknowingly wanders across a border into a combat zone—where all the guns are aimed at him.

All hospital patients, and especially the first-timers, are strangers in a strange land. They are in desperate need of a reliable guidebook to help them tiptoe safely through the medical minefield and make it back home intact. Sort of a *Mobil Guide to Medicine,* a *Bedside Baedeker.*

That's what this book is. It could be subtitled *Hospitals on $5,000 a Week (More or Less).*

You should know as much as you can about what is happening to you. You need to be a part of, and a partner in, your own care. You have a right to be alerted to the upcoming twists and turns on the bumpy hospital road ahead.

Keep this book with you as you would your passport. Refer to it often. Use the information in it to extract the very best from your "trip." Read it so you can avoid the dangers that often walk hand in hand with the medical miracles.

Take this book to the hospital with you.

BON VOYAGE! BUT BEFORE YOU GO...

I

A 1980 U.S. government report estimated that out of every eight hospital admissions, only one was medically justified.

A well person is at risk in a hospital, for the probabilities of overdiagnosis and needless treatment there are formidable.
Patients should avoid hospitals whenever possible.
Thomas Preston, M.D.

If you were planning a trip overseas, you would almost certainly read up on your destination before leaving. You would try to get a feel for the cities and towns you would be visiting, find out beforehand about any necessary inoculations or medical tests, try to memorize a few handy foreign-language phrases. You would familiarize yourself with native customs and food and dress, and the prices of goods. You would determine the climate—meteorological and political—and know where to go for help or where to register complaints.

Doesn't it seem odd to seek out more information about an upcoming vacation than for an upcoming hospital stay? Doesn't it seem odd to have more information about your seven days and eight nights in Aruba to get a tan than your three days and four nights in General Hospital to have an operation that could save—or end—your life? It is odd. More than that, it is quite dangerous to your health.

YOUR DOCTOR BOOKS
THE TRIP

Just as a travel agent makes your vacation reservations, a doctor books you into the hospital. What makes the doctor even more important is not that he might be treating you but that he is your only way in. Unlike a fancy hotel (half the price, or less, of a mediocre hospital), hospitals do not take direct reservations from potential guests.

You visit your doctor because something is physically bothering you and worrying you, or because it is time for a checkup. You talk, he pokes. You sweat, he mumbles. "Do I have something?" you whisper. "I want to run a few tests and maybe have somebody else take a look at this . . ." is the response.

And then he reaches for the phone to buzz his secretary and tell her to make an appointment with a specialist or even to go ahead and secure a bed for you in a hospital. You are willing to do whatever he says, pursue any course he lays out for you. He is your doctor, after all. He knows what's best for you. You trust him. Right?

Well . . . Can we talk?

The doctor-patient relationship is a paradox. It is at once the strongest and the weakest link in the medical chain.

It is the strongest link when a good doctor provides the personal touch, the encouragement, and the caring that can get a patient to rally all of his or her innate healing powers. It is the strongest link when the doctor carefully assesses and suggests various forms of therapy and offers guidance on possible mid-course corrections for the patient. It is strongest when both the doctor and the patient see each other as equal partners in care.

It is the weakest link because doctors do *not* always know best— they just know something about medicine. They are highly skilled technicians who have become knowledgeable (some more than others), if not expert, in one focused area of human endeavor. They are

Many, perhaps most, problems that come to medical attention are quite simple [and] easily diagnosed. . . . the truth is that most conditions with which the physician is confronted require no knowledge that is beyond the grasp of any intelligent human.

Ashley Montagu

not necessarily smarter than their patients, nor do they have the corner on morality or integrity. They are human beings who have gone to school to learn a type and style of disease treatment.

Doctors' hold on what will work for you is tenuous at best. They will tell you that their decisions are based on scores of years of experience with well-documented success and sound scientific studies that cannot be denied. In fact, the U.S. Government Office of Technology Assessment reports that 80 to 90 percent of doctors' treatment methods are not based on scientifically proven principles, and the results are not guaranteed to be reproducible time after time. Nor have they been proven effective.

If you should presume to suggest a possible alternative to your doctor's methods—a new treatment or therapy or concept you heard about or read about—don't expect it to be warmly embraced. Many doctors are not the least bit receptive to new ideas that might unsettle their established norms for treatment or those that challenge methods of diagnosis that are, for them, chiseled in stone. They suffer from what Norman Cousins calls "hardening of the categories." A bypass of such doctors may be called for.

You have the right to information. You need to exercise that right. And you have residing within you the ultimate power that comes from the confidence that knowledge brings. You can say yes, and you also have the power to say no.

You might not have as much medical education as the doctor, but you do have your brain, your voice, and your instincts. You also have a unique advantage: You are inside you. You live with yourself day in and day out. You know how you feel and behave and react, and have for years. You have a longer, more intimate history of yourself than your doctor does. You are the expert on you. Use that expertise. Though you might sometimes be your own worst enemy, more often you are your own best friend. You certainly know enough to ask questions and make decisions. You know plenty.

A GUIDED TOUR—OR
ARE YOU BETTER OFF
TRAVELING ON YOUR
OWN?

Most vacation tours are led by a full-time guide, but occasionally the guide turns the group over to someone who specializes in a particular attraction. Your family doctor can take you only so far in diagnosis and treatment,

then he too might recommend that you see a specialist who has more experience or training in treating your condition. Before you agree, there are many questions that need to be answered.

Here is an early opportunity to take responsibility for your health care and make the doctor-patient relationship into the partnership that is so necessary. If your family physician recommends a specialist, then here is what you need to find out:

"Why Do I Have to See a Specialist?"   Or put another way, "I'd like a good explanation of what you think is wrong with me." Ask for—demand, if necessary—a complete and understandable point-by-point diagnostic portrait. Maybe your doctor can't or won't explain things clearly to you. Or he might respond resentfully to your questions with, "If you don't trust my judgment, then perhaps you should find yourself another doctor you *can* trust." Take that advice. Find yourself another doctor who can and wants to explain things, one you *can* trust, and who trusts *you.* Going to a specialist should not be a casual next step routinely taken in every medical situation.

"Why This Kind of Specialist?"   Again, it's information you are after. You need to know about the specialist's area of expertise, and what is involved with the performance of that specialty. Knowing this will help you determine whether you want to see the specialist at all. That *is* an option. You don't *have* to see a specialist (or see *that* particular specialist) immediately if you are not convinced that consultation is justified. Let your doctor know that he must make a very good case for every step taken in your medical care.

Because purchasers of health-care services regard quality as extremely important, I suspect that in a more competitive market, consumers will demand *and get* information that will enable them to identify more easily the most highly qualified physician-providers. For example, in a more competitive environment, consumers may insist upon getting such information as a physician's year of graduation from medical school, place of residency, and the names of hospitals where the physician has admitting privileges before selecting a physician. Of course, this is precisely the type of information with which physicians judge their peers.

Michael C. McCarey, Associate Director, Federal Trade Commission,
Bureau of Consumer Protection

"Why This Particular Specialist?" Why Dr. Jones and not Dr. Smith? Is Dr. Jones the best person for the job? Are you being sent to Dr. Brown because he is an excellent representative of his profession? Or is it because he and your doctor are country club buddies or old fraternity brothers who have an arrangement, each recommending the other? While there is nothing wrong with friends referring patients to each other, you want to feel confident that competence is the basic reason for the referral.

So when your doctor says, "I'll have my receptionist make an appointment for you with Dr. X," ask "Why Dr. X?" Ask if Dr. X is board-certified; that is, has he or she taken extra training and passed the rigorous examination administered by a national board of professionals in that specialty field. Although there are some inferior doctors who somehow manage to become board-certified, and there are some excellent doctors without board certification, board certification is a good sign that the person is up-to-date on the procedures, theories, and success-failure rate in this speciality. Don't be afraid to ask your doctor to recommend two or three board-certified specialists. That gives you an option you might find useful.

Tell your physician you want to think about it for a while before making any appointment. Use that time to ask around about the specialists whose names you have been given. Ask people you know if they've heard about them. Call the Medical Licensing Board in your state and see if any complaints have been lodged against any or all, or if any are currently in litigation. Check back issues of your local newspaper for articles about the doctors, good and bad. See if their offices are in a section of town you'd want to travel to or are accessible with relative ease. Call their offices and ask the doctor questions. The kind of response you get will tell you a lot.

Take as long as it takes—within the time limits dictated by your condition—to feel certain that you want to have the tests done, and which particular specialist you want to do them. Don't be intimidated if your family doctor appears exasperated by your deliberateness. Don't let yourself be pushed into anything.

The oversupply of physicians is altering the very superstructure of the medical delivery system, so finding a suitable specialist—and, for that matter, a suitable primary physician—is about as difficult as finding a nice-size wave in the Pacific. If your doctor can't or won't suggest other specialists, in case you decide against the one offered, find one on your own. They are listed in the yellow pages. Also, you can call the organization that certifies that particular specialty and ask for the names of a few doctors in your area.

"What Will You Be Looking for in the Results of These Tests?" This is a key question. It requires your family physician to let you in on the process, diagnosis, and prognosis and to justify the need for further testing. If the doctor's response to this question is something like "We won't know until we take a look," screech those consumer brakes. He should know what the tests are expected to reveal.

"Will the Procedure Be Painful, and Is It Dangerous?" Don't hesitate to ask this question. It doesn't mean you are a weakling Milquetoast crybaby if you do. If the test might cause more pain (or might lead to complications more dangerous) than the condition itself, you should think twice about having the test.

"How Much Will It Cost?" If the answer is "Don't worry, your insurance will cover it," find out what the charge is anyway. Just because your insurance covers the visit and procedure, that doesn't mean you don't pay. You do. We all do—eventually. And why add extra dollars to America's astronomical annual medical bill just because there is no direct expenditure involved from you? Shop around for the best doctor at the best price.

"How Much Time Will It Take?" This might seem to be a selfish and trivial question at first glance. To decide against having essential medical care simply because you don't want to juggle your schedule would certainly be foolish. However, if an examination or testing procedure is of questionable diagnostic value and to have it performed means losing work time, some much-needed pay, and maybe even your job itself, then the matter of time—how long, what time of day, and whether multiple visits are involved—is a consideration. When you have the information, discussions with your family physician and employer will help you to determine if you can afford to—or afford not to—pursue a certain medical course.

Instead of sending you to a specialist, your doctor might want to send you to a hospital lab or perhaps a private clinic to have tests performed requiring radiation or ultrasound or some type of invasive technique. A specialist might do so, too. If so, ask all the questions mentioned above, and ask this one, too.

"Do the Potential Advantages of the Tests Outweigh the Tests' Risks?" The tests themselves might be dangerous or cause serious problems as a side effect. Have your doctor give you a rundown on the possibilities.

Finally, there is a question you must ask. It may be the single most important query one could pose at any and every level of dealings with the medical system, and it should be asked every time a procedure is recommended.

"What Will Happen if I Don't Have This Procedure Done?" If your doctor answers "Then you'll die," you will probably experience an overwhelming desire to undergo that test—*after* getting a second (and even a third) opinion, of course. On the other hand, your doctor might say, "Well, nothing really. We'll just have to keep an eye on things so they don't get worse, and reevaluate the situation every three to six months or so." And then you've saved yourself time, money, and grief. What could you possibly lose by asking? And you could gain a great deal.

WAITING FOR CONFIRMATION

No matter how impatient you might be to finalize your plans, you can push your travel agent only so far in speeding up the confirmation of your tour. You will hear when everything is in place, not before. The procedure is similar when you try to determine whether or not you will be heading for a stay in the hospital. Your doctor is the agent. All pertinent information is funneled through him. You wait for the doctor to tell you what the next step is.

Assume you have asked your questions and received entirely satisfactory answers. You have gone to the library and read up on your "case," had your specialist's examination, or you have been tested at a lab or clinic of some sort. Now you want to know the results.

Although the specialist may know, he probably won't tell you unless you demand the information from him, or unless you told your family doctor up front to arrange with the specialist to give you the results.

Despite your insistence, you may have to get the information from your family doctor anyway—which could mean another office visit and another fee. It could also mean waiting days, or even longer, to receive "that call" from your doctor's receptionist. And then the phone rings. "The doctor wanted me to call. Your tests were negative."

On the other hand, the tests may not have come up negative. "That call" may not be quite so brief. The doctor himself may get on the line to ask you to come in to go over the results.

You will go in at the designated time. You will be expecting bad news. And to one degree or another, you will get it.

The word "hospital" comes up. Possibly, the word "surgeon" comes up. And then the doctor reaches for the telephone to make arrangements for you. . . .

IS THIS TRIP
REALLY NECESSARY?

There is always a moment of doubt as you write out the check for the whole tour and give the travel agent carte blanche to finalize the arrangements. Is this the trip you really want to take? Is it worth the money? Did you make the best choices from the options presented? You want to be sure.

Giving the doctor the go-ahead to finalize your hospital trip should cause some doubt, too. Take time to be sure.

What you need to consider before any hospital reservations are made for you is whether hospitalization is really required for your situation. Some of the questions you asked before going to the specialist—What do you hope to find? Do the advantages outweigh the risks? What will happen if I don't have this done?—can be asked in deciding whether your ailment needs to be treated in a hospital.

Once again, just because your doctor says you belong in the hospital doesn't mean you positively do. Many hospitalized patients should not be in the hospital at all. In fact, says Dr. Thomas Preston in *The Clay Pedestal* (Seattle: Madrona Publishers, 1981):

> It is estimated that seventy to eighty percent of the people who go to doctors have nothing wrong with them that wouldn't be cleared up by a vacation, a pay raise, or relief from everyday emotional stress. Only ten percent require drugs or surgery to get well, and approximately ten percent have diseases for which there is no cure.

Some of America's doctors and many of America's patients— along with the government and a growing number of America's

businesses, who are paying a big chunk of America's medical bill—
have recognized this truth. Current statistics show that utilization
of hospitals is down and the number of empty hospital beds is up.
And the death rate has not risen in proportion to the diminishing
use of hospitals.

A hospital ought to be the place your doctor sends you when all
else fails, when there is no other choice and no better place to
continue your care. Discuss your situation in depth with your physician and do research on your own to help determine if a hospital
stay is called for in your case.

Another of the prehospital checks and balances is the second
opinion, which might confirm the original diagnosis (and perhaps
the need for hospitalization). It could also contradict the first doctor's conclusions and thus precipitate some doubt about the need
for hospitalization. You might require a third, tie-breaking
opinion.

Making these opinion rounds may mean extra time, trouble, and
expense. But consider this: The results of an eight-year study conducted by Cornell Medical Center showed that 25 percent of patients who were told they needed surgery were subsequently told
by a second doctor that they *didn't* need it. A majority of them chose
to believe the second doctor, didn't have the surgery, and lived very
nicely without it.

Do not limit the search for a second opinion to procedures that
involve surgery. Many types of therapy performed in a hospital are
risky or invasive even though they are not surgical. Ask another
doctor for assurance about the need for any procedure that concerns
you.

A lot of second-opinion doctors recommended by first-opinion
doctors turn out to be professional ditto marks and not all that
valuable in terms of exploring your problem independently. In
other words, they may be reluctant to disagree with the friend who
recommended them. So find yourself a doctor for a fair and original
second opinion by asking around or calling a local hospital for
referrals. Check the *Directory of Medical Specialists* in your local library's
reference section. In addition, the government sponsors a toll-free
phone-in information and referral service called the Second Surgical
Opinion Hotline. The number there is (800) 638-6833 (in Maryland,
[800] 492-6603).

For current needs or future reference, you might want to write for
the Department of Health and Human Services' free booklet *Thinking of Having Surgery?* The address is: Surgery, Consumer Information
Center, Dept. 59, Pueblo, CO 81009.

DAY-TRIPPER

Some people do not feel comfortable sleeping in an unfamiliar room, not to mention a strange bed. They ask their travel agents to book day trips as often as possible so they can return to home base for a good night's sleep after seeing the sights. Your doctor might be able to book your care in the same way. Check out the possibility of outpatient services and same-day, ambulatory surgery.

As an outpatient, you arrive at the hospital's outpatient clinic, or a freestanding ambulatory care center, at the appointed time. The staff does for you what needs to be done. Then you go home. An inpatient would stay in a hospital room at least overnight.

Today nonsurgical outpatient treatments include procedures that once entailed expensive stays in the hospital—for example, chemotherapy. Advanced techniques, plus the cost-containment urgings of government, industry, and private citizens, have led to increased outpatient offerings. Opting for treatment as an outpatient or electing the increasingly popular home care—whether initially or as a method to abbreviate a hospital stay—might easily reduce one's medical bill by half.

There are clouds behind the silver lining, however. Some people use *hospital* outpatient services when they could do just as well or better with their family doctor, internist, or pediatrician. A study conducted at Brandeis University has shown that many people who use these hospital outpatient departments pay more, because of higher overhead, and because hospital physicians tend to order more tests. Bear in mind that more tests do not necessarily mean more accurate diagnoses.

Another outpatient clinic drawback is excessive waiting time. At least half the people in a clinic will wait for more than an hour to see a doctor, according to a study performed at the New Jersey Medical School in Newark. Why? "In some cases, the doctor is unavoidably late," the researchers said, "in other instances, physician tardiness indicates a surprising disregard for patients' feelings."

The benefits of having surgery the outpatient way are more clear-cut. Time and money spent are kept to a minimum, relatively speaking. If you factor in the room charges you are not paying, and the dubious extra lab tests not performed on you, you save in many ways. A conservative estimate of potential savings nationwide due to outpatient treatment is more than $1 billion annually. And it is growing every year.

Some Outpatient Surgery Options

Some of the most popular, safe, and effective same-day surgeries are:

- ▶ dilation and curettage (D&C)
- ▶ tubal ligation
- ▶ various orthopedic operations
- ▶ breast biopsy
- ▶ tonsillectomy and adenoidectomy
- ▶ hernia repair
- ▶ some types of plastic surgery

- ▶ cystoscopy
- ▶ cataract extraction
- ▶ varicose vein removal
- ▶ drainage procedures for glaucoma
- ▶ excision of skin or tissue lesion

There are scores of others. Your ailment might be among the same-day possibilities.

Third-party payers—the health insurance companies, such as Blue Cross/Blue Shield—have joined the movement to push outpatient services. This is ironic when you consider that it was the "Blues" who kept outpatients at a disadvantage for years by refusing to reimburse any but inpatient charges. This position takes on new meaning when one remembers that Blue Cross was invented by the hospitals themselves during the Depression, has historically been a friend of hospitals, and for many years included hospital administrators on the Blue Cross boards of directors. Now that they are beginning to change their tune, after lots of outside pressure was placed on them, the Blues and other health insurers are strutting around taking bows for being revolutionary cost-containment pioneers.

Still, to their credit, they are coming around. Through some very nifty maneuvering and pressuring of their own, the Blues in some states have been playing a large part in controlling and eliminating unnecessary hospital stays.

To take one example, in the mid-1980s Blue Cross/Blue Shield of Michigan kicked off a program that earmarked nearly 250 types of minor operations that they strongly recommended be performed on an outpatient basis. "Strongly recommended" translated into "economically encouraged" in the following manner: The doctor who performed the designated operation on a same-day basis received 125 percent of his usual-and-customary fee; if he performed the surgery on an inpatient basis, the remuneration was just 75 percent of the usual fee.

Even though the savings in claims payouts by the Michigan Blues came to only a little more than 1 percent annually, that translated into $30 million, which is still a fair piece of change. Other states, including California, New York, Wisconsin, Kansas, Iowa, and Hawaii, introduced similar programs. Today, such programs are commonplace and not just with private insurers.

The Health Care Financing Administration, the federal agency that runs Medicare, has been in the forefront of the trend toward outpatient surgery. Most senior citizens have seen this change already. Procedures that used to require days in the hospital are now done in hours, thus allowing more senior citizens to be home and active, rather than hospital-bound and possibly at further risk.

Of course, if you do not have health insurance, same-day outpatient services make even more sense.

Dear PMS,

I was tripped on a jogging trail by a Great Dane, fell, and fractured the little finger on my left hand. I waited two weeks before going to the clinic. The crooked finger had already healed. I only wanted to know what to do to get back some flexibility.

When I got the notice that they had paid for my "surgery," I called the local Blue Cross/Blue Shield office and explained that no surgery had been performed. With curt bureaucratic efficiency, my informant said that "surgery" was what the doctor chose to call "surgery."

Right out of *Alice in Wonderland*.

I cannot send you the Blue Cross notice for the amount they paid that local bonery for x-raying and putting a piece of Scotch tape (right off the desk of the secretary) on my finger. I kept it for a while as a conversation piece but found that no one found it unusual or even interesting.

W. G. M., Arlington, Virginia

Checkpoints for the Potential Outpatient

Here are some things to investigate before becoming an outpatient:

▶ If you decide, in conjunction with your medical
professional, to have the procedure done at a freestanding,

walk-in surgical clinic, make sure it is a professional, properly inspected facility. Visit the place. Look for sufficient space and privacy in the recovery room, as well as general overall cleanliness and professional ambience. Ask what you will be charged, and what services are included in that charge. Ask if it is an accredited ambulatory health-care facility; this isn't a critical question, but it might be an indicator. The organization that accredits ambulatory facilities is: Association for Ambulatory Healthcare, 9933 Lawler Avenue, Skokie, IL 60077-3702 (Phone: [312] 676-9610). You might want to give a call to your local department of health or your state's department of hospital facilities licensing to see if any complaints have been leveled against the clinic. Check back issues of newspapers, too. Find out if the physician serving you is board-certified in the specialty he practices.

▶ There is no such thing as minor surgery. Sudden emergencies can and do happen during all types of operations. Make certain that the place you choose, whether connected to a hospital or not, is located near emergency facilities—just in case.

▶ Find out what happens if you do not recover completely enough to be sent home safely that same day. This is especially important if you are using a freestanding facility without hospital affiliation. Are there provisions for hospitalization, or are you on your own? Will they call an ambulance for you or will you have to make any necessary arrangements yourself?

▶ Make sure ahead of time that your health insurance policy includes ambulatory-care coverage. Determine whether it recognizes the procedure you are having as one that can be performed in an outpatient facility, and that your insurance company approves of and deals with the facility you are using. Nearly 90 percent of all health policies cover and actually encourage same-day surgery. Yours, though, might be one that does not. Find out.

Your decision on whether to be an inpatient or an outpatient will be based on advice you get, monetary considerations, courage, pioneering spirit, and, perhaps ultimately, convenience. The quick, one-stop "operations while-u-wait" concept is pretty appealing if you are the kind of person who can't be bothered with an unnecessary and time-consuming layover. And you get to sleep in your own bed that same night. This is, for most of us humans, a great selling point.

At this point you have seen your doctor, gone to a specialist (possibly more than one for a second or third opinion). You have explored the possibility of outpatient medical treatment or same-day surgery. With any luck, everything has been ironed out.

However, if those second and third opinions jibe with the original diagnosis, and if the treatment for your ailment isn't a same-day procedure, you must consider a hospital stay. There is much to consider—a whole load of information, tips, advice, and warnings to sift through before you submit to Admissions.

THE PRIVILEGED CLASS
AND ITS CASTLES

Some countries require that a traveler have a visa to enter. The embassy of the host country grants it. Hospitals also have a sort of visa requirement for entry. A doctor who has "privileges" at the host hospital must secure permission for you to be admitted.

The concept of privilege resolves a mutual need in the doctor-hospital relationship. A physician needs a place to send sick patients, and a hospital needs sick patients to fill beds; a deal is struck. The doctor is given privileges allowing him or her to place patients in the hospital and to use the institution's facilities to care for those patients.

Not all doctors want privileges in all hospitals. On the other hand, most hospitals do not dispense privileges to just anybody with a medical-school diploma. A game of "do you, don't you/will you, won't you" goes on, until a physician gets the place or places he wants, and the hospital assures itself of a legitimate, reliable, and continual source of new income. If you live in a community where there are two, three, or more hospitals fairly close to each other,

Dear PMS,

As a physician and a member of the People's Medical Society, I would like to relate to you an incident of which I was recently part of:

I had accompanied my sixty-four-year-old father to the hospital for a routine outpatient barium enema and abdominal ultrasound tests, which his doctor had felt were indicated due to his recent symptoms. Upon arrival at the cashier's window prior to the tests, we were informed of the charges. These were $86 for the barium enema and $240 for the ultrasound. When we informed the cashier that my father's physician had quoted the ultrasound to only cost $80, she rebuffed that that was for a "routine" abdominal ultrasound and that our doctor had called and specifically asked them to take a look at the pancreas, gallbladder, and the kidneys, and so this accounted for the triple charge.

Boy, was I mad! A routine abdominal ultrasound should look at all those organs, and the most that could be additionally required would be about five minutes of technician time and a few extra pictures—certainly not costing triple the charge in either time or materials.

However, and this is my point, my father had complete insurance coverage and was in a hurry to get back to work so, like most people would, he paid these outrageous charges, and if it wasn't for my incessant anger, he would have allowed the medical establishment to get away with another outrageous and uncontested rip-off.

Several days later, my father returned to the scene of the crime to have some forms filled out and again began to question the triple charge for his ultrasound. This time he apparently spoke to the correct person in the hospital administration and will soon be getting a refund check in the mail totaling $160.

Moral of this story: (1) *Be informed.* Ask questions and do not be intimidated by doctors, cashiers, or administrators. You have a right to know. (2) If you feel you have been wrongly treated, *speak up!* Do not let injustices pass by just because you have insurance and it doesn't come out of your pocket. It does come out of your pocket when you pay your next insurance premium.

J. K., M.D., Philadelphia, Pennsylvania

your doctor might have privileges in more than one of them, perhaps all of them.

How does the doctor select the one for you? Of course, he should base his choice on which of his privilege hospitals is best suited to handle your condition. Clearly, if you are suffering from coronary artery disease, he shouldn't be reserving a bed for you in a maternity hospital. If a hospital chosen for you seems to be an odd choice, it could be that the appropriate hospital has refused affiliation to your doctor for one reason or another. Check on that.

If the best hospital for your condition has no bed available, the doctor might attempt to put you in the second-best place, if he has privileges there. Provided your medical situation isn't all that critical, tell your doctor you will wait until he can get a bed for you in the best hospital.

Your doctor should also try to find the best possible hospital relatively close to your home, for your convenience. This is a courtesy to you, not a professional requirement. However, his doing so—or not doing so—may speak volumes about other aspects of his care.

How Some Doctors Choose
Hospitals for Patients

If your doctor has privileges at more than one hospital, but automatically, and without consulting you, books you into one specific institution, there may be a couple of reasons for it.

▶ He might be putting you in a place where the rest of his hospitalized patients are so that he can see all of you quickly, easily, and without having to drive to another hospital. Such a choice, if made primarily for his convenience, might jeopardize the quality of your care.

▶ He could be operating under a quota arrangement, which requires that the doctor deliver a predetermined number of patients to the hospital each year. With hospitals now losing large numbers of patients, and with shorter stays of those admitted, a doctor may be actively pressured to maintain a brisk admissions tempo. If he does not, he loses his privileges at that institution and sometimes he loses the hospital-supplied office in which he maintains his daily practice. That might be why more of a given doctor's patients end up in Hospital A than in Hospital B, even though B might be better for them. It is also conceivable that some people who shouldn't be going into the hospital at all are admitted, needlessly treated, and perhaps harmed, all in the name of meeting that quota.

So before you accept your doctor's choice of a hospital, find out about other hospitals he *could* be sending you to, the ones he has privileges in. You can ask about this on your first visit. (You should ask this of any doctor you use or are considering using.) If the doctor has privileges at only one hospital, and it is not to your liking, discuss this with the doctor and ask his help in coming up with an alternative. Or look for a doctor of comparable ability with admitting privileges at a hospital you prefer. You will find that all your efforts—questioning, demanding, investigating—are worth it in the end.

If the doctor has privileges in several hospitals, ask why you are being sent to this specific one. "Because I send all my patients there" is an unacceptable answer. You are not all patients, and all patients are not the same. Furthermore, it is rare to find one hospital that is all wonderful things to all patients. "Because it is the best hospital in town" is an answer that calls for clarification. Is it better in every single department than all the other available hospitals? What makes it "best"? How does the doctor know it is the best? Most doctors see a relatively small portion of any hospital they send patients to, and that for just a few hours a day.

"Because it is the best hospital in town *for you*" is the answer you should hear. What is it that makes it best for you? Get specifics. Best nursing care? Cleanest rooms? Extensive patient education programs? Superior recovery rates? All the best necessary equipment? Ask and keep asking until you get satisfactory answers.

PICKING THE SITES

Travelers en route to France, Japan, Brazil, or any other country must decide on what type of experience they want there. Will it be big cities with museums and grand hotels and restaurants, or small towns with rural inns and country fare? Will it be razzle-dazzle or relaxation? You know what you like. Hospitals come in various types, too. It is important that you understand what your choices are.

A Specialty Hospital or a General Hospital?

The two major categories of hospitals in the United States are specialty hospitals and general medical-surgical hospitals.

A specialty hospital takes care of only one kind of medical condition or one type of patient. It might admit only those patients with cancer, orthopedic problems, or only children, for example.

The selling point of these hospitals is that they concentrate on a single disease or condition or type of patient, day in and day out, and presumably the staff becomes expert in dealing with it. There is no better place for someone in your condition than an institution that works on that condition solely, or so the argument goes.

Studies do indeed show that hospitals get better at a procedure they perform often, and the results are usually better, too. No surprise, really. But a high rate of successful cesarean births or hysterectomies at a particular hospital does not mean you should enter without concern. The number of successes may be meaningless if these procedures are being performed more often than necessary. It has been documented by several studies that some facilities perform far more of one procedure than a hospital only a few miles away with the same number of persons entering with the same conditions. We may not know exactly why, but avarice, convenience, habit, or the hospital's policies and aims have been prominently mentioned. Check it out. Do not enter a hospital that might conceivably put its needs ahead of yours.

Another drawback in some otherwise excellent specialty hospitals is limited emergency facilities. For example, if you are in a hospital that specializes in orthopedic surgery and you go into cardiac arrest during an operation, the hospital may be able to do nothing more than stabilize the coronary emergency. It might not have the facilities, technology, or manpower to do much more. You might have to be rushed to another hospital to take care of this unexpected development.

General medical and surgical hospitals aren't necessarily better in terms of efficiency or proficiency than specialty hospitals, but they are equipped to handle a larger variety of medical eventualities. These facilities are what most people envision when they hear the word "hospital." They are, in effect, a conglomeration of little specialty hospitals under one roof. Still, a general hospital occasionally sends a patient to a specialty hospital for better, more focused, and more knowledgeable care.

Community Hospital or Medical Center?

Community hospitals, as the name implies, commonly dot the landscape of residential areas. They become, they like to think, one of the neighbors. Through their administrators or community relations staff, they invite you to just drop in and spend some time with them. Maybe you have received a newsletter from one near you. Such hospitals may have as few as 50 beds or as many as several hundred. A good-size community hospital has around 250 beds, and it provides nearly every sort of department and facility. It also has virtually every kind of expensive technology that might be required for the best of what hospitals have to offer. The selling point of such places is that they are large enough to give you big-time medicine, yet small enough to provide personal attention.

The selling point medical centers stress, on the other hand, is that they are big institutions, and because of this they see many different kinds of patients and are able to treat rare conditions that might stump most community hospitals. These medical centers are usually affiliated with a university. They consider that a plus because it implies that all the newest ideas, machines, techniques, and drugs are available to the practitioners. Many experts, world-famous in their fields, roam the halls of these hospitals.

But that is only half the story. Certainly, a big hospital is good for providing the doctors with lots of patients to see, work on, and learn from. But for a patient hoping for a relaxed and easy recuperation or personalized care, a medical center or other large hospital is probably not the place. And don't forget, all that elaborate equipment they have is there to be used, and the staff will surely find ways to use it. If not, the doctors must answer to the trustees who authorized the large expenditures for the supermachines.

While medical centers have just about everything that could possibly be called on to take care of your condition, your condition might just be too "commonplace," too "boring" to interest the "best" people. Experts and eager young doctors come to these hospitals to pioneer the new medical frontier, to be in the eye of the healing hurricane, which they see as modern medicine. The odds are that they will find your very typical gallbladder operation something less than an exciting challenge. You might find yourself feeling like a second-class citizen, relegated to the second-string medical-surgical team, because you have the misfortune of suffering from too mundane an ailment.

If you do decide on a medical center, don't go there simply because some world-famous authority is on the staff. You might never see him, or he you, while you are there. This physician-researcher-scientist-personality may be too busy with his work or his next grant proposal to see patients. You might enter thinking you will be getting the attention of the Great Man himself, but instead you see flocks of his disciples fluttering around your bed. The attention might not be bad (it might be very good), but it is not what you had in mind when you were admitted. They advertised steak, and they served you hamburger.

A hospital's size is not always a reliable clue to the kind of treatment you can expect there. You might have a warm and caring experience at a 750-bed leviathan of a medical center, and you might be treated like yesterday's oatmeal at a 100-bed community hospital. Obviously, you need more information if you are to make a wise choice. You need it to protect yourself from costly mistakes, costly in terms of your pocketbook and your health.

Teaching or Nonteaching Hospital?

The arguments for going to a teaching hospital are just about the same as the ones for going to a medical center: expertise, the newest technology, the latest knowledge. In fact, many of the best and best-known teaching hospitals are university medical centers. These hospitals exist as much for the education of the medical students at the university as they do for the care of the patients. Many patients are convinced that the only reason they have been admitted is because the students, interns, and residents need patients to work on and learn from. In this way, going to a teaching hospital is like getting a trim at a barber college, except that a bad haircut grows back for a second chance. So be prepared to be used as a teaching tool if you become a patient at a teaching hospital.

Like medical centers and university-related hospitals, some community hospitals and specialty facilities also have good teaching programs, attracting top students as well as excellent specialists from around the world. These community hospitals are considered the most sophisticated, best-equipped, most desirable places in that category. The fresh, young, eager students are more than happy to attend to you and show off what they know to you and their fellows. One thing you'll never be in a teaching hospital is lonely.

However, this cub-pack form of medicine is just not for everybody. Sure, it's nice to get attention, but how much do you need? How much can you take? Eight different white-coated interns might visit you, one by one, all before lunch. Each will ask the same questions, ask to see the same incision, maybe draw the same amount of blood until you are almost anemic. It may be quantity care, all right, but is it quality? It can be confusing and frustrating, and a certain continuity of care is sorely missed.

There are teaching rounds, too—times during the day when the students, interns, and residents will converge around your bed, and you will be on display for all to see and comment on. This is a school session, and you have become today's show-and-tell. It can be awkward, embarrassing, even demeaning. It is one thing to have your body exposed to a single examining physician behind drawn curtains; to show all to dozens of prying eyes is quite another.

Don't be surprised if the instructing doctor presents your case to the group by speaking about you in the third person, discussing your personal problems as though you weren't there, as though you were some unfeeling inanimate object. That is one of the darker, more dehumanizing aspects of the teaching-hospital experience. You don't have to take that kind of treatment. Demand respect—accept nothing less. Only then will such demeaning medical behavior end.

Beyond annoying depersonalization, there is also the matter of cost. Teaching hospitals have greater expenses than nonteaching hospitals. They usually pay a decent salary to postgraduates-in-training. They must pay what it takes to attract top-flight experts.

Dear PMS,

After an episode of headache, vertigo, and confused speech that lasted for a few seconds, my internist thought I should be checked out for a possible light stroke. He found nothing wrong—blood pressure low for my seventy years (about 120/80) and pulse and reflexes normal. However, he thought I should see a neurologist. In the neurologist's office a blood sample was taken, and when my blood pressure was checked it was again shown to be a healthy low. All reflexes were exceptionally good. The diagnosis was "probable migraine." A series of tests were set up with other doctors: one with an eye specialist, one for an EEG, one for a brain scan, and one for a sonargram, which was to be administered by the surgeon who would perform an endarterectomy, if indicated. In addition, I was to undergo an arteriogram at the local teaching hospital.

This same neurologist also prescribed 150 mg per day of Persantine and 80 mg of Inderal. Knowing that my husband was taking a maintenance dose of 20 mg per day of Inderal, I asked what would become of me inasmuch as my blood pressure was already on the low side. His reply was that Inderal is good for migraine. Two weeks later I was in the hospital, still on Inderal; my blood pressure was found to be dangerously low.

On the day that I had the arteriogram, I asked the neurologist what the next step would be if the arteriogram did not indicate the need for surgery. His reply this time was, "I think you should have the surgery anyway." All other doctors concerned agreed that surgery was not indicated. Although the overmedication and the insistence on an unnecessary endarterectomy was the opinion of only one doctor, they do illustrate two aspects of medi-

The research that doesn't earn any money directly for the institution must be underwritten. Enormous sums must be paid for new technological marvels. And fewer patients at teaching hospitals pay their bills, compared with nonteaching hospitals. No wonder the average cost of care in a teaching hospital can be as much as twice that in a nonteaching hospital.

A further explanation for higher cost, in the opinion of some medical professionals we spoke to, is the tendency for inexperienced doctors to order too many tests and unnecessary procedures. They are understandably anxious about what they need to do to pin down a diagnosis, stabilize a condition, or lay down a paper trail for good defensive medicine. So they tend to do a lot. They are, after all, just learning. But bear in mind that they are learning on you.

Does all the care and all the attention the patient receives in teaching hospitals add up to a superior experience? A major University of Chicago study showed greater patient dissatisfaction with teaching hospitals than with nonteaching hospitals. That seemed to surprise the researchers, who noted that "because higher-quality

---

cal care that are making it more and more difficult for the layman to rely with confidence on the opinion of some physicians.

All of the procedures, except for the arteriogram, had taken place at a private hospital in our university town. The arteriogram was performed at the local university teaching hospital, where I, as a private patient, had been assured that the specialist on duty would perform the procedure. Most of us know that teaching hospitals are just that, and we expect that residents, interns, and students will perform certain functions under the constant supervision of the teaching doctor in charge. In my case the supervising doctor came in, said a few words to the resident who was doing the work, and went to the other side of the room. I saw him again briefly only as I was being wheeled to the exit. Not once did this doctor introduce himself, call me by name, speak to me, or in any way indicate that I was a human being to be treated with respect and compassion. It was obvious that to him I was just another statistic. This is degrading and demoralizing to a patient, especially one who is undergoing a serious treatment.

If that doctor had taken a few seconds to introduce himself, to call me by name and, in this case, to introduce the resident, that could have removed some of the natural anxiety I felt in the situation.

Teaching hospitals are busy places, yet they are where most members of the medical profession send their patients. Courtesy takes only seconds, but the result lasts a long time. Discourtesy breeds dissatisfaction and disillusionment.

N. W., Charlottesville, Virginia

care is associated with teaching hospitals, and because patients are referred to teaching hospitals for care unavailable in nonteaching institutions, it was assumed . . . that the data would show patients more satisfied with the quality of care in teaching than nonteaching hospitals." Yet this was not the case.

A teaching or nonteaching hospital? Your condition, your personality, the role high-powered technology can play in treating your ailment, the need for uncommon sophistication among the caregivers, your pocketbook—these are factors to consider in making the decision. Think it over carefully, weighing what you know now. It is an important choice.

THE KNEE

We are attending rounds with the usual group: attending, senior resident, junior residents, and medical students. There are eight of us. Today we will learn how to examine the knee properly.

The door is open. The room is ordinary institutional yellow, a stained curtain between the beds. We enter in proper order behind our attending physician.

The knee is attached to a woman, perhaps 35 years old, dressed in her robe and nightgown. The attending physician asks the usual questions as he places his hand on the knee: "This knee bother you?"

All eyes are on the knee; no one meets her eyes as she answers. The maneuvers begin—abduction, adduction, flexion, extension, rotation. She continues to tell her story, furtively pushing her clothing between her legs. Her endeavors are hopeless, for the full range of knee motion must be demonstrated. The door is open. Her embarrassment and helplessness are evident.

More maneuvers and a discussion of knee pathology ensue. She asks a question. No one notices.

More maneuvers. The door is open.

Now the uninvolved knee is examined—abduction, adduction, flexion, extension, rotation.

She gives up.

The door is open.

Now a discussion of surgical technique. Now review the knee examination. We file out through the open door.

She pulls the sheet up around her waist.

She is irrelevant.

by Constance J. Meyd

Osteopathic Hospitals

The osteopathic hospital (staffed with doctors of osteopathy, or D.O.'s) differ little these days from the allopathic hospital (staffed with medical doctors, or M.D.'s). Despite the legal and public relations wars, both types of hospitals provide well-rounded doctors and primary care physicians, as surgeons and specialists. In fact, some hospitals offer privileges to both D.O.'s and M.D.'s.

There are far fewer osteopathic hospitals than allopathic ones. Osteopaths and their hospitals tend to serve smaller, more rural communities than do M.D.'s and their hospitals.

The biggest differences between the two are historical and philosophical. Osteopathic medicine holds that the body is an interrelated system—the body structure affects organic functioning and vice versa. Thus, along with the usual, familiar bag of medical tricks, D.O.'s use manipulative therapy, whereby muscles, bones, joints, nerves, and tissue are in some way manipulated or have pressure applied to them in order to effect some beneficial change in a patient's condition. Whether such manipulations, used alone or in conjunction with other therapies, are indeed of any value is the crux of what remains of the M.D.-D.O. squabble. Misinformation leads the public to confuse osteopaths with chiropractors (who do not have medical degrees), and anti-osteopath propaganda by some M.D.'s and medical organizations doesn't help either. That compounds negative perceptions of osteopathic hospitals.

If the doctor you prefer is a D.O., and if he plans to send you to a hospital, the least of your worries is that it might be osteopathic. That it is a hospital is what ought to concern you. A hospital is a hospital; whether it is allopathic or osteopathic makes little difference. The same good things—and the same awful things—happen in both.

THE GOVERNING BODY—
WHO RUNS THE PLACE?

Something all foreign travelers should check on is what type of government or leadership is running the country they plan to visit. Knowing this helps the visitor understand why there may be a high tax on souvenirs, soldiers on every corner, or a ban on photographing government buildings. Knowing who owns and runs a hospital is equally as important.

You might say, "Who cares who owns the hospital I end up in, just so long as I get all the best care and get well?" But you should know that the level of care, the recovery rate, and the costs at a hospital are strongly influenced by that hospital's owners.

All sorts of people and organizations own hospitals. Most of us, at one time or another, have seen, visited, or had dealings with hospitals owned by religious orders, universities, governments (federal, state, county, or municipal), or health maintenance organizations and other kinds of health plans. For many years doctors have owned hospitals, either singly or in groups. Those are often of good-to-excellent quality, but doctor-owned hospitals do represent conflicts of interest. The potential for fraud, excessive costs, price-fixing, and overutilization is obvious. It is enough to warrant your concern.

Sometimes an owner or ownership group might buy and run a few hospitals in a fairly defined, fairly small and limited region. Such privately owned, for-profit proprietary hospitals are not uncommon. And over the years they have grown in number. In her book *The Economics and Politics of Health* (Chapel Hill: University of North Carolina Press, 1982), Rita Ricardo-Campbell noted that "of the 6,637 short stay hospitals in 1977, 14 percent were profit-making, but these had only about 8 percent of the acute general hospital beds. By 1982, for-profit hospitals were one-third of all hospitals and about one-fifth of acute, general care hospitals."

In 1988, the American Hospital Association published the following numbers:

TOTAL NUMBER OF HOSPITALS: 5611

	Number	Percentage of Total
For-profit	828	14.8
Not-for-profit	3278	58.4
Government-owned	1509	26.8
Hospitals in systems (multisystems)	2572	45.8
Independent hospitals	3039	54.2

OWNERSHIP BY SYSTEMS: 303 SYSTEMS OWN 2572 HOSPITALS

	Number	Percentage of Total
For-profit	64	21.2
Not-for-profit	239	78.8

TOTAL HOSPITAL BEDS: 949,781

	Number	Percentage of Total
Beds in systems	435,422	45.8
Beds in independents	514,359	54.2
Beds in for-profits	148,084	14.7
Beds in not-for-profits	801,697	85.3

What is happening in the for-profit hospital business (and never forget it is a business) is the rise and monumental growth of corporate chain ownership. Whereas privately owned hospitals split the profits among the various owners, the corporately owned, national chain hospitals distribute the wealth to shareholders who expect solid returns on their investment.

The corporations run their hospitals as they would any other business—for maximum profits and earnings. It is a bold change from the hospital's traditional image as a financially imperiled do-gooder to that of a commercial entity with one eye on the ledger and the other on healing. This has led critics to claim that chain ownership is changing for the worse the way medical services are delivered. And, according to Stanley Wohl, M.D., author of *The Medical Industrial Complex* (New York: Harmony, 1984), in the early 1980s about 33 cents of every health dollar spent in America ended up in stockholders' pockets. Today that figure is significantly higher. It is projected to continue growing.

Obviously, the corporations see the hospitals, nursing homes, and other medical properties they own or operate (and some own nonmedical businesses as well) as good investments with good returns. Ill health is a growth industry. They treat these holdings like any other: They must make money. These corporations are accused of promoting overutilization of technology, overtesting of patients, and overpricing of dispensed goods, all in an effort to improve the bottom line. And among all physicians in the United States, nearly half admit their patients to these hospitals.

For-profit chains certainly aren't *all* bad. For example, they have brought hospitals to places that never had them. They have also helped to keep hospital care in some communities by purchasing or contracting to manage a failing local institution, refurbishing it, and putting it back in profit-making operation.

The for-profit chain hospitals saw themselves as the answer to medicine's financial woes. The theory went that if all decisions came from one office, the national headquarters, if supplies and technology were brought in massive quantities at reduced rates, if new hospitals were constructed using more or less a single design, then costs would be less and the savings would be passed on to the patient.

But that didn't happen, because the laws of supply and demand don't seem to function in medicine. Despite the bulk buying, despite the clone construction, despite the centralized decision-making, corporate-owned hospitals actually end up costing the consumer *more*—23 percent more, according to one survey—than a not-for-profit establishment. Among the reasons: too many tests, and astronomical markups. Paul Starr, in his Pulitzer Prize–winning book *The Social Transformation of American Medicine* (New York: Basic Books, 1982), states that "national data also indicate that, for every bed-size category, for-profit hospitals have higher costs than the overall average for community hospitals."

Then, too, since making lots of money is a major consideration, new hospital construction and purchases take place in generally suburban, generally affluent areas where people have more of that money to spend. As a result, the needy have little access to these facilities.

Corporations that make the technology, the drugs, and the other materials of hospital life walk hand in hand with corporations that own and run hospitals. As Stanley Wohl writes: "The suppliers now own shares in the hospitals that buy the machines from them; they also own shares in the physician groups that prescribe the use of the machinery for their patients. The present freewheeling system leaves open the possibility of unholy alliances."

And the for-profit style of operating hospitals is spreading to other sectors. These days there isn't much difference between the for-profit hospitals and the so-called nonprofits. Many nonprofits make lots of profits, call them "excesses," and spend them on expanded salaries, new construction, and technological equipment, among other things. The nonprofits have one enviable advantage: tax-exempt status.

Ricardo-Campbell cites evidence that nonprofit hospitals "often subsidize their more expensive cases by overcharging for the simpler, routine cases." In that way, she says, "some in-hospital patients help pay for, or cross-subsidize, other patients."

A recent development among nonprofits is the creation of holding companies. The nonprofit hospital corporation, which in the past was comprised solely of the hospital itself, can, in the holding-company setup, own and operate any number and any type of profit-making business: hotels, theaters, restaurants, office buildings, malls. "We are now becoming business people, not just hospital people," explained a spokesman for New Brunswick, New Jersey's Middlesex General–University Hospital, now called the Robert Wood Johnson General–University Hospital, when it formed a nonprofit holding company. Besides, there are nonprofit hospitals that are managed by profit-making companies.

But what is wrong with hospitals making extra money? What is so bad about chain operation hospitals? Alvin R. Tarlov, M.D., of the University of Chicago's Pritzker School of Medicine, told the Massachusetts Medical Society on May 18, 1983:

> In brief, the facilities through which about half of all health costs are expended are assuming the characteristics of a mature industry with aggressive activities centered on mergers, capital development, investment, and profit. One might wonder whether the social purpose, which motivated the community hospitals of the past, will emerge with any influence in these newer structures, or whether a loss of social purpose will affect the outcome of services to patients.

In 1990 many public officials are wondering the same thing. Communities such as Burlington, Vermont, and Allentown, Pennsylvania, are challenging the tax-exempt status of many nonprofit hospitals. It's the old "If it smells like a profit . . ."

Before your doctor makes arrangements for you to enter a certain hospital, find out who owns it and how that ownership might affect your care and its cost. Whether your concerns are political, personal, or financial, you should know the setup before you become a patient.

THE TOUR LURES

Travel agencies stop at nothing to get your business before some rival does. They promote their tours with gusto, sending out fancy four-color brochures with idealized descriptions and slick pictures of luxurious accommodations, gourmet meals, delightful natives, impressive sights, and irresistible financial savings. The world of hospital hype is becoming equally as slick and "sale"-oriented. But don't expect to find bargains.

Normally, competition means lower prices. But not when it comes to hospitals. Despite increasing competition, prices have not declined.

Public and private, for-profits and not-for-profits are all competing for patients, because filling those beds means hospitals can
charge for their use and for services performed for and on the people
occupying those beds. Hospitals used to need a 70-to-80-percent
occupancy rate to break even. And if all they were providing were
plain old-fashioned medical care, they would still need high occupancy. Now hospitals are doing better than even with occupancy
rates as low as 50 percent. In today's climate of soaring medical
inflation, businesses and insurance companies are working to cut
down on medical usage and hospital stays. For the hospital that
wants to keep its profits above water, it's showtime!

Lures range from the superficial (new paint job, prettier lobby,
maybe a new name) to the intense (new wings, more operating
rooms, new on-site birthing centers, and infant intensive care units).
Multimillion-dollar machinery is bought to match, or one-up, the
purchase by another hospital in town. Each can advertise its very
own nuclear magnetic resonance scanning device.

How au courant. How wasteful. How ultimately expensive it is
for the community to have two of these things; the consumers' bills
will reflect the cost of that redundant piece of high tech. Wouldn't
it be much more economical for one machine to be shared by both
or a few hospitals? But each hospital wants to make its own reputa-
tion as a big leaguer, the top hospital, and it uses your dollars to do
it.

Like other advertisers, hospitals, each offering basically the same
product, sell the sizzle, not the steak, when marketing their product.
Campaigns utilize heartwarming buzzwords like "care" and
"touch." Billboards and newspaper ads show kindly, square-jawed
doctors patting cute little tow-headed children on the head. Television, radio, and direct mail all present soft and soothing messages
about coming to Hospital A for what will surely be the best darn
time of your life.

▶ Bethesda Hospital in Chicago offered free transportation, a
$5,000 line of credit, VIP treatment by staff and
administrators (shouldn't we be getting that kind of
treatment anyway?) and membership in the "select" Silver
Key Society—all of this and more if you would agree to
have elective surgery performed there before Christmas.

▶ A hospital in Halstead, Kansas, provided free room and
board to patients admitted for diagnostic testing.
Presumably the $135 a day loss would be made up if they

found something that called for expensive treatment—in their hospital.

▶ Some hospitals have hotellike units to entice patients, who are not quite sick enough to require hospital care, to stay anyway instead of opting for home care. The "hotel" rates rival the best, and additional medical services are strictly à la carte at a cost that can quadruple the room charge.

▶ To increase hospital utilization rates, some institutions offer a "money-back guarantee." If service is unsatisfactory, if the staff is rude, even if the food doesn't meet expectations—you can get a deduction from your bill. It is shrewd, because most people don't take advantage of such offers. Product manufacturers have known this for years. Even if you did get your money back, would it make up for any serious threat to your health or life during your stay?

▶ Mt. Sinai Hospital in Minneapolis sold the sizzle *and* the steak. It is one of many hospitals that provide gourmet menus for their "customers," with such items as Poulet à la Marengo, Fruit de Mer St. Jacques, and Châteaubriand for Two. And dessert. *Très élégant!* And only ten to fifteen dollars for guests. Gift certificates available. *Bon appétit.*

▶ Oh yes! Let's not forget "health fairs." These are those clever marketing gimmicks so many hospitals offer nowadays. The idea here is that they lure you to a shopping mall or some other convenient gathering place and offer a black bag full of medical screening tests. Everything from cholesterol levels to vision tests are provided, along with some booths filled with literature about dieting and exercise. Actually, they are misnamed. They should be called "sick fairs" since they really are designed to find a disease with which you are afflicted. And, surprise, it just so happens that the friendly, sponsoring hospital has a program you can enter to correct, or ameliorate, your just-discovered malady.

Two factors complicate and intensify the competitive situation: DRGs (diagnosis-related groups) and the rise of ambulatory care centers.

The DRGs are the almost five hundred categories of illness devised by the people at Medicare as a way to reduce the federal government's medical care costs. Each category of illness merits a predetermined hospital stay and has a ceiling on how much money can be paid to a hospital for that stay or procedure. In effect, Medicare stopped the open-ended fees and charges of the past. In theory, at least, this has cut hospitals' earnings and emptied beds at a brisker pace. Hospitals now find themselves competing for the available patients to fill those beds. It also means the potential for more cost-shifting. If the hospital gets less from Medicare per procedure than it did before DRGs, the likelihood of the non-Medicare patients paying more increases.

At the same time, freestanding ambulatory care centers are popping up in prime locations. Among these are the "docs-in-the-box" and urgicenters, places to go when you can't get in to see your doctor or when you need minor surgery. Sometimes these businesses compete with hospitals; sometimes they are owned by hospitals and act as satellites that send the sicker patients to the Mother Ship facility.

Suddenly, the medical market is a free-for-all, with private practice doctors being hurt the most in every possible scenario: patients lost to docs-in-the-box, in-office procedures lost to ambulatory centers, autonomy lost to a corporate-determined privilege system. To get back in the game, some doctors have even resurrected the house call.

It seems like a buyer's market. But appearances can be deceiving. Despite everything, plenty of money is being made in the medical business. It still takes a savvy medical "shopper" to find the best facility practicing the best medicine at the best price.

LE GRAND TOUR—A
HOSPITAL TOURIST'S
CHECKLIST

Travelers attend lectures and travelogues, read pertinent literature, or seek out people who have already toured the places they want to go. They want help in preparing a checklist of things they might need or should be aware of. Hospital travelers should do the same. Often they have the distinct advantage of having the medical travel site nearby for a pretrip drop-in.

There is no way to know what a hospital is really like except by giving it a good once-over in person. Seeing is believing. It is something you ought to do when you move to a new town or do now, even if you have been living in the same community for years. You never know when you are going to need a hospital, so don't chance being stuck in the wrong one for lack of investigation.

Ask your doctor which hospitals he or she has privileges in. Check those out first, then look into others that interest you.

Don't just barge in, clipboard in hand and a Ralph Nader scowl on your face. Call and ask to speak with the hospital's administrator or someone in the community relations department. Explain that you are new in town and want to see the facility because you have heard so many *wonderful* things about it. Tell them you expect to have some surgery done soon, perhaps there, and you would like to get a feel for the place. Tell them anything you think will get you in.

You will probably get a quick walk-through (if that) with some minor-level administrative employee or a hospital volunteer by your side. He or she will point you in all the "right" directions, telling you very little—the way Western journalists get a tour of North Korea. Another way to get information and more than a passing glance at the place is to visit a patient and ask about the food, nursing care, and other features of the hospital experience that only a patient knows firsthand. Wander around a bit, as though you belong wherever you happen to be in the building at the moment. Better yet, take this book to the hospital with you. We gave it that title for a good reason. With this book prominently displayed, your tour will most likely be more comprehensive and attentive. The hospital people will know you mean business.

Here are some important things to observe and to mark down on your inspection tour:

I. Physical Features

1. Is the building neat and well maintained?   *Yes*   *No*

2. Is the hospital located within easy walking distance of public transportation?   *Yes*   *No*

3. Is there an area outside where patients can sit?   *Yes*   *No*

4. Is that area neat, well maintained, and safe?   *Yes*   *No*

5. Is the lobby clean and well furnished?   *Yes*   *No*

6. Are patients permitted to use the lobby?   *Yes*   *No*

7. Are emergency exits well marked?   *Yes*   *No*

8. Is fire-fighting equipment (such as fire extinguishers) prominent?   *Yes*   *No*

9. Is there a sufficient number of smoke detectors?   *Yes*   *No*

II. The Rooms

1. Are the rooms neat and clean?   *Yes*   *No*

2. Is there sufficient light?   *Yes*   *No*

3. Are there windows?   *Yes*   *No*

4. Are there curtains on the windows?   *Yes*   *No*

5. Do the windows provide a pleasant view?   *Yes*   *No*

6. Can the windows be opened to let in fresh air?   *Yes*   *No*

7. Is the room nicely furnished?   *Yes*   *No*

8. Is the room air-conditioned?   *Yes*   *No*

9. Do the rooms have individual thermostats?   *Yes*   *No*

10. Do patients have enough personal space?   *Yes*   *No*

11. Are the beds too close together?   *Yes*   *No*

12. Is the television set equipped with earphones for patient privacy?   *Yes*   *No*

13. Are there grab bars by the toilet and bathtub?   *Yes*   *No*

14. Do the tubs have nonslip surfaces?   *Yes*   *No*

15. Do bathrooms and toilets allow for sufficient privacy?   *Yes*   *No*

16. Are the room's lights fluorescent?   *Yes*   *No*

17. Are the rooms very far from the nurses' station?   *Yes*   *No*

18. Do the rooms and halls smell of human excrement?   *Yes*   *No*

19. Do they smell of heavy perfume?   *Yes*   *No*

20. Do the nurses take very long to answer a patient's summons?   *Yes*   *No*

21. Is the call button within easy reach?   *Yes*   *No*

22. Can the call button be turned off only at the patient's bed?   *Yes*   *No*

23. Are there call buttons in the bathrooms and bathing areas?   *Yes*   *No*

24. Does each patient have a water container and a clean glass at hand?   *Yes*   *No*

25. Are the halls noisy?   *Yes*   *No*

26. Are the linens changed frequently?   *Yes*   *No*

III. Personnel and Policies

1. Was the administrator or his representative courteous and helpful?   *Yes*   *No*

2. Did he see you promptly?   *Yes*   *No*

3. Was he open to your questions?   *Yes*   *No*

4. Was the staff generally friendly toward you?   *Yes*   *No*

5. Do there seem to be enough nurses, nurses' aides, and orderlies on duty?   *Yes*   *No*

6. Are they neatly dressed?   *Yes*   *No*

7. Do the patients seem at ease with the staff?   *Yes*   *No*

8. Do the staff speak to the patients in respectful, unpatronizing terms?   *Yes*   *No*

9. Are the hospital staff doctors on the premises, or nearby?   *Yes*   *No*

10. Are visiting hours liberal?   *Yes*   *No*

11. Are patients given reasonable leeway in deciding when to go to bed?   *Yes*   *No*

12. Are there limitations on outgoing or incoming telephone calls?   *Yes*   *No*

13. Do the published rules and regulations seem reasonable to you?   *Yes*   *No*

14. Are children permitted to visit?   *Yes*   *No*

15. Is there a quiet, private place outside the room where patients can be with visitors?   *Yes*   *No*

16. Are there accommodations in the hospital for relatives to "sleep in" near the patient?   *Yes*   *No*

17. Are religious services held on the premises?   *Yes*   *No*

18. Are all religious beliefs accommodated?   *Yes*   *No*

19. Is there a library, circulating or otherwise, with recent magazines and a good selection of books?   *Yes*   *No*

20. Does the hospital provide a patient's bill of rights?   *Yes*   *No*

IV. The Food

1. Are fresh fruits and vegetables served?   *Yes*   *No*

2. Does the hospital prepare meals from scratch, instead of using frozen or prepackaged meals?   *Yes*   *No*

3. Do patients have a choice of meals?   *Yes*   *No*

4. Are dining hours set for the convenience of the patients rather than that of the staff?   *Yes*   *No*

5. Do the meals arrive hot?   *Yes*   *No*

6. Are patients given sufficient time to eat their meals?   *Yes*   *No*

7. Does the food appear appetizing to you?   *Yes*   *No*

8. Are provisions for special diets available?   *Yes*   *No*

9. Can the kitchen accommodate special diets not medically prescribed (for example, vegetarian, kosher)?   *Yes*   *No*

10. Is the kitchen basically clean by your standards?   *Yes*   *No*

11. Does the kitchen staff appear neat and clean?   *Yes*   *No*

12. Do the menu offerings vary sufficiently?   *Yes*   *No*

13. Does the meal being served match the one listed on the menu?   *Yes*   *No*

Notes

_____

_____

_____

_____

_____

_____

What About Hospital Policies?

While you are still on the premises and have somebody of authority
at hand, here are a few more questions to ask:

Is the Hospital Accredited?   To seek accreditation is a voluntary
act for a hospital. However, many U.S. hospitals do volunteer for
inspection by the accrediting agencies, resulting in about 75 percent
of them being accredited.

In the accrediting process, conducted by either the Joint Commission on Accreditation of Healthcare Organizations (a private organization established by doctors and hospitals themselves, formerly
the Joint Commission on Accreditation of Hospitals) or the American Osteopathic Association, teams of investigators arrive at a hospital that has either applied for the first time or is up for renewal,
which occurs every one or two years. A long list of items—from
nursing care to the hospital administration, food service to medical
records—is studied and inspected to see if the standards are sufficiently high.

The stated aim of accreditation is to set and promote high levels
of quality, and to reward those institutions that achieve those levels.
Since every legitimate hospital has to be licensed, accreditation can
help the consumer avoid the subpar, though licensed, hospitals.

Recently, consumer pressure has brought about a marked change
in the way hospital accreditation is being handled. The public recognition that hospital accreditation was more concerned with process and administrative procedure rather than patient outcome data
or other information related to quality has forced the accrediting
bodies to change their way of reviewing facilities. So as we enter the
1990s, we are just beginning to see accrediting bodies looking at the
type of data that will truly affect consumers. Of course, an exposé
in the *Wall Street Journal* about hospital accreditation practices didn't
hurt matters.

Unfortunately, though the objective standards are examined, crucial subjective standards may be overlooked. Of course, it is reassuring to know that the lab meets all accrediting specifications—but what good is that if the pervading atmosphere of the entire facility is distinctly unpleasant? Accreditation procedures might uncover minor glitches in the emergency room, but they don't always pick up major deficiencies in the humaneness of its character.

It can't hurt that the hospital you are going to is accredited. Your basic needs will probably be met, and that is *something.* At least the hospital has met a nationally established standard. But that seal of approval doesn't tell the whole story.

Will You Have Access to the Hospital's Medical Library? The books there (such as the *Physician's Desk Reference,* with information about drugs, or the *Merck Manual,* with in-depth descriptions of diseases) could answer many of the patients' questions, and probably calm many of their fears. But use of the library is usually restricted to the medical staff. Ask about access to the medical library; or, barring that, ask if medical books or journals could be routed to your room on occasion. Don't be intimidated if they tell you the books are over your head. You will find that under the Latin book cover is a text written in English, most of which you can follow. Ask for a dictionary, too, to help out.

IS THERE A CPR-SAVVY DOCTOR IN THE HOUSE?

Don't depend on it. Whatever else full accreditation means in terms of hospital staff competence, it doesn't mean that all the doctors on staff know how to perform that major lifesaving technique, cardiopulmonary resuscitation (CPR). A letter in the medical journal *Lancet* of March 12, 1983, stated that the Joint Commission on Accreditation of Hospitals "no longer requires that every physician on a hospital staff receive CPR training." The authors, three professionals on staff at Warren Hospital in Phillipsburg, New Jersey, continued, "We understand that the regulation was changed from a requirement to a suggestion because of protests from doctors."

Are the doctors in your hospital required to know CPR? If not, why not? An excessive reliance on technology instead of hands-on procedures such as CPR could be the difference between life and death in an emergency situation.

Does the Hospital Offer a Wide Range of Practitioners? New, slightly more enlightened guidelines forced on the Joint Commission on Accreditation of Healthcare Organizations allow hospitals to open their privilege gates a crack. However, it does not mean that they all do it. These guidelines give so-called limited license practitioners—psychologists, dentists, and other non-M.D.'s—the right to admit patients into hospitals independently, without M.D. supervision or direction.

That independence is not, however, all it seems to be. If you are admitted by a non-M.D., you will have to be examined immediately by an M.D., (and, of course, pay for it) and have your general medical condition monitored by one (and also pay for that).

The concerned progressive hospitals have always had a more loosely swinging privilege door and a varied contingent of attending and consulting practitioners, reflecting the needs and desires of the communities they serve. Find out if the hospital you are interested in is current and ecumenical in its thinking.

Is There an All-R.N. Nursing Staff? The best hospitals have moved in this direction, replacing practical nurses and others with the more highly trained and, theoretically, more expert registered nurses. It is considered by those in the medical world to be a good thing for consumer and facility alike if a personnel overhaul of this sort has taken place or is going on.

NOW APPROACHING YOUR DESTINATION...

There are always last-minute arrangements to be made before you go on a trip. You have to stop the paper delivery, arrange for the cat to be fed, leave destination addresses and phone numbers with a neighbor, engage transportation to and from the airport, and take care of innumerable other details. Departing for the hospital involves lots of last-minute arrangements.

It's nearly time for you to leave. In a day or two you will be in the hospital.

We hate to burden you with even *more* things to think about and *more* arrangements you need to make before you go, but these, too, can be crucial to your well-being.

Dear PMS,

Why is it that doctors who charge $25 to $35 a visit to their offices, and have to cover their own overhead from it, charge from $40 to $100 a visit at a hospital for much less time spent with the patient and little overhead? This seems to me to be gouging.

R. A. G., Agoura, California

Things for You to Iron Out
with Your Doctor

▶ Will he be the doctor in charge of your care in the hospital? If not, why not? Who will be? Ask to meet that other person ahead of time, so you can decide if you approve and if you feel confident about him.

▶ Will your doctor be making regular visits to you in the hospital? If not, why not? If so, how often? Every day? Every other day? Twice a day? What time of day—morning or evening, or both? Will the visits be long enough to really determine how you're doing? If the visit is just to say hi, is there a charge for such a visit? By the way, what does he charge for each visit?

▶ Ask your doctor if he charges an admitting fee and/or a release fee. Many doctors do. They bill you as much as $70 to $100 just for putting you in the hospital. They usually aren't present at the hospital when you are admitted, or anywhere nearby. The admitting fee is sort of a luxury tax levied on you: their luxury, your tax. Doctors defend the admitting charge by saying it covers the cost of their taking an initial in-hospital history and an initial workup. But even if you are a longtime patient, have just been given a thorough physical exam by the doctor in his office (complete with lab tests), and the doctor has all the data, he will still want to do another, in-hospital physical exam, complete with lab tests. Wasteful. Redundant. But lucrative.

The release fee is utter thievery. You pay him another $50 or so for signing your release form. He is rarely even present for your checkout. He does nothing for the money.

Discuss these fees with your doctor. Ask why they are imposed. Ask him if they can be eliminated. And ask him what happens if you refuse to pay them.

▶ Find out who will handle your aftercare once your surgery or other procedure is done. Will it be your family doctor, the surgeon, somebody else? It is vital to know.

▶ If the doctor monitoring your case is planning to go on vacation while you are in the hospital (you will have to ask to find out), who will be covering for him? Make an effort to meet that person.

Your Talk with the Surgeon and the Anesthesiologist

If you are admitted for surgery, you will, of course, meet the surgeon ahead of time. That is absolutely essential. Make an appointment to see the surgeon as many days in advance of the operation as possible. It should not be some fifteen- or twenty-minute chat the night before you go under the knife. If you can't pin him down, find another surgeon.

You and your surgeon have a lot to talk about. For example, what will happen in the operating room? (Knowing is better than not knowing.) Ask how many times he has performed this operation in the past year. If it's under ten, try to find another surgeon. If it's the first time, say thank you and leave. Ask the experienced surgeon about his complications rate, including infections. Ask about the fee. It is separate from and in addition to your hospital bill. Make sure he does the answering about fees. Don't let him shuffle you out to his nurse or receptionist on this one. If the doctor is afraid to lower himself to talk bucks, maybe you should seek another care-giver. Find out if he is actually going to do the operation. Many big-name, big-dollar surgeons allow their schedules to become so overloaded that these stars may only do part of the surgery. Their assistants do the rest, with an occasional supervisory glance from Dr. Well-Known, the surgeon of record. Insist that he do your operation. Get it in writing.

Most of all, see the surgeon in advance so that you have time to get a feel for the person. Your emotional reaction to him is just as

Dear PMS,

It is greed when the patient foots the entire bill of the operating room. The surgeon and his crew use the facility and pay zero. The doctor uses the clerical help who keep the records of the patient. Yet the doctor pays zero and the patient pays all.

They respond that then the doctor would just turn around and charge the patient. Be that as it may. But then the patient could go one-on-one with the doctor on the billing. It's easier to fight one person than an organization such as a hospital.

J. C. P., Wayne, Pennsylvania

valid as your rational reaction. If he just doesn't "feel" right, if he seems less than professional in any way, if he doesn't fill you with confidence that you are going to be in good hands, then don't use him. Even if he's brilliant and board-certified (another thing you should ask him about), if he's wrong, he's wrong. Find somebody else. Having "informed" faith in your surgeon—going into the operating room with the conviction the you will be coming out OK—is 75 percent of the ball game.

The same goes for the anesthesiologist or anesthetist, who is tough to get ahold of ahead of time or any time—but it is vital that you do so. Patients rarely choose anesthesiologists; the surgeons do or the hospital does or it's the luck of the draw. Most patients see their anesthesiologist—the person who, as much as anyone else in that operating room, could do them the greatest good and the severest harm—only the night before the operation. He will slip into your room, make brief introductions, and start asking you questions about your health history. The idea is to find anything in your physical makeup that could conceivably cause trouble when you are put under the anesthetic: allergies, heart problems, high blood pressure, low blood pressure, and so on. Questions done, the anesthesiologist usually makes a speedy retreat.

That really is not enough. To be fair to both you and the anesthesiologist, you should seek him out ahead of time. Ask your doctor or your surgeon to tell you who your anesthesiologist will be. Ask for help in making an appointment with him. With that help the tracking-down process becomes a bit easier. Anesthesiologists are independent vendors, so to speak. They sell their expertise to many hospitals. They are elusive and tough to corner. And always busy. That is why they earn more money than almost any other kind of physician (median annual income: $160,000). But it is worth the effort to search for them and pin them down for even just a half hour or so. It is so much better to give them your medical history when you are not in a hospital bed at night, tired and scared and distracted to the point of forgetfulness. Discussing matters when you are closer to your best will help the anesthesiologist to do his or her best on the day when it really counts

Ask which kind of anesthesia will be used on you. General or local? Gas or injection? Why one and not the other? What dangers are there?

Ask some of the same questions you asked the surgeon. What is his fee? (Like the surgeon's, it is also a charge separate from the hospital bill.) What is going to happen in the operating room, and just afterward in the recovery room? Will he be there giving the anesthesia to you? Many anesthesiologists have such a large and geographically wide practice that they can't be at every operation they are responsible for. They hire help. An entirely different anesthesiologist might stand in for the person you met and talked to.

In some hospitals anesthetists (nurses with some advanced training) often do the job instead. Your anesthesiologist may merely check in by phone from whatever other hospital he happens to be working in at the moment. An emergency situation could arise, one that only the anesthesiologist could handle, but he could be on the line to another hospital or too far away to make it in time. So tell your anesthesiologist that you want him in the operating room with you, monitoring your progress in person. Accept no substitutes. Get it in writing.

As with the surgeon, if during your discussion with the anesthesiologist something just doesn't quite seem "right" about him, arrange with your family doctor, the surgeon, or the hospital to have another, equally well-trained, equally experienced board-certified anesthesiologist work your surgery. And meet that person ahead of time.

CHECKING IN

Every seasoned traveler goes by one inflexible rule: arrange as much as you can before leaving home—the airline seat over the wing, the salt-free meal on the plane, the hotel accommodations away from the elevator and

on the ocean side, some cash in native currency. The person about to enter the hospital can plan ahead, too, and resolve a host of potential problems before signing in at the admissions desk.

The next step is arranging for your admission. You could, as many people do, wait until the day you are scheduled to be admitted, and just waste a lot of your time sitting in the waiting area. You might even have to spend an extra, and expensive, day or two in the hospital just to have all the admissions tests performed on you. Or, being the wise medical traveler that you are, you *could* take care of all this bureaucratic bother in advance. Just about anything that has to do with the admissions process can be handled ahead of time, at everybody's leisure and convenience.

Call the admitting office and ask when the best time would be for you to stop by, ask questions, and sign papers. Make an appointment. Take care of as much as you can over the phone, so that your stop-off will be a brief one.

▶ Ask the admissions person about your insurance coverage. Determine the extent of that coverage, and what papers you need to bring along with you (insurance card, social security card, Medicare or Medicaid, etc.).

▶ Ask what kind of information you need to bring along with you if you are uninsured, and if you have to pay in full in advance. If it is not necessary to pay the entire bill or a large percentage of it up front, ask what the payment policy and billing practices are in that hospital. Some want your money in regular installments over the course of your stay. Others want it before you walk out the door, still others bill you afterward. You ought to know what's what so that financial arrangements can be made. Ask if the hospital accepts credit cards. Which ones? Up to what amount?

▶ Ask about room rates. What is the difference between a private and a semiprivate room? What is the availability of each type of room on the day you are scheduled to be admitted? Can you reserve it now?

You will probably have to make a choice: private or semiprivate. Both have pluses and minuses. A private room will be quieter. You won't have to put up with roommates who smoke, are loud, get lots of phone calls, get lots of noisy and annoying visitors. Roommates can cause irritations that get in the way of your speedy recovery.

On the other hand, roommates give you somebody to talk to, to comfort or be comforted by, to measure your rate of recovery against. Nurses will come into a room more often when there are several patients in it to take care of. Sometimes a roommate can be a lifesaver, literally—for example, by ringing for the nurse for you in an emergency. In addition, semiprivate rooms tend to be closer to the nurses' station. Whichever you choose, and for whatever reasons, make a reservation in advance.

When you call or stop in at the admissions office, be sure to have identification on hand (social security card, insurance card, driver's license, checkbook). You will also need your doctor's and surgeon's names and phone numbers, the date of your planned admission, and the reason for your hospitalization.

Find out what time of day billing begins, and what units of time billing is broken down into. If it is cheaper to arrive the morning of operation day rather than the night before, then do so. You save money and get to sleep in your own bed an extra night. If it is cheaper to arrive at noon rather than 10 A.M., then do so. Ask when meals are served; you might miss the last one of the day and not see any food till the next morning.

▶ Ask about ordering special diets and make arrangements for their preparation.

All of this can be done conveniently by phone or during a pread-mission visit to the hospital. Your telephone dealings should be followed, if there is time, by a written confirmation of all points covered in your discussions. Be sure you get the name of the person you have been dealing with. If anything is wrong, you have time to get it fixed. It is advisable to call the day before you enter the hospital to double-check all arrangements and see if there is any-thing else you need to arrange for or know. If this is done before-hand, admissions should be a breeze.

As for tests, you could wait until you get to the hospital to have them. But why pay hundreds of dollars a day for a room if all that takes place is a few brief tests punctuating a lot of expensive thumb-twiddling? Nearly every test can be done on an outpatient, preadmission basis, to save you time and money. Make arrangements with your doctor or surgeon to clear the way for your tests to be performed in this fashion.

The more you do ahead of time, the shorter your stay, the smaller your bill, and the more in control of things you are.

A few final thoughts:

▶ Don't allow yourself to be admitted on a nonemergency basis on a Friday afternoon or evening. You will just languish, expensively and in no particular comfort, until Monday. Most of the labs that would be performing your diagnostic workups don't do those things on weekends. Wait until Monday; better yet, Tuesday, some experts say. By Tuesday the hospital is back in gear after the weekend and the end-of-the-week blahs haven't hit yet.

▶ Try to avoid going into the hospital in July. That is when the new interns arrive. Possibly the worst time to be a patient is when that special someone coming toward your bed is a new intern trying to become a doctor.

ALL ABOARD!

No smart traveler leaves home for an extended period without making a last-minute check. Are the tickets and passports handy? Do you have the travel agent's phone number in case there is a problem? Will somebody take in the mail? Water the plants? Are you thinking this way about your trip to the hospital? You should be.

Today is the day. Even though you have done so much already— all the planning, all the organizing—there are still last-minute loose threads to tie up before you go. Who will feed the cat, water the plants, take in the mail, watch the house? Did you stop the newspaper delivery? Did you put timers on the lamps? Have you put your personal papers in order and told a trusted friend or relative where they are and what to do with them, just in case? If it is advisable, have you given someone you trust power of attorney?

Do you have a way to get to the hospital? Have you also arranged for getting home afterward? Plan to get to the hospital early—there is bound to be a wait or a snag somewhere in the admitting process, so allow time for it. Think twice about driving to the hospital yourself. Hospital parking lots are notoriously expensive and may be unsafe. By all means avoid using an ambulance unless you need the care or the speed. Fees of $100 or more for the shortest of ambulance trips are standard.

If you are still packing, don't close your bag just yet. Here are some last-minute do's and dont's:

▶ Do label all the personal items you intend to bring.

▶ Don't bring too many personal items, or items of real or sentimental value, even though they are labeled or engraved with your ID. It is possible that one or more of them will be stolen.

▶ Don't bring more than about five dollars in cash.

▶ Do leave rings, watches, and other expensive jewelry at home or in a safe-deposit box. You will not be permitted to wear them to surgery, and they could vanish while you are in the operating room. If having pretty personal adornments is your way to perk yourself up during your stay, bring some inexpensive costume jewelry.

▶ A child who wants his security blanket should have it by all means. Tag it well, keep track of it, and alert the staff to keep an eye on it.

▶ Do bring photographs of loved ones. They help.

▶ Do pack pajamas, robe, slippers, toilet items (including toilet paper—you never can tell), comb, brush, shampoo, razor, deodorant, eyeglasses case (leave your contact lenses at home), dental floss, nail clippers, nail file, a book or magazine, a TV guide (you will be watching a lot), pens or pencils, stationery, stamps, and a small, quiet clock. This list is long but you won't need a steamer chest to carry all these things, and you will be happy you brought them.

▶ Don't bring electrical appliances that need to be plugged into a wall socket. Using them is against most hospital's safety policies (an errant spark can do a lot of damage when oxygen is in use nearby), and they often raise hell with the high-tech machinery.

▶ Do bring a list of the medications you take, along with the dosage and how often you take them. If you bring the actual medicine or vitamins or special foods with you, have your doctor make a note in your hospital medical record that he is permitting you to have these things and that he would like the nurses to find a storage place for them.

▶ Do take this book to the hospital with you.

Now you know what to say; you know what to do. You have the basis for making the good, sound decisions that smart medical consumers make.

A TOUR
OF THE
ISLANDS

Hospital Land is not one unified country, but a federation of island states (Ireland and England, for example: X ray and Emergency, for example), each with its own territory, rules, leaders, history, and hubris. They don't all get along, these separate and different realms; sometimes they are at war with each other. Sometimes they are at war within themselves. Sometimes they don't know who they are at war with, but they know it's got to be somebody. Maybe you.

But every day, wars or no wars, these governing bodies get together and have security council sessions and general assembly meetings, and they worry about finances and budget cuts and native rumblings and the tourist trade. And every day they do what they each know how to do and sell the native crafts of their islands to those who will buy.

This is what makes Hospital Land the place it is today.

Before you settle in for your first exciting night in the Land That Never Sleeps (so why should you?), a brief tour of some of the major islands—a quick overview of some places we won't be stopping at and others we'll visit at greater length later—is highly recommended.

All aboard!

ADMINISTRATION

To all outward appearances, administrators run the show—and up to a certain point that is the case. They can make some internal policy decisions, they can hire and fire, they can do a lot of things that upper-middle management can do in any type of corporate setup. They take responsibility and feel the heat, and they get some of the credit.

51

But in reality administrators are hired hands in the hospital bureaucratic hot seat. They answer to powerful masters. In the traditional formulation, hospital administrators are hired by and serve at the discretion of the hospital's trustees or board of directors, a band of rich and/or influential people who get together on occasion to show that the capital *P* in Philanthropy also stands for *P*ower. The trustees see it as their civic duty to run the institutions that help the less fortunate—which, in most cases, can be defined as being everybody but those on the board—and to make decisions for the community based on the wisdom they have accumulated, along with their money, over the years.

In the newer formulation, the administrator is an executive of a corporation that owns hospitals, or of a holding company that has a hospital as one of its properties. The administrator (sometimes these days called executive director or president) answers to corporate bosses who may be a thousand miles away in centralized corporate headquarters, keeping track of hundreds of other administrators: their nationally distributed surrogates.

The administrator is the most powerful on-site employee, and as such is the court of last resort for your complaints, requests, and demands. Many administrators can't be bothered with patient matters; they have a business to run. So they push off such annoyances on other hospital workers, who may not have the power to do what you need. Other administrators understand that a satisfied customer will come again (especially important in these days of empty hospital beds). Such a customer is also less likely to slap the friendly hospital with a mean old lawsuit. For these reasons some administrators make themselves or their office staffs accessible to at least listen to what patients are saying. These administrators don't want customers or employees making waves large enough, or getting publicity splashy enough, to catch the eyes of the board of trustees or corporate headquarters. They want promotions and raises and bonuses, not a dressing-down. Therefore, they may be amenable to your requests, if the threat of litigation or media exposé is in your arsenal and you let them know it. So, let them know it.

ADMISSIONS

This is about the only place in the hospital where anybody will admit anything. In this case it happens to be you.

Life in America is the pursuit of liberty.

Life as a patient in an American hospital is marked by submission to custody.

When you enter a hospital, you cross a border and leave many of your freedoms behind. Almost everything about your life in a hospital is decided by the institution, by the people who operate that institution, and especially by the history of medical practice on which hospital work is based.

The word "custody" truly does describe the spirit of institutional medical care. My dictionary says "custody" means "immediate charge and control (as over a ward or suspect) exercised by a person or an authority." Doesn't that definition capture some of the flavor of the hospital experience?

Of course, the custodianship of hospitals is benign. You are being protected and controlled during a time of sickness or injury for your own good. I will concede that. The intention of hospital custody is to protect and help you.

But is an environment almost completely lacking in personal freedom really necessary for the repair of injury and the recovery from illness? Wouldn't it be better for attempts to be made to create health in the same environment of liberty and self-reliance in which most people live their normal lives?

I think "Yes" is the right answer to that question. And many people agree, including a growing number of physicians and even some hospital administrators. The idea of health freedom is gaining ground.

But freedom for the patient comes slowly, mainly because doctors for centuries have been reluctant to get patients' full and informed consent for everything they do. Only recently have patients even been given a consent form to sign. (The mere phrase "informed consent" dates back only to 1954, to a case between Stanford University Hospital and a man paralyzed by a new medical diagnostic procedure.)

The Hippocratic oath set the trend for silence by saying nothing about a need or obligation for doctors to even converse with patients. And in his other writings, Hippocrates went even further, according to Jay Katz, M.D., in his important book *The Silent World of Doctor and Patient* (New York: Free Press, 1984). He points out that Hippocrates told doctors to work "calmly and adroitly, concealing most things from the patient while you are attending to him."

Ever since hospitals were invented a few hundred years ago, they have functioned less efficiently than they might behind that shield of silence. Now the hospital is being reborn under the pressure of rising consumer desire to extend liberty from traditional areas such as freedom of expression and religious practice into all phases of economic and personal activity. Hopefully, if enough people needing hospital care decide to pierce the shield of silence surrounding the medical experience, hospitals will change for the better.

If you are to give your informed consent to everything that happens to you in a hospital, you need to know more about hospital life than most doctors think you need to know. True informed consent means far more than knowing what kind of operation you are going to have performed on you and agreeing to have it. If you are to be informed about hospitals, you need to know almost as much about them and how they function as you know about your own home.

The purpose of this book is to help you get that inner knowledge of your own personal hospital experience—both before and as it occurs. Charles Inlander and Ed Weiner describe *Take This Book to the Hospital with You* as a guide to your possible future travel to and through a hospital. I feel it is more than that. It is also a guide out of the old style of custodial hospital care into a new and healthful era of personal freedom during medical treatment.

Bob Rodale, Founder
People's Medical Society

Even if you have taken care of tests and some paperwork in advance, you will still have to sit down with an admissions worker and sign a few more forms. You will find out early on that the admissions people are less interested in seeing that you are taken care of than they are that the hospital is taken care of. Nearly everything you sign, in one way or another, seems to give the hospital some extraordinary power or lets the institution off the hook. It is the job of the admissions department to make sure you have either enough money or a recognized insurance plan to cover the cost of your time there and that everything is all nice and tidy and legal.

Among the forms which you or your designated or legal representative will sign are those that give your consent to a number of actions you wouldn't under any other circumstances let anybody get away with (before signing any consent, see the consent form in chapter 4, "What the Wise Traveler Knows"). There may be nothing you sign—or the hospital signs—that mentions your rights or outlines the hospital's responsibilities.

Once all the signing is done, identification shown, your "reservation" confirmed, and money matters settled to somebody's satisfaction (not necessarily yours), you will be assigned a room. Make sure it is the kind of room you want or the room you may have reserved. If it is not, ask for an explanation. If the reason is legitimate, either take the room offered with the stipulation that you are to be moved when a room more to your liking opens up, or wait in the hospital or at home (if the wait will be long) until you get what you ordered. Ask to see someone with more authority if the reason given for the mix-up is lame, or if none is offered. Call your doctor, explain what is happening, and ask him to help. He might have the muscle to get you that room.

A plastic identification bracelet will be snapped onto your wrist by the admissions person. The bracelet has some basic information and an ID number, along with your name and that of your doctor. It is a way for technicians to know they are giving the right test to the right person, for surgeons to double-check on who is getting cut, and for nurses to make certain they are giving the right medication to the right patient.

Now, all signed and sealed, you need to be delivered. A hospital employee or a volunteer worker will lead you or wheel you to your room.

EMERGENCY

Not everybody enters the hospital in an easygoing, take-your-time-and-think-things-over manner. Sometimes the need for a doctor or a procedure is sudden and surprising. You take yourself (or are rushed) to an emergency room (ER), where you are seen by a physician: a private practice physician on call, an intern or resident, or an emergency medicine specialist who is on staff or who works for a firm that runs the hospital's emergency programs under a contract arrangement. You might be examined, treated, and dismissed. In fact, that is the usual scenario.

Only about 5 percent of the people who seek care in an emergency room are admitted to the hospital. Your own personal doctor may be the one who admits you and then later attends to you. If you don't have a family doctor, someone at the hospital will become your doctor. This is the old way for young doctors to build practices: be on call or moonlight at an ER and pick up patients who don't have a family physician. It is called "obligation and privilege."

About 90 percent of the people who go to emergency rooms for care should not even be there. They are not experiencing an emergency or anything that could not wait until the next day when an appointment could be made with a private practice doctor.

Don't use an ER as "your doctor." A Seattle-based emergency

Dear PMS,

Our twenty-four-year-old daughter injured her knee quite badly during a softball game. All precautions were taken by her coach, so an ambulance was called and her leg was placed in an air bag before she was taken to the emergency room of the local hospital.

Too bad the same care was not followed up at the hospital. The typical long wait to be seen by a doctor; only a doctor never came. It was an emergency room technician who recommended an X ray and who wrapped her leg, without even cleaning the ground-in dirt of the open wound. Worse than that, he told her to keep it wrapped for a week. Anyone else might have followed his ill advice, as they would not know how to rewrap the entire leg. Fortunately, my daughter is an athletic trainer, and so she removed the wrapping that evening and washed the wound.

Keep in mind, she was never seen by a doctor, but a doctor's signature was placed on the hospital release form. That signature gave him just cause to send my daughter a bill for $50 for his services. What a rip-off.

A. G., Glengary, West Virginia

Dear PMS,

I recently had the occasion to go to an emergency room, and wasted an hour waiting to be treated, was in the treatment area less than one hour, and was billed $60 for being there and $176 for drugs—one injection for rabies.

In my opinion, they're no better than some SOB who would steal your hubcaps.

W. C. B., Downingtown, Pennsylvania

physician explained why in an article that appeared in the February 19, 1981 issue of the *New England Journal of Medicine*:

The cost of ER care is much higher than that of equivalent office care. ER's are parts of hospitals, and their construction must adhere to the costly specifications of building codes. They are equipped to handle all contingencies, requiring expensive equipment that is used infrequently. They must be staffed around the clock, substantially increasing the number of paid personnel. Their personnel are underused; they spend much of the time wasting time.

The pace is hurried and impersonal. Most ER's lack privacy, and care is suboptimal. The patient's contact with a particular physician is the patient's first, and probably the last. The meeting is hasty and the treatment superficial. Arranging follow-up care is difficult, and there is little likelihood that patients will arrange it on their own. The seriously ill patient has an excellent chance of receiving good care, but such patients are in the minority; the majority of patients are short-changed by a system that is poorly suited to their needs. In short, ER's are inefficient means of providing primary health care.

Waiting times are long, and the ER employees can be surly and uncaring. The place is hardly a paragon of desirable ambience, yet it does a profitable business.

People continue to use the ER as a kind of "7-Eleven" of medicine: It might not have your brand, but it is close, and it is open, and the higher cost is just the trade-off for the convenience. Besides, insurance of some sort will pay the bill.

While most hospitals have emergency rooms, many are contracting out for someone else to run them. It's sort of franchised medical care. Companies with headquarters on one side of the country are actually operating emergency rooms on the opposite coast in community or teaching hospitals that used to run the ER's themselves. For hospital management it may mean one less administrative headache. For the patient it may cause confusion or even care not up to the standard they had when they were an inpatient.

To go to an emergency room for less than emergency reasons is a waste of your money (an ER visit can be three times as expensive as an office visit) and the doctor's time. Also, it takes up space and manpower needed for people with real life-or-death problems.

Dear PMS,

When he came home from the emergency room, where he'd gone for cleansing of a surgical scar that had become infected, my boyfriend brought with him a little paper bag with several changes of gauze pads for him to use over the next couple of days. He said the "nice nurse" had "given" them to him.

I am sure that she was a nice nurse, but she certainly had not given him the sterile pads. When he received a copy of the bill, he saw that he had been charged for each and every one of them, at 75 cents a piece! Obviously, we could have done better at any drugstore.

What I find annoying is that he was not *asked* whether he wanted to purchase these sterile pads, and pay 75 cents for each one. The bill was not that large. But it's the principle of the thing. Where else is a customer provided with goods that he hasn't requested, and then charged for them at exorbitant rates well after the fact? This is indicative of the kind of inflationary practices that hospitals are becoming so well known for.

J. J. H., Brooklyn, New York

If you or a loved one has been taken to the hospital experiencing a life-threatening emergency medical situation—a heart attack, a severe allergic reaction, seizures, a serious injury, poisoning, etc.—you have the right to speedy attention. You have the right to know the diagnosis, even if it is of a preliminary nature.

Under normal circumstances it is not advisable for you to accompany a sick or injured friend or relative into the treatment area. You might get in the way, and you might faint on viewing the emergency procedures and end up on a cot next to your friend (it is not an infrequent occurrence). It is agonizing to sit in a waiting area to find out if your husband or mother is still alive, but it has to be that way. However, if the patient is a child or an adult who cannot communicate for one reason or another, or if you witnessed the accident or collapse and can provide details useful in determining the course of treatment, then you have a right—a duty—to be in the treatment area. The doctors, nurses, and assistants may try to force you out, but be firm. Explain why you feel it is crucial for you to be there. Don't get violent or abusive. They are within their rights to call the police and have you arrested. Say your piece, stay as long as you feel you are needed, then go back into the waiting room and let the doctors do their job.

Several years ago a People's Medical Society member accompanied his friend to the emergency room. She was incapable of communicating her problem or the details of events that occurred just prior to his bringing her to this Michigan facility. He entered the treatment area with the individual and was advised that he was to leave. Despite pointing out that he had vital information that would possibly aid in her treatment, he was still ordered to get out. He refused and was arrested. Later he sued the hospital. He won and the hospital was ordered to post a sign in the emergency room indicating the circumstances in which it is permissible to enter the treatment area. A victory for medical consumerism.

In some states, hospitals that refuse emergency treatment to the critically ill can be charged with criminal liability. These laws resulted from increased instances in which ambulances diverted patients from one hospital to another, sometimes farther away, because the patients were poor and the first hospital didn't want to have anything to do with them. Many such "hot potato" patients died.

Never allow yourself or a loved one to be transferred from a private hospital ER to a public hospital ER because you have no insurance or that person has none. A study by Oakland, California's Highland General Hospital, the University of California at Berkeley's School of Public Health, and the Research Group of the Committee to Defend the People's Health showed that such transfers "are common, may be hazardous, and disproportionately affect the poor and minority group members." Of the 103 transferred patients reviewed in the study, "transfer resulted in substandard care for 33 of these patients, either because they were at risk for life-threatening complications in transit or because urgently needed diagnosis or therapy was delayed." Assert your rights. Call your lawyer if you have to. Stand your ground.

One thing more: The rise of independent, proprietary stand-alone emergency clinics or emergicenters, (some call themselves "urgicenters") as they are called, could be an alternative to using the hospital ER for less than emergency situations. You owe it to your-self to at least check on such establishments. Inspect the facilities, note the hours they are open, and ask about the procedures they can perform.

LABORATORIES

Whenever a bit of you is removed or measured or explored or scanned for the purpose of determining what might be going on inside you, one or more of a hospital's numerous labs are involved. The pathology lab will peruse cells and blood and urine. Radiology will X-ray you. Nuclear medicine will scan portions of you after you have had a radioactive solution put into you. Technicians will either work on these tests personally or merely prepare a machine to do the work. The technicians are well trained, adequately paid, and susceptible to a whole cartload of diseases and infections that can be transmitted from the specimens they handle every day and from the patients themselves.

Lately, hospitals have been entering into deals with independent laboratories. They invite these laboratories to take on the lab concessions. It is a cost-cutting, profit-enlarging move for the hospi-tals. They no longer have employee and maintenance costs; instead, they get a fat rental fee and perhaps a cut of the income or a big flat fee up front. For the laboratory companies, it is a big money-maker.

But for you as a patient the main concern is who orders the tests and how well they are executed. Health benefits, as well as financial savings, can accrue to you as a result of keeping close tabs on these tests.

Too many tests are ordered in hospitals. Among the reasons are the inexperience of the younger medical staff (interns and residents) and their fear of a malpractice suit if something is overlooked; the overuse of consulting physicians who order tests of their own, repeating prior tests; and a hunt-and-peck philosophy of trying to find what is wrong with the patient, among others. Not only are about two-thirds of all tests of no benefit to the patient, according to Dr. Thomas Preston in *The Clay Pedestal,* but "a normal person who has twenty or more tests has a less than thirty-six percent chance of being judged normal by all the tests." Some abnormality, however insignificant, is bound to surface and be seen, or misidentified as indicative of some disease or illness. Of course, this can lead to unnecessary treatment of a nonexistent condition.

Even doctors themselves are owning up to performing unnecessary tests. In a 1989 telephone poll of 1,004 physicians who work in the United States, conducted by the Gallup Organization for the American Medical Association, 75 percent said they felt the threat of malpractice suits causes them to do tests that they otherwise believe are not needed.

Of course, we have been unable to uncover a poll that asked consumers how many times a doctor has told them that the test being ordered is to protect the doctor rather than the patient.

Many tests that you had done in an outpatient setting before your formal admission to the hospital are repeated unnecessarily once you are in. One study showed that of nearly 250 patients who

---

X-RAY EXCESS

Upon admission, when the doctor or nurse or attendant on duty aims you in the direction of the X-ray room for "routine" chest pictures, stop right there and say no. Then say why.

The American College of Radiology (ACR) has urged that chest X rays be eliminated as a routine procedure for hospital admissions, tuberculosis screening, and as part of preemployment physicals. The ACR found that most such X-ray sessions usually turn up very little, if anything, so it just isn't worth the cost and the risk. Many of these X rays and other tests are taken as much for your physician's fiscal health as for your physical health. Only if a person's health or medical history warrants it, or if a worker is regularly exposed to chemicals or health hazards that could affect the lungs, should hospital admissions chest X rays be added to the rest of the numerous routine examinations. Too many of these are already unnecessary and excessively costly as well.

had tests performed in the week before entering the hospital, 71 percent of the tests were repeated, and in 14 percent of those patients there was absolutely no justification for the repeats. Those tests most duplicated were routine hemoglobin determinations and urinalyses.

A Few Tips on Tests

▶ Check with your doctor to make sure a test or retest is necessary. Why does it need to be done? Wasn't it done before? Is this a retest because the first was flawed or inconclusive, or is there something new and important to be gained? If the first test was ruined in a lab or because of equipment failure, do you have to pay for it? Make certain that the tests and retests ordered for you are not, in Norman Cousins's words, "more an assertion of the clinical capability of the hospital than of concern for the well-being of the patient." And don't allow yourself to be whisked away by some attendant for another test unless you are absolutely sure you should be having it.

▶ If tests need to be done over and over—and especially if these tests can be hazardous to you, such as those involving nuclear medicine and repeated exposure to radiation—call a halt. The problem might be with an inept or impaired technician. Get a new one. Better yet, tell your doctor about your anger and your fear of more such tests, and see if they are in fact required any longer. File a formal complaint with the hospital administrator, keeping a copy for yourself and your attorney.

▶ Don't tolerate bad or rude treatment from laboratory personnel. Don't tolerate unnecessary pain. The technicians work for you, not the other way around. It is your right to get off the table or undo the apparatus and get yourself out of the testing room if you are not being treated with courtesy, consideration, and professionalism.

▶ If you should desire a second opinion on interpretation of test results, ask your doctor to find you an independent expert outside the hospital. Otherwise (especially if the labs in the hospital are run by a private company leasing hospital space) the test evaluator might be the same person who gave the first report, or a fellow employee who might not want to contradict a coworker.

MEDICAL SERVICE

The picture we all have of a hospital is of a labyrinth of halls, giving off onto honeycombs of rooms, and everywhere doctors swarm. Unless you are in a university medical center, that is not what you see. If you are in a community hospital that is also a teaching hospital, you will see young interns and residents throughout the day. But if you happen to be in a nonteaching hospital, there is a very good chance that you will see nary a physician all day, except for the brief blur of your personal doctor as he or she quickly slips in and out early in the morning. Such hospitals might not have a physician on the premises at all; instead, there is a list of doctors who are on call to rush over in case an emergency arises. Otherwise, the nurses do everything.

The classification and hierarchy of doctors in the average hospital goes something like this, in descending order:

Attending Physician. This is the doctor who admitted you, probably your regular doctor who has admitting privileges at the hospital. This doctor is responsible for your continuing care in the hospital, and he or she orders tests and pharmaceuticals for you. The doctor runs your therapeutic show. This independent private practice doctor is one of a group of similar doctors who are the reigning physician powers at the hospital—despite the fact that they are not there most of the time, except for daily rounds and a few other duties incumbent upon them as attending physicians. (Such duties include the occasional instruction and monitoring of residents and interns, or being on call at the emergency room perhaps every fifth weekend.)

House Staff. This is what the interns and residents are called. In a teaching hospital they are all over the place and will be taking care of your medical needs in lieu of the attending physician (but under the watchful eye of the nervous nurses). They are the eager beavers.

The interns are fresh out of medical school and in their first year of postgraduate training. This is on-the-job training for them, and you are the lucky work project. A resident is a new doctor who has been through internship, decided on a specialty, and is in training at the hospital for a few or more years. Interns and residents are graduates of medical school with a degree of doctor of medicine. (They may or may not be licensed.) They aren't experienced doctors. That is why they rotate from unit to unit, service to service, picking up new skills by working on you.

Medical Students. They are in their third or fourth year of medical school, and they tag along after the interns (which tells you how low in the pecking order they are) and the residents, who in turn tag along after the attending physicians. Medical students have had little or no clinical experience. They are in the hospital to absorb as much information and observe as many technical and manual skills as they can. Unfortunately, they also absorb the callous antipatient and antinurse attitudes that are passed down the chain of command, from attending to house staff to med student, and become a part of the genetic makeup of a doctor. As Dr. Thomas Preston writes:

> From the beginning, students learn to subordinate the rules of normal human interactions to the tenets of the profession. . . . the criterion becomes not what is best for the patient, but what a well-trained physician should do. . . . The waitress-in-training is judged by how well she serves the customer; the physician-in-training is judged by how well he serves the profession.

Medical students are not doctors. They can't and shouldn't treat you. Yet they are often called "Doctor" by their superiors as part of the socialization process within medicine. This is dangerous, and one medical student, in a letter to the *Journal of the American Medical Association,* took his superiors and the system to task for it.

He had come to realize, he wrote, that "addressing medical students as 'Doctor' in front of patients or other health-care personnel is misleading and could even be dangerous. . . .

"A nurse who thinks a medical student is a physician by virtue of the title 'Doctor' used in introduction might ask for or accept orders for patients without proper authorization," the student wrote. "In addition, a patient might consent to examination or treatment by a misidentified 'physician' that he would *not* consent to from an accurately identified medical student. There might even be a basis for a charge of fraud under such circumstances."

This student identified himself to patients as "Vic Wilson, the medical student working with Dr. X." He said patients seem to like this, and those who want a "real" doctor thus have the opportunity to get one.

> When I was a resident, I was told by a very kindly professor who was trying to help me, "You know, your problem is that you talk to patients too much. But I'm sure you'll learn how not to."
>
> **Michelle Harrison, M.D.**

> Postgraduate medical training—internship and residency—really does change our doctors, and not always for the better. As they master clinical skills, many also become more arrogant, authoritarian, and cynical. They learn to scoff at any alternative to their own approach to medicine, calling it "the lunatic fringe." The ceaseless demands of the profession put many at risk of severe psychological problems. They learn to think in terms of "the liver in 464"—the disease rather than the person who has it. They learn to overlook the hazards of their own technology and the petty indignities to which patients are routinely subjected.
>
> **Tom Ferguson, M.D.**

"I believe," he summed up, "that the practice of addressing medical students as 'Doctor' is a disservice to the student, who is then obliged to masquerade as someone he is not, and to the patients, who are denied the right to know the qualifications of those treating them."

Know who is treating you. Ask. Look at the name tag or badge the individual is wearing.

NURSES

Doctors may make the money, administrators may sign the checks, trustees may break ground for new buildings—but nurses run the show. Of everybody you deal with during a hospital stay, nobody is as important, can do more for you (and to you), and can be more a colleague-in-arms than your nurse.

Registered nurses (R.N.'s) are at the top of the nursing status ladder, having had more education, more clinical experience, more on-the-job training than the licensed practical nurses (L.P.N.'s), who might have just a year of nursing school (whereas many R.N.'s have baccalaureate degrees in a four-year college nursing program and sometimes a master's degree). Next down the chain are the nurses' aides and orderlies.

It is because of these levels of skill and experience that the all-R.N. hospital is considered the best and most medically responsive place for a patient to be. Beyond that, the primary nursing system is to be desired. When you have been brought up to the unit after admission, checked in with the unit secretary, and have been shown to your room, you are introduced to your primary nurse, one of a number assigned to that unit. He or she is *your* nurse (shared, of course, with other patients) and provides continuity of care. In the primary nursing system, you don't have a whole slew of different people each doing a different task. Rather, your primary nurse (and that nurse's associate, who covers when your nurse is off-duty) will do almost everything for you, except for minor or particularly distasteful duties, which are given to the lower-level nurses and to candy stripers and other volunteers. These lower-stratum folks act as gofers and errand boys, take patients to X ray and other departments, take patients on walks, etc. These and similar activities are considered to be beneath an R.N., and they won't do such tasks if they can possibly be avoided.

It is the primary nurse's job, during your first day in the hospital, to take a history and tailor a nursing care plan to your needs. Your job is to work with your nurse in making that plan, arranging a schedule, and developing some sort of rapport. There may be no rapport, and that is unfortunate. However, if there is hostility, you can ask for a new nurse, even demand one if necessary. If you have only one nurse working with you, it has to be somebody you get along with. The reverse is also true. Your nurse might reject you and ask for a change in assignment. This is your nurse's right. The primary nursing system is a good one, but it is a delicate one and relies a great deal on the right patient-nurse personal chemistry and mutual respect for its success.

Two of the reasons why doctors and nurses don't exactly get along might be a lack of this same personal chemistry and mutual respect. In fact, in Hospital Land, theirs is the longest-running, most bitter, and potentially most explosive civil war.

The seething resentment between some doctors and nurses has to do with changing roles, professional recognition, and concern for you, the patient. Men are now nurses; women are now doctors. And we live in a time of changing male-female relationships. The traditional roles of dominance (male doctor) and submission (female nurse) that were gender-related as much as professional, are now topsy-turvy. Both sides feel cheated and angered in dealings with each other. And nurse-practitioners—sort of doctors, yet sort of nurses—are in the middle and the target of envy and frustration and resentment from both sides.

Lewis Thomas, M.D., in *The Youngest Science* (New York: Viking, 1983), writes: "The doctors worry that nurses are trying to move away from their historical responsibilities to medicine (meaning, really, to the doctor's orders). The nurses assert that they are their own profession, responsible for their own standards, coequal colleagues with physicians, and they do not wish to become mere ward administrators or technicians."

Doctors resent the growing professional autonomy of nurses. In a poll of nurses 83 percent said that if the doctor won't tell patients about therapeutic alternatives, they will. Nurses spot mistakes on charts and note them; they see doctors' therapeutic missteps and refuse to carry them out. Things like this drive the doctors crazy, because they see their presumed omnipotence eroding badly.

Meanwhile, for all the direct nursing and administrative functions they perform every day, the nurses are paid far less than doctors. In some cases they are paid less than the interns and residents they suffer and tutor, and who in return treat them like natural inferiors. While a medical student, Perri Klass described the "prestige-sensitive medical world" in a *New York Times* column: "One of the ways that doctors learn to be doctors, it seems, is by learning that they are not nurses and must not stoop to nurses' work. . . . It wouldn't do a medical student any harm to see the hospital from the point of view of a nurse."

Your nurse is with you more and does more for you than any other medical practitioner; the doctor saunters in, spends a few minutes with you to evaluate and/or prescribe, strolls out, and gets money, credit, and prestige for that. Your nurse gets the bedpan— and may even get chewed out by the doctor if anything is not up to snuff, even if the problem was a result of following that doctor's orders.

It is all a battle of status. You should not allow yourself to be drawn into it—you can't win—unless the competitive situation between your doctor and your nurse gets in the way of your care and recovery. If that is the case, let both of them know you won't stand for it, and it has to stop. If necessary, change your nurse or doctor, whoever is worth less to you.

Just remember: The person who can help you more than anyone else within the hospital walls, who is there for you more than anyone else, who will look out for you and bend the rules for you, is your nurse. It is wise to cultivate a nurse's friendship. Then all

sorts of consumer rights doors, leading to secret passages of empowerment, can open for you.

PATIENTS'
REPRESENTATIVE

The patients' representative is one of the better ideas hospitals have
had—or have had forced on them—in recent years. Possibly ever.

The patients' representative is sometimes known as a patients'
advocate, although that term is sometimes used to describe anyone
(a friend, relative, or guardian) who looks out and speaks up for a
patient. A patients' representative is a hospital-employed consum-
erist go-between. The job of the patients' representative is to make
the alienating environment of a hospital seem more human and
responsive to the worried and befuddled patient.

Some do and some don't. Some are merely public relations tools,
happy little homemaker types who think, or who have been told,
that a patient's complaints can be neutralized with a smile and
noncommittal phrases uttered in a soothing, cheery tone. Such patients' representative don't represent anything but the contempt the
hospital who employs them has for earnest, concerned patients.

The "real" representatives act as ombudsmen, workers within the
establishment, who will listen to your complaints and suggestions,
assess the situation, and pass along your thoughts with their own
analysis to the proper authorities for action. Presumably, the patients' representative's voice is heard more clearly by doctors and
administrators than your voice could be. The representative then
reports back to you. In this way the patients' representative (often
a nurse, but not always) should be an educator, a rights activist, and
a hospital version of a State Department envoy involved in shuttle
diplomacy.

If your hospital has a patients' representative—and more than
three thousand hospitals do—you should be introduced to him or
her, as soon after admission as possible. Find out the representative's name, in-hospital phone extension, working hours, office lo-
cation, and home phone in case of emergency. (This last might not
be made available. If not, ask if he or she is on call during evening
hours, or if there is a backup representative on the premises.) A
good patient's representative is readily available and probably

makes regular daily rounds. During your initial chat ask questions about the representative's background and qualifications, and what he or she can do for you. In this way you might be able to determine whether your patients' representative is a mere pillow fluffer or a real feather ruffler.

The patients' representatives see their job as that of lessening patient stress and keeping tempers under control. They are good corporate team players, creating a positive feeling in the community toward an institution that presumably cares enough about people to institute such a service. They move information quickly through the proper channels to the proper people and save lots of people lots of time. Many patients' representatives are part of their hospital's risk-management department, which means they monitor "incident reports"—reports of occurrences that might lead to malpractice cases—and then they try to defuse the situation to avoid the lawsuit.

It is a good idea, this patient representation, but there are some dark sides to it. Patients' representatives can be an obstruction by keeping your complaints to themselves so as to shield "busy" administrators from such petty annoyances. They may also be the ones who answer your angry letters, and the administrators, the people who can change conditions, might never see what you wrote.

Even the most conscientious, dedicated, helpful, and skillful patients' representative (and that describes many of them) is in a bind. He or she gets paid by the hospital and may be reluctant to place his or her job in jeopardy by espousing an unpopular position or opposing a powerful staff member. The patients' representative is part of the administration. Certain lines are drawn and may not be safely crossed. The question to be asked is the one put forward by Seymour Isenberg, D.O., and L. M. Elting, D.O., M.D., in *The Consumer's Guide to Successful Surgery* (New York: St. Martin's, 1976): "When it comes to the nitty-gritty, do patient representatives bite the hand that feeds them or the one that is held out for help?"

Despite the drawbacks and the possible political impotence of some patients' representatives, it is well worth giving them a try. You may be lucky enough to deal with one who has a relatively free hand, and who has a good working relationship with doctors, nurses, heads of departments, and the administrative office. If you are not that lucky, then the patients' representative might not be a part of the solution, but rather only a part of the problem. That means that when it comes to your rights, you will have to go to bat for yourself.

PHARMACY

The pharmacy is where the drugs come from. Period. And that would pretty much take care of this section, except that all hospital pharmacies are not alike. Some are not as safe for you as they should be. Here is how to tell if your hospital cares enough to provide at least the framework of a good, efficient pharmacy:

Is There a Pharmacy on the Patient Floors? It is better for everybody if each patient floor has its own dispensary. This makes for quick service (especially in an emergency) and lets the nurses and doctors work with the pharmacist and not just order drugs from some anonymous room somewhere. It also allows the pharmacist to get involved more directly in patient care (if the doctor's ego will permit it) by talking to patients, taking pharmaceutical histories, making notations on the chart, and determining firsthand if what has been ordered by the doctor is correct. The pharmacist can be a valuable member of the health care team. Having the pharmacy right down the hall also allows you to stop by during a midday stroll to ask questions about your prescriptions that only a pharmacist can answer.

In some hospitals the pharmacy is still a centralized bureau stuck somewhere in the basement, where it is not doing nearly as much good as it could do.

Are All Intravenous Admixtures Made by the Pharmacist? It is often necessary for somebody in the hospital to add, let's say, potassium to the intravenous solution in quantities that your condition requires. Sometimes the nurses do it, and that could mean big trouble. It is not that they get the quantities wrong, although that does happen, but rather that when they open the IV bags to add to the solution, they also expose the solution to any and all germs flying around the hospital. And then those microorganisms get dripped into your bloodstream, causing some very serious repercussions. The IV solution remains sterile—and you remain safe (or, at least, safer)—if the pharmacist makes the admixture under a laminar flow hood. This device blows sterile air over the pharmacist's hands and the IV bag, keeping unwanted bugs away from the proceedings.

Does the Pharmacy Have a Unit Dose System? Unit dose came into being in the 1960s and describes a method of dispensing in which an individual supply of medication is made up for each

A CAPSULE SUMMARY: HOSPITAL DRUG OVERCHARGES

It is not very often that we civilians get a behind-the-scenes look at the way hospitals make their money. But in 1983 Neil D. Rosenberg, medical reporter for the *Milwaukee Journal,* happened to be present at a staff meeting held in one of his town's hospitals. What he saw and heard about that institution's drug-pricing system—a system, he said, that is "not altogether unlike those at other hospitals"—confirms what a lot of us have suspected. And then some.

What follows is a chart of some commonly prescribed antibiotics, their actual costs, wholesale costs, and what a patient in that Milwaukee institution—and others—would have expected to pay. Today, with medical inflation, the numbers may easily run to five times the amounts shown.

The hospital's explanation for these mind-boggling markups was that the drug income pays for the administrative, housekeeping, and maintenance departments, none of which produces any revenue on its own.

Well . . . maybe. But, then, what do the exorbitant room charges pay for? Or any of those other outlandish charges, overcharges, and "phantom charges"—the ones where people get charged for goods and services they never received?

Another thing Rosenberg discovered was that doctors, many of whom haven't the foggiest notion of what things cost, end up unwittingly socking it to their patients. For example, a doctor treating a pneumonia caused by gram-negative bacteria might go for the new state-of-the-art antibiotic cefoperazone. The chart shows that a ten-day treatment would have cost

patient and is replenished every twenty-four hours. Each drug prescribed for the patient is in a unit-for-use form; that means if you are to get 500 mg of a certain drug four times a day, a drawer in the pharmacy with your name on it will contain four separately wrapped, properly labeled 500 mg tablets of that drug. The drawer is then delivered to the nurses' station. At the end of the twenty-four hours, the drawer should be empty—a proof of sorts that you received all your medication. If there is something left in the drawer, somebody goofed. Unit dose, in other words, is a stab at quality assurance, with a number of checkpoints along the way, the last of which is the nurse, who should check to see if it is the right drug just before giving it to you. Ideally, you are the last checkpoint, making sure that you are being handed your medication.

Time was (and still is in some very traditional hospitals) when the doctor would write up an order for medication for a newly admitted patient—say, that same 500-mg tablet, four times a day—and the

the ill consumer $1,510. But if the doctor went with the equally effective antibiotic gentamicin instead, the same job would have been done at half the price.

It's just that doctors don't know this. They need to learn, and your questions can help them do that. Ask if there is a less expensive viable alternative to drugs when a doctor prescribes them. You could save a bundle.

Antibiotic	Average Wholesale Cost ($)	Average Actual Cost ($)	Charge to Patient Per Dose* ($)
Penicillin (2 million units)	0.39	0.61	14.35
Ampicillin (500 mg)	1.22	2.69	15.50
Gentamicin (80 mg)	0.74	3.82	21.70
Cefazolin (1 g)	3.11	6.42	21.70
Cefoperazone (1 g)	9.50	11.28	30.50

*Charge includes pharmacy fees of $9.

Chart reprinted from the *Milwaukee Journal* (July 23, 1983). Used with permission of the publisher.

pharmacy would send up thirty tablets at a time, a week's supply or so. The trouble with this, of course, is that sometimes the dosage was changed the very next day or the day after, or it might even have been canceled. But the unused drug would still sit on the shelf, encouraging the chance for an error to happen with it, the chance for it to go bad or to get "lost." There were no unit dose drawers; the nurses just rooted around the shelves, trying to come up with the drug and dosage to match the order noted in the chart.

Unit dose systems aren't perfect. When using them, medication errors occur somewhere between 3 and 5 percent of the time. A horrifying figure—until you realize that the national average for medication errors is at least double that.

Does the Pharmacy Get a Carbon Copy of the Doctor's Orders? This is important. In some hospitals the pharmacy doesn't get a copy. Instead, a nurse may read the order over the phone to the pharmacist. The nurse may misread or misinterpret an order. The names of many different drugs are spelled similarly, sound alike when spoken, and may even be prescribed for the same disease. For those reasons the better hospitals try to avoid errors and protect patients by providing the pharmacy with carbon copies of orders. The best hospitals use computer or facsimile systems, sending the order electronically and accurately from nursing area to pharmacy.

How Limited Is the Formulary?   In pharmacy lingo a formulary is the list of drugs available in a hospital. Not every drug and every brand is bought by every hospital pharmacy. There are, for example, ten or so brands of tetracycline drugs on the market. A hospital probably stocks only two. It would be uneconomical to stock them all, but the selection should be adequate. If your doctor orders a drug for you that isn't on the formulary—a drug you have taken for years, feel comfortable with, and are comforted by—some hospital pharmacies will get that drug for you, but you will be charged for the full bottle no matter how little you use. Others with "closed" formularies will not order it for you. They will substitute, unmindful of your feeling upset and mistrustful when you get a green pill instead of your usual pink. The wider and more inclusive the formulary, the less chance of such problems.

Does the Pharmacist Get Involved in Patient Education, and Medication Instruction at the Time of Discharge?   In many hospitals nurses handle patient education. In the better hospitals, pharmacists will get involved, especially when it comes to instructions about medications to be used after you are discharged. The pharmacist can help to teach you about the supplies you need to buy at a drugstore after you leave the hospital.

SPECIAL CARE UNITS

There are people alive today who wouldn't be if they hadn't been rushed to an intensive care unit or cardiac care unit, where they were plugged into the latest beeping and flashing monitoring equipment, pumped full of the latest lifesaving drugs, and watched with the greatest caution by nurses and medical specialists (known as "intensivists") in that field. There is no denying that quick action and reaction, a far better than average practitioner-to-patient ratio, plus constant care can make a difference. No other activity in a hospital, except perhaps for exotic surgeries and transplants, represents medicine at its most modern.

That may be why intensive care units (ICUs) have become a lightning rod for criticism—most of it kept within the walls of the hospitals and academic institutions, and away from the eyes and ears of the medical consumer. The questions aimed at the use of ICUs, the barbs and brickbats, and real moral dilemmas, are at the cutting edge of ethical discussions about medical care today.

If you are told you need ICU care—or, more likely, if you are in bad shape and your family is informed that you are headed for the ICU—the odds are that the go-ahead will be given (unless your choice is to discourage any measures that seem to be lifesaving, and instead to die peacefully with dignity; see "Dying, Death, and Beyond" in chapter 4, "What the Wise Traveler Knows"). In times of sudden stress and anguish we follow the normalized paths and the most authoritative-sounding voices. The ICU has been well publicized, has gained an excellent image, and acts as a security blanket for frightened family and patients. We can't second-guess our decisions in moments of such turmoil, and those decisions usually turn out for the best, or as well as possible.

But there is information that one can have and ought to have *before* being confronted with an ICU-or-no-ICU decision. Here are some of the facts, figures, and controversies swirling around intensive care:

▶ More than 95 percent of acute care hospitals have intensive care facilities, and a number of these have more than one. In 1960 only 10 percent of hospitals with 200 beds or more had ICUs.

▶ The average charge for daily ICU care is now $1,324. The average cost is over $25,000 per stay, and has gone as high as $500,000 for very ill patients. ICU billings make up about 1 percent of the gross national product of the United States.

▶ On any given day, there are an average of 47,200 patients nationwide occupying ICU beds.

▶ Despite the number of ICUs in America, and despite their great costs, experts today still argue over their benefits. Detractors insist that ICUs are overused and/or improperly used, that patients are put in there who shouldn't be there, and much of what is done for them is pointless. It is startling that something so expensive and so labor-intensive, something that attracts so many of the best people practicing in the hospital and is used so often in the course of treatment, is still being evaluated in terms of its basic worth.

A conference on critical care medicine held at the National Institutes of Health concluded, according to a report in *Family Practice News,* that "nobody really knows how much intensive care units are accomplishing in saving lives or improving the quality of survival for critically ill patients." It's a little late in the day for that sort of uncertainty, but that is the way of much of the medical world: Ready, fire, aim.

Life-threatening conditions that are reversible is one type of problem that is resolved more readily from a stay in the ICU. Others include some victims of accidents and drug overdoses, and some patients with neurological disease. Beyond these, and a very few other categories, "there is no acceptable evidence that care in the ICU improves more lives than it harms," claims Eugene D. Robin, M.D., a professor of medicine and physiology at the Stanford University School of Medicine.

A study at George Washington University Hospital and fifteen other hospitals with ICUs indicated that as many as 25 percent of ICU patients shouldn't be in there, either because they are too healthy for intensive care or too ill to benefit from it. For those who are too sick, or are terminally ill, the ICU merely delays the inevitable. And it does so at some pain and loss of dignity, and certainly at an expense that might be three times higher than regular hospital care. The too-healthy will certainly get lots of attention but also risk the hazard of too much attention: too many tests and the chance of catching a new disease, both of which outweigh any potential benefit of ICU care for them. There are other ICU hazards and drawbacks: The artificial, no-day and no-night atmosphere of the ICU can disorient patients and cause sleep disorders; the ICU environment with its hustle and bustle can terrorize patients, thus affect their recovery, and possibly even literally frighten them to death. The patients can also suffer from the care they receive from impaired ICU personnel, who have a high rate of early burnout.

An ICU study published in the December 11, 1981 *Journal of the American Medical Association* showed that "for nearly half (49 percent) of the admissions and during two-thirds (65 percent) of the nursing shifts, the emphasis was on close nursing care and observation, not intensive treatment." Furthermore, the researchers found, 86 percent of patients admitted for monitoring "never required active treatment before discharge." The study concluded that "a substantial portion of ICU services may now be directed at monitoring stable, noncritically ill patients."

"The ideal ICU patient appears to be one who needs very sophisticated monitoring and intensive care for a short period of time and has a good chance of survival and subsequent enjoyment of life at least for several years," states Robert Wilson, M.D., of Wayne State University in the April 8, 1983 issue of *American Medical News.* "In many respects, postoperative surgical patients, especially those with trauma, fulfill the requirements for the ideal ICU patient."

All this is saying is that ICUs can be crucial to the survival of *some* people suffering *some* conditions. But many others are put into the ICU who could do just as well—and do it much less expensively—in a regular room with a regular nurse. If there is time to discuss this with your doctor or the doctor of the friend or relative who needs care, then do so. Talk about it even after the person is in the ICU. It could shorten the stay there.

▶ Similar doubts exist concerning two specialized care units, the coronary care unit (CCU) and what used to be called the infant intensive care unit (IICU), now the neonatal intensive care unit (NICU). Most studies show that people who are victims of heart attacks and other heart conditions have the same mortality rates when placed in a CCU as in a regular hospital unit. In fact, many studies show that people do *worse* in the CCU. And in one British study 20 percent of heart attack victims treated at home died—but that is better than the 27 percent who died during treatment in the CCU. "The better the study, the less benefit that has been shown to result from CCUs, is what Leon Gordis, M.D., of Johns Hopkins University told a *Medical World News* writer.

The NICU indeed sustains the life of many young children, especially premature newborns and those with massive deficiencies. However, its technology creates, in many cases, moral and ethical dilemmas never conceived of just a decade or two ago. Critics of the NICUs suggest that the infants might sometimes be put on life support because doctors don't want to lose a case. They are saying, in effect, that because science can do it, it must be done, and they think the child can make it, often in the face of statistics to the contrary. Some do make it; many don't. Many of those who die had been kept alive in a painful, half-life limbo for a very short time and against parents' wishes; many who died do so not from their diseases or their very premature state, but from the effects of the treatment they received to keep them alive.

The moral and ethical dilemma becomes even greater because a large number of those who live must spend their lives deformed, retarded, or worse. The cost is astronomical and the psychological toll on parents is immeasurable. To some parents the cost is insignificant when put against the value and sanctity of a human life, and they are willing to do whatever it takes to give their newborn the best life it can have, however small the quality and brief the duration. Other parents are not prepared or even aware of the commitment medical science has imposed on them. Peggy Stinson, mother of a deathly ill premature infant who suffered the attempts to save him, wrote about her devastations in *The Long Dying of Baby Andrew* (Boston: Atlantic Monthly Press, 1983), coauthored by her husband, Robert. In the book, she stated her belief that "if every doctor who makes a unilateral decision to go all out to save a desperately premature child were thereby made adoptive parents of that child, we would begin to see some important policy changes in the IICU's."

The situation is only going to get more complicated before it gets better. The 1980s brought us the well-known case of Baby Jane Doe, the handicapped infant whose parents were sued by the U.S. government in an attempt to override the parents' wishes and require more aggressive treatment of the infant.

The Baby Jane Doe case and the Baby Doe case two years before brought the issue of parents' rights versus the rights of seriously ill newborns to the attention of most Americans. Baby Doe was allowed to die without treatment at the request of his parents even though his

life-threatening condition could have been treated. Baby
Doe had Down's syndrome. The effects of these cases
extend beyond the rare instances of severely handicapped
infants to the more common ones of premature but
otherwise normal infants. The rights of parents to give or
deny consent to treatment for newborns and very small
children are now being questioned. Courts and legislatures
do not always assume that parents will act in the best
interests of their children—and this shift in emphasis from
parents' rights to children's rights will have important
consequences to both parents and children.

All medical practitioners have become wary of these
potential conflicts and, when disagreements arise, often
seek to obtain court permission to treat a child without
parental consent.

▶ Some people are admitted to ICCs not because they need
the full extent of intensive care services but because they
need a specific piece of technology, and that machine and
the skilled operators who run it happen to be located in the
ICC.

▶ The cost issue is bringing the most difficult and complex
ethical issues surrounding ICUs to the fore. If
cost-containment is a general goal of the medical, business,
and private sectors, which services do you cut first? Some
eyes are looking at ICUs, trying to figure out who should
get the care and who should not. Approximately $22 billion
a year is being spent on ICU care. It's estimated that about
half of that is spent for people who probably won't and
usually don't pull through. Thus, the specter of medical
rationing is raising its ugly head, as is that of selective
treatment, or triage.

The new fixed-rate, diagnosis-related-group (DRG)
payment concept instituted by the Medicare system is
putting the squeeze on, too. Money is no longer rolling in
on demand, as it used to; now the hospital will get only a
set amount for a condition, no matter how long the patient
needs to be in the hospital, no matter if that patient is in a
general hospital room or the ICU. Any profit incentive for
putting a Medicare patient into the ICU is gone. This could
mean rationing and possibly poor medical treatment. The
doctors and nurses in charge of ICUs will have to make

sharper determinations about who can and who can't benefit from intensive care. They might be forced to play God, with money as the major determinant.

WHEN IN ROME . . .

3

Travelers quickly learn that accommodations are seldom what they are cracked up to be, that the English of the "English-speaking guide" might be incomprehensible, that fellow travelers are not always pleasant companions, and that service sometimes takes a real nosedive just when it is needed most. The wise tourists change what they can—and put up with the rest. As a hospital guest, you can expect to swim in the same rough waters, so it makes sense to prepare yourself for the challenges that will surely come your way.

THE LANGUAGE

Legend has it that the Tower of Babel was a hospital. And as soon as all of the people scurrying about on the upper tower began speaking a language that no one else could understand, they were sent down to speak to the patients.

Since that misty prehistoric time, it has been the custom of the Hospital Land natives to speak in a strange tongue. They don't think their language is unusual; they certainly don't think that they are difficult to understand. In fact, they think they make perfect sense; it's you who are a little slow on the uptake. We know better, but we humor them because, after all, it is their island.

By letting medical personnel get by with jabbering in their native tongue, however, we do them and ourselves a grave disservice. We don't get the information we need. They never learn that we want the information. Worst of all, they don't feel any pressure to develop ways to tell us what we want to know, clearly and succinctly.

Those among the medical ranks seem to enjoy reeling off a string of long and technical words or phrases that leave the layperson scratching his or her head in wonder and total confusion. These medical folks also have their own set of abbreviations and acronyms, their own coded messages. They use a language that sets up barriers and puts down patients.

There are theories about why medical professionals do this. Some say it is a way to maintain an elitism, a secret society atmosphere around the practice of medicine. Others say it is just kind of fun and addictive when one has been seduced by it. All professions (which, as George Bernard Shaw reminded us, are conspiracies against the laity) have a jargon, some people point out, and medicine's is no more dark, deceitful, or dangerous than any other.

Perhaps. But speaking in technical tongues is yet another way for doctors and nurses to assert and maintain power by keeping information to themselves and away from the person most concerned and most in need of it. You.

The popular science magazine *Omni* recently ran an article in which one doctor gave his reasoning for medical mumbo-jumbo. In effect, he said, it is developed and used, consciously or subconsciously, by some physicians to "cloak inexperience and bumbling with an air of sophistication and competence. Even more important, it hides the inability to make firm diagnoses."

First there are the technical tongue twisters. To come to terms with the terms you come up against, flip to the back of this book. You will find a glossary that should help a lot, plus a key to translating almost any medical term.

Decipher the Abbreviations

One thing medical folks just love to do is abbreviate, especially on your chart and medical records. You see, they think no one else, except another doctor or nurse, will ever have occasion to look at what is scribbled there, and they all know the code. But you don't. And when you look at your chart and records (something you ought to do regularly), you are once again shut off from what your doctor is thinking about you, about your condition, and about your prognosis. It is one more obstacle blocking your participation in your own care.

Smash that obstacle with the following list, a collection from many sources of abbreviations frequently used in records, on forms and prescriptions, and even in everyday chatter. If something you see or hear doesn't appear on this list, ask your nurse, doctor, patients' representative, or some other person in the know to translate. If they won't tell you, or they casually brush off the request, persist. Threaten to go to the hospital administrator if you have to. If you really think they are trying to hide something from you, threaten to bring in your attorney.

One reason hospital personnel might not want to level with you is that the message could be a real embarrassment for them if interpreted accurately. Sometimes the descriptions medical people use in referring to their patients and their patients' conditions are couched in a colorful code that is hard for the uninitiated to crack. For example, "LOL" is noted next to your name on your chart. You ask your nurse what it means. She turns a couple of shades of crimson. "LOL" is medicode for "Little Old Lady." This signals those reading the record that you are a nice, perhaps cheery, certainly passive, unquestioning, and utterly compliant female senior citizen.

If you hear that the patient next door "boxed," that means he or she died. Cute. A "gork" is a brain-damaged person, a vegetable.

A "gomer" is, according to one medical lexicographer, the nickname given to a "real dirtball patient." It is the acronym for "Get out of my emergency room."

In medicode a "delightful" patient is one who does anything anybody tells him or her to do and never asks questions. The same goes for those patients described as "pleasant."

A "turkey" is something quite different. A turkey is *you*—a patient who asks a lot of questions, demands respect, knows his or her rights, and won't stop wanting to be a part of his or her own healing care. In other words, a smart and careful medical consumer. This is somebody many doctors and nurses happily could do without. Turkeys of the world, we salute you.

Here are abbreviations you might encounter in records, on forms or prescriptions, or in hospital chatter:

a = before

aa = of each

a.c. = before meals

ad = to, up to

ADL = activities of daily
living

ad lib = as needed, as
desired

AF = auricular fibrillation

agit = shake, stir

A.M.A. = against medical
advice

Ap. = appendicitis

Aq. = water

ASHD = arteriosclerotic heart disease

B.E. = barium enema

b.i.d. = twice a day

Bl. time = bleeding time

BM = bowel movement

BMR = basal metabolic rate

BP = blood pressure

BRP = bathroom privileges

Bx = biopsy

C. = centigrade

c̄ = with

CA = cancer

CAD = coronary artery disease

cap(s) = capsule(s)

CBC = complete blood count

CBD = common bile duct

CC = chief complaint

cc = cubic centimeter

CCU = coronary care unit

CHD = coronary heart disease; or congenital heart disease

CHF = congestive heart failure

Chol = cholesterol

Cl. time = clotting time

CNS = central nervous system

comp = compound

cont rem = continue the medicine

COPD = chronic obstructive pulmonary disease

CSF = cerebrospinal fluid

CV = cardiovascular

CVA = cerebrovascular accident

CVP = central venous pressure

CXR = chest X ray

d = give

D&C = dilation and curettage

dd in d = from day to day

dec = pour off

dexter = the right

dil = dilute

disp = dispense

div = divide

DM = diabetes mellitus

dos = dose

dur dolor = while pain lasts

D/W = dextrose in water

Dx = diagnosis

ECG or EKG = electrocardiogram

EEG = electroencephalogram

emp = as directed

ER = emergency room

F. = Fahrenheit

FBS = fasting blood sugar

febris = fever

FH = family history

Fx = fracture

GA = general anesthesia

garg = gargle

GB = gallbladder

GC = gonorrhea

GI = gastrointestinal

GL = glaucoma

gm = grams

gr = grains

grad = by degrees

gravida = pregnancies

gtt = drops

GTT = glucose tolerance test

GU = genitourinary

GYN = gynecology

h = hour

HASHD = hypertensive arteriosclerotic heart disease

Hb or Hgb = hemoglobin

HCT = hematocrit

HHD = hypertensive heart disease

HOB = head of bed

HPI = history of present illness

h.s. = at bedtime, before retiring

Hx = history

ICU = intensive care unit

I&D = incision and drainage

IM = intramuscular

I.M. = infectious mononucleosis

I&O = intake and output (measure fluids going into and out of body)

IPPB = intermittent positive pressure breathing

ind = daily

IV = intravenous

IVP = intravenous pyelogram

L = left

liq = liquid

LLE = left lower extremity

LLQ = left lower quadrant

LMP = last menstrual period

LP = lumbar puncture

LUE = left upper extremity

LUQ = left upper quadrant

(m) = murmur

M = mix

m et n = morning and night

mg = milligrams

MI = heart attack (myocardial infarction)

mor. dict. = in the manner directed

M.S. = morphine sulfate

neg = negative

N-G = nasogastric

no. = number

non rep; nr = do not repeat

n.p.o. = non per os
(nothing by mouth)

NS = normal saline

NSR = normal heart rate

N & V = nausea and
vomiting

O_2 = oxygen

o = none

O.D. = right eye

o.d. = once a day

O.L. = left eye

OOB = out of bed

OPD = outpatient
department

OR = operating room

O.S. = left eye

OT = occupational therapy

OU = both eyes

P; $\overline{P}$ = after

Para = number of births

Path. = pathology

p.c. = after meals

PE = physical examination;
or pulmonary embolus

PI = present illness

pil = pill

p.o. = per os (by mouth)

Post. = posterior

post-op = postoperative,
after the operation

PR = pulse rate; or, rectally

p.r.n. = as needed, as often
as necessary

Prog. = prognosis

pt = patient

PT = physical therapy

PTA = prior to admission

Px = prognosis

q. = every

q.h. = every hour (q.4h. =
every four hours; q.8h. =
every eight hours; and so
on)

q.i.d. = four times a day

q.n. = every night

q.o.d. = every other day

q.s. = proper amount,
quantity sufficient

q.v. = as much as desired

R = right

rbc = red blood cell

RBC = red blood cell count

rep = repeat

RHD = rheumatic heart
disease

RLQ = right lower
quadrant

R.N. = registered nurse

ROM = range of motion

RR = respiratory rate; or
recovery room

RT = radiation therapy

rub = red

RUQ = right upper
quadrant

Rx = prescription; or therapy

s̄ = without

S&A = sugar and acetone (a urine test for diabetics)

SC = subcutaneous

Scop. = scopolamine

SH = social history

SICU = surgical intensive care unit

sig = write, let it be imprinted

sing = of each

SOB = shortness of breath

sol = solution

solv = dissolve

SOP = standard operating procedure

SOS = can repeat in emergency

ss = half

S&S = signs and symptoms

SSE = soapsuds enema

stat = right away, immediately

sub Q = subcutaneous

suppos = suppository

Sx = symptoms

T&A = tonsillectomy and adenoidectomy

tab = tablet

TAT = tetanus antitoxin

tere = rub

TIA =transient ischemic attacks

t.i.d. = three times a day

tinc or tinct = tincture

TPR = temperature, pulse, and respiration

Tx = treatment

ung = ointment

URI = upper respiratory infection

ut dict = as directed

UTI = urinary tract infection

VD = venereal disease

VS = vital signs

WBC = white blood cell count

WC = wheelchair

YO = year old

↑ = increase

↗ = increasing

↓ = decrease

↙ = decreasing

→ = leads to

← = resulting from

♂ = male

♀ = female

A lot of people are easily bowled over and impressed by professionals who liberally sprinkle around the technical jive talk without ever once looking back to see if their words are being picked up and understood by the laypeople who are paying the bills. Don't let that sort of talk impress you—not in television repairmen, not in appliance salesmen, and certainly not in doctors. Your body and your life are at stake. Even the most revered medical figure who can't (or, worse yet, won't) speak in an understandable fashion is wrong. Wrong, because by not communicating in your language, he or she isn't helping you to help yourself, and you are your best healer. Tell your doctor that you want to be spoken to in everyday, direct, and totally honest English. Don't accept less. Communication is the most important first step in a healing relationship.

LODGING

The Ritz it's not. But what did you expect? Plush carpeting? A mahogany credenza? A mint on the pillow?

Maybe not, but you *are* paying three to five times as much as you would for a good hotel room. Is it unreasonable to expect price and quality in Hospital Land to be compatible roommates?

To be fair, it is not practical for your hospital room to have all the look and feel of a suite at the Plaza. For one thing, such accommodations are costly to furnish and maintain. You certainly would not want to be paying more than you already are just to have a gilt-edge mirror and an alabaster toilet-paper holder.

Admittedly, comparing hotel rooms and hospital rooms is like comparing first class and steerage. Still and all, hospital rooms really don't need to be quite so basic and dismal as they are. Slightly cheerier, more amenable surroundings certainly couldn't hurt the healing process, and the cheerless hospital rooms we all know too well certainly can't be helping it.

You might be surprised to learn that a goodly number of the hospital employees and attending physicians interviewed for this book see nothing all that wrong with the rooms you get at hospitals these days. One particularly stark, antiseptically futuristic intensive care unit room was deemed "beautiful" by a physician on his rounds. Even rooms that look like detention cells for political prisoners get high marks.

This points up an important fact about your hospital room. Though you are paying for it, it was designed neither for your comfort nor your aesthetic pleasure. It was designed for the doctors'

and nurses' convenience. That you might want pleasant surroundings to mitigate the otherwise unpleasant aspects of your stay is
truly a minor consideration.

Let's take a look at the typical room and its amenities. Not very
pretty. But here are some tips on how you can improve it.

The Windows. In a hospital there is no guarantee that you will
feel no pain; you can almost be sure, however, that you will *see* no
pane. Many hospital room windows are frosted, dirty, too small,
ill positioned, unopenable, and/or blocked by drawn curtains.
What good is a window that sheds no light, has no view, and
cannot be opened? Just another example of how hospitals are designed for the convenience and cost efficiency of the institution
(big windows need to be washed, sunlight fades fabrics) and not
the comfort of the patient.

Being able to gaze out a window onto a pleasant scene is not only
a happy state of affairs for the patient, but it may actually be
therapeutic and economically sound, too. A researcher at the University of Delaware who studied records of patients at a suburban
Pennsylvania hospital found that "23 surgical patients assigned to
rooms with windows looking out on a natural scene had shorter
postoperative hospital stays, received fewer negative evaluative
comments in nurses' notes, and took fewer potent analgesics than
23 matched patients in similar rooms with windows facing a brick
building wall." Some people don't even have a brick wall to
look at.

Ask that the curtains on your room's windows be drawn and the
shades pulled up. Ask to be placed in a bed near that window so
you can look out of it and not just at the privacy curtain pulled
around the bed of your roommate. If the windows are openable, and
the weather is nice outside—and if your medical condition allows—
get those windows open to let in some non-climate-controlled air.

If it is important to you to be near a window, to look outside, to
breathe fresh air, to see a tree and not the air-conditioning duct
work on the roof of the hospital annex, insist on it.

The Floor. It is usually a neutral-colored vinyl tile; carpeting
would wear out, would be more difficult to keep clean, would need
periodic and costly replacing, and it would slow down fast-moving
carts and gurneys.

The vinyl is almost always cold (that is why slippers were on the
bring-to-the-hospital list) and can be dangerous because it is frequently slick. When water or other liquids have been spilled on it
and form hard-to-see patches, it becomes as slippery as a hockey
rink. Wear the slippers and be careful!

RESENTMENT IS BUILDING

"It recently occurred to me that we have reached a crisis in idiotic and inhuman architecture," began a letter in the *Canadian Medical Association Journal*.

The target of the wrath was hospitals.

The thought came to the writer as he looked at a bleak, uncomfortable room for laboring mothers. "The three beds were along one wall, so that the mother looked at an entirely blank wall. What were the architects thinking of?"

The answer: pleasing the big shots. "Top management . . . gets a window and often a corner," the letter writer noted. "The architect meets the administration and board of management; hence administration and boardrooms have windows and taste."

The letter writer concluded that what it really all boils down to is money, a certain "financial reflex action" on the part of the architects and probably the hospital administrators. "The outside, the view of the landscape and sky, is free. Accordingly, unless and until they can figure a way to charge money for looking at it, the buildings will remain windowless.

Dirt, plain and simple, is another underfoot hazard. Dust and grime lurking on the floors, in the corners, around chair legs, are breeding grounds for organisms that can enter open wounds and cause infections that might add days to your stay.

If your room is noticeably messy, alert the maintenance person, and watch to be sure the problem is taken care of to your satisfaction. If that does no good, complain to your doctor, nurse, patient's representative, or any hospital higher-up who can get things moving.

The Walls. The good news is that hospitals are slowly but surely doing away with institutional green walls. The bad news is somebody has invented institutional orange. There are other similarly dreary shades of paint and wall coverings proliferating as well.

You can't do much about the walls themselves, but you can improve what is on them. Suppose your room is decorated with some sort of wall art—a print, a poster, a reproduction of a painting, or an original—that is not to your liking. Having to stare at a bad or annoying work when you are confined with it can really get to you. This is not petty nit-picking. It might even agitate you to the point of slowing down the healing process. Talk to your roommate about your feelings and see if he or she agrees. Then call in the nurse and ask to have the offending piece removed. If that is against hospital policy, don't make a fuss. Nod understandingly. Then have one of your first visitors unhook the monstrosity and shove it deep into your closet. Should anybody notice its absence, play dumb. Return it to its place when you leave.

You might want to consider bringing some art of your own (possibly a poster or something religious, if you believe that will help you pull through) to replace that offending object if your stay will be longer than a few days. First, ask the hospital staff for permission to do so, with a promise that your picture will hang from the hook already on the wall. It wouldn't be nice to pound another hole into the nice new institutional pink surface.

In sections of hospitals where young people are placed, their home bedroom art, featuring the latest teenage idols and heart-throbs, is often put up around their hospital room. It helps to make the scary and alien hospital world seem a bit more "right" and homelike. Adults can benefit from it just as kids do.

Be sure to mark the piece with your ID and don't bring anything you could not bear to have stolen.

The Ceiling. You will come to know this ceiling as well as you will ever know anything during your hospital experience. While waiting (or which there is plenty), while reading, when you awake each morning, when you open your eyes post-op—there it will be, bland and featureless.

There are several things you can do to improve your overhead view. Ceilings are just walls hung above you. You can have a poster or mobile attached for your stay. It gives you something to ponder besides white acoustic tile.

Some folks—maybe you—are bothered by headaches and eye aches from the hum and flicker and "cool" shades of fluorescent lighting. If your room is lighted by flourescent tubes and you are fluorescent-sensitive in some way, get those lights turned off and kept off. Explain the situation to your doctor and the nursing staff. Ask for an extra table lamp or two with incandescent bulbs (perhaps three-way) as a replacement. The room will immediately feel cozier and a little more homelike. A little. Also ask that the curtains and shades be pulled away from the windows, so that you can use natural lighting as long as the day allows.

If your roommate just loves fluorescent lighting, explain your situation. If that doesn't help, demand a room change. A private room may be the only viable alternative. It will probably cost you extra, and the availability of such rooms is limited. If you can afford it and it is worth it to you, be persistent.

The TV. What did hospital patients do before the advent of TV? History tells us that they read books, wrote letters or poems or essays, related to the people around them, thought about things. Thank goodness television was invented—and not a moment too soon.

Television in a hospital room is an electronic baby-sitter, a mind-distracter, and a paradox: a boring way to chase away boredom. As paradoxes go, it is not a cheap one. You have to pay rent for that set, and it can add up over a long stay. It is up to you to find out the price and determine if it is worth it to you.

Ideally, each occupant has his own set. If you must share a single TV set with others in a room, pray that you and your roommates can agree on programs and on quiet times minus TV noise and flicker. Conflicts over TV—"Masterpiece Theater" versus "Wheel of Fortune"—can lead to real anxieties and bad feelings among all those in the room. Wars have started over less. If an amicable agreement cannot be achieved, get your room changed.

Extra Charges. Be careful about asking for anything extra in the hospital, because you might be charged an arm and a leg for it. That goes for just about anything you might innocently request, or receive as a kind gesture during your stay. Even a Band-Aid. In the hospital, there is no such thing as a free anything.

The Bed. It will be a typical hospital issue. It goes up, it goes down, it bends. The mattress is semicomfortable and the pillow is worse. But be careful about asking for a second pillow—even if you always sleep two-high, because you might be charged some exorbitant amount for it, for the reasons given in the preceding paragraph.

Bring your own pillow from home? Might be a good idea. But beware: While you are in the bathroom, the bed might be changed and all the linen—including your favorite pillow—will end up in the laundry room, never to be seen again.

You will notice the set of rails attached to the side of your bed. They are raised to protect hospital patients—especially the elderly—from getting hurt by falling out of bed. But Howard S. Rubenstein, M.D., an internist and chief of the allergy clinic at University Health Services, Harvard University, has warned that a large number of hospital patients are injured while trying to climb over these rails to go to the bathroom.

"Why are bed rails routinely used in the United States in caring for the hospitalized elderly, despite a lack of evidence that they protect the patient, and despite abundant evidence suggesting they may be hazardous?" asked Rubenstein in a 1984 *Medical World News* essay. Then he suggested, "Their use may stem more from fear of liability than from consideration of patient welfare." Just who are hospitals protecting?

In England, Rubenstein noted, the people who run hospitals have concluded that routine use of bed rails for elderly patients is not a good idea. British health investigators discovered that "the risk of an elderly patient's falling without the 'protection' of elevated bed rails was low."

Does your hospital's policy require bed rails up at night? For everybody? Will this potentially get in the way of your habits, not to mention your personal freedom? Do the rails being up make you feel claustrophobic? Are they in some way demeaning to you? Discuss it with your doctor, nurse, and patients' representative. Don't sign any forms that release the hospital from liability for falls from bed that you might have. Don't sign *anything* in a hospital unless you are sure that it is to your advantage.

The Buzzer. In most up-to-date hospitals the buzzer or call button is now part of a little control panel, located somewhere around the bed, that might also control the television and adjust the bed.

Call buttons signal the nurses' station, and some allow the person at the station to ask you what you need through a speaker by your bed.

Once you get settled in your room, try out the buttons. If there is a break in the communications link between you and the nurses' station, it is crucial to find out now, not when you really need help. But don't just hop into bed and start pushing buttons. Tell the nurses that you will be testing your control panel, so they can help you determine if anything is out of order.

Don't spend time in a bed whose bedside call button doesn't work. If it cannot be fixed immediately, get another bed. (Check the call button in the bathroom, too.)

The Telephone. Hospitals have varying telephone policies. At the time of admission, have all applicable phone-related add-on charges explained to you in detail. Some hospitals permit you to make outgoing calls all day and all night, while others cut off phone service at a certain nighttime hour. Most don't allow incoming calls past midevening. Find out what your hospital does. Check on the charges for phone calls, both those you make and those you receive. Some hospitals actually charge *you* for the calls made to you by someone else. It might be cheaper to bring your own cellular phone, if you have one.

When you are settled in the room, make sure the telephone works and find out if everybody in the room has his or her own phone. If sharing is involved, it could be a problem, especially if you are rooming with a phone hog. Even when there are individual telephones, a roommate who is always on the phone, speaking loudly,

laughing coarsely, and chatting feverishly about very personal affairs can drive you nuts. Have the nurse ask the loudmouth to keep
it down.

Your telephone is also a link to the hospital departments. Got a
problem? Get on the horn and call the patients' representative or the
administrator's office.

Your phone can act as a call button backup system, too. If nobody
at the nurses' station responds to your buzz, pick up the phone and
call them. They will probably think it is a doctor calling, pick it up,
and be surprised (if not entirely delighted) to hear that it is you.
They may tell you never to do that again, but don't listen to them.
Always use the buzzer first, but if you get no response after three
rings or five minutes, phone the nurses' station. If that doesn't work,
and if it is important enough, call your doctor at his office or home
and describe what is happening. It won't make you friends, but it
will get things moving—especially if you mention that your next
call will be to your lawyer.

It is painfully obvious that there is no comparison between hotel
rooms and hospital rooms. In a hospital, the accommodations are
less plush, less comfortable, and less quiet; in a hotel, room service
isn't in the habit of showing up at 1 A.M. to take your temperature.
Some people find that recovering in a hotel room (at least for the
tail end of the recovery period) is a far better experience than spend-
ing that time in a hospital. Norman Cousins, former editor of the
Saturday Review, now at the UCLA Medical School, felt that way. He
discovered that the hotel cost was only a third of what it would have
been in the hospital. The "benefits were incalculable," he said, and
"the sense of serenity was delicious and would, I felt certain, contribute to a general improvement." It is something to think about.

But most of us who are in the hospital can't or won't do what
Cousins did. We stay in the hospital. Therefore, it is up to us to fight
for the best possible room they can provide—and to change rooms
if what we get isn't what we need. The hospital folks won't like it
(there is lots of paperwork and other red tape involved in moving
you even one room over), and they will try their darndest to talk
you out of it or tell you it is impossible. Stick to your guns. You are
paying for it.

THE NATIVES

The medical world keeps coming up with new medical specialities
as quickly as they come up with new things to find wrong with you.
Any number of these specialists might end up consulting on your

case (remember the questions to ask about specialists in chapter 1), and many times it is money well spent. The surgeon who calls in a cardiologist to determine if your heart is strong enough to keep on ticking through the administering of anesthesia, an operation, and the recovery period (and seeing the bill for all of this), is doing you an important service. Sometimes, though, it's the ol' "you scratch my patient, I'll scratch yours, and we'll both collect some scratch from the insurance company."

It is important to know exactly what each specialist does—by specialty. Who does what where? Why should you be billed for the opinion of an ear specialist when the problem is in your foot? Granted, such a conniving consult doesn't happen often, but it does happen. If it happens to you once, that is once too often. You can protect yourself from such fraud by consulting this list of the hospital's native subcultures: physicians from head to toe.

The Headhunters

1. *Plastic Surgeon.* Restores and rebuilds body parts damaged or destroyed by accident or disease; corrects or improves structures that don't live up to the individual's or society's standards. The indicator in the illustration points to the face and head because plastic surgeons do much of their work in this area: rhytidectomy (face-lift), blepharoplasty (eyelid surgery), rhinoplasty (nose job), otoplasty (change of shape or display of ears), hair transplant, dermabrasion and chemical peel (removal of skin layers to make wrinkles and scars fade or disappear), mentoplasty (restructuring of jaws and chins), skin grafts. Of course, plastic surgeons also rework problems in other parts of the body, breast enlargement or reduction (mammaplasty) and "tummy tucks" among them.

2. *Otorhinolaryngologist.* This is the ENT—ear, nose, and throat—specialist who explores problems and treats disease in those three interrelated portions of the body.

3. *Psychiatrist.* The psychiatrist is involved in examining, treating, and preventing mental illness. (Do not confuse this specialist with the nonphysician psychologist.) A psychiatrist's repertoire may include everything from the noninvasive (psychoanalysis) to the pharmaceutical; his or her observations and diagnoses may determine that the problem may be relieved only through surgery.

4. *Neurologist.* This doctor is involved with the diagnosis and treatment of nervous system disorders.

5. *Neurosurgeon.* Surgery on the nervous system (the brain, spinal cord, and nerves) is this doctor's field of expertise.

6. *Ophthalmologist.* The ophthalmologist diagnoses and treats diseases of and injuries to the eye. He or she can perform cataract removals and retina reattachments, among other operations.

7. *Allergist.* As the name implies, this specialist is involved in the diagnosis and treatment of allergies. Allergists often subspecialize in a single allergy. The indicator in the illustration (page 96) points to the nose as the allergist's primary area of expertise, because hay fever and other conditions caused by airborne substances do make up a lot of his or her practice. However, this specialist also examines and treats asthma cases and skin problems all over the body (for example, hives and contact dermatitis).

The Body Politic

1. *Nephrologist.* Deals with diseases of the kidney.

2. *Cardiologist.* This specialist diagnoses and treats heart disease. He or she may perform cardiac catheterization (snaking a catheter through a vein or artery and on into the heart to take certain measurements and examine heart structures) and pacemaker implantation. The cardiologist may also oversee the administration of stress tests, among other procedures.

3. *Endocrinologist.* This specialist's field includes the diagnosis and treatment of disorders of the endocrine glands. Although the indicator in the illustration points to the general head and neck area—where the pituitary, thyroid, and parathyroids are—endocrine glands in other parts of the body include the ovaries, testes, thymus, and the pancreas's islands of Langerhans. (The islands of Langerhans secrete insulin, which explains why endocrinologists are involved in the treatment of diabetes.) They also treat problems of obesity.

4. *Thoracic Surgeon.* This doctor performs operations on the heart and major vessels and the lungs. Surgical procedures on the trachea and esophagus also fall within the scope of this physician's specialty, as do operations to repair hiatal hernias.

5. *Gastroenterologist.* Diagnoses and treats problems of the stomach and intestines, the gastrointestinal tract.

The Southern Contingent

1. *Urologist.* Diagnoses and treats diseases of the urinary system, as well as the organs of reproduction in men, such as the prostate.

2. *Gynecologist.* Diagnoses and treats problems associated with the female reproductive organs.

3. *Obstetrician.* Specializes in the medical aspects of and intervention in pregnancy and labor.

4. *Proctologist.* This physician deals with diseases of the anus, rectum, and colon.

5. *Orthopedist.* This doctor's domain includes the treatment and correction, usually surgically, of deformities or damage to the musculoskeletal system. Although the indicator in the illustration (page 96) points to the leg area, orthopedic surgeons (sometimes referred to as orthopods) work on bone, muscle, and ligament problems all over the body.

The Society at Large

1. *Anesthesiologist.* This is the physician responsible for the safe dispensing of anesthetics, usually to patients undergoing surgical procedures. The anesthesiologist monitors the patient's condition and vital signs vis-à-vis the anesthesia.

2. *Dermatologist.* Skin problems, diagnosis and treatment thereof, are the specialty here.

3. *Emergency Medicine Specialist.* One of the newest of board-certified specialties, this doctor's focus is on the medical expertise required in emergency room situations.

4. *Geriatrician.* Deals with diseases of the elderly and problems associated with aging. Besides looking at and treating strictly medical conditions, the geriatrician gets involved in the psychological and social well-being of the elderly patient, and in that way acts as a sort of medical social worker.

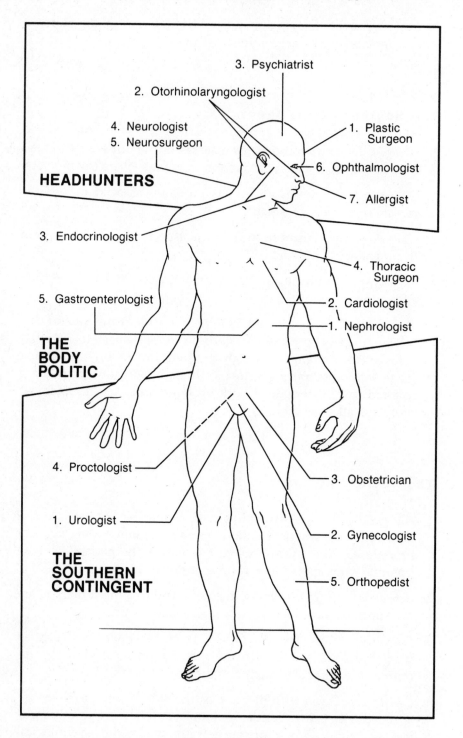

HEADHUNTERS

3. Psychiatrist

2. Otorhinolaryngologist

4. Neurologist
5. Neurosurgeon

1. Plastic Surgeon

6. Ophthalmologist

7. Allergist

3. Endocrinologist

4. Thoracic Surgeon

5. Gastroenterologist

2. Cardiologist

1. Nephrologist

THE BODY POLITIC

4. Proctologist

3. Obstetrician

1. Urologist

2. Gynecologist

THE SOUTHERN CONTINGENT

5. Orthopedist

A *gerontologist* is a physician-scientist who studies the aging process.

5. *Hematologist.* This specialist diagnoses and treats diseases and disorders of the blood and blood-forming parts of the body.

6. *Immunologist.* This doctor's wide-ranging specialty takes in the study and treatment of problems of the body's immune system, which may include allergies, infections, and life-threatening diseases, such as AIDS (Acquired Immune Deficiency Syndrome).

7. *Internist.* Specializes in the diagnosis and nonsurgical treatment of diseases, especially those of adults. While internists may set up practices in which they act as highly trained family doctors, they often subspecialize in many other areas.

8. *Oncologist.* This doctor deals with tumors and other cancers; he or she is sometimes also a hematologist.

9. *Pediatrician.* This specialist diagnoses and treats diseases of childhood, and monitors the growth, development, and well-being of preadolescents.

10. *Radiologist.* Specializes in the study and use of various types of radiation, including X rays, in the diagnosis and treatment of disease.

11. *Rheumatologist.* The concerns of this physician include the diagnosis and treatment of inflammation, deterioration, and other painful problems (such as arthritis) having to do with the joints and connective tissues.

DRESS

The hospital gown is to clothing what the Volkswagen Beetle was to automobiles: kind of short, not all that pretty, but efficient—and air-cooled, too. The hospital gown is also the great equalizer. The mightiest plutocrat and the lowliest beggar look pretty much the same in one.

Not for the modest, the hospital gown is easy to put on (although it's difficult to tell which end is up, which side is front, and how many portions of your anatomy can be covered at any one time), easy to take off, and easy for authorized hospital personnel to get into to take your temperature, your blood pressure, some of your bodily fluids, and more than a smidgen of your dignity. It's one more example of a hospital product designed for *their* convenience, not your comfort.

But what can you do? A hospital gown does speed up routine pokes and probes. It is uncannily efficient. Still, if wearing the darn thing with its peekaboo lines embarrasses you, don't wear it all the time. Or wear two of them. Put one on their way, with the open part in the rear; put the other one on the way normal human beings wear a robe with the open section up front. That way the pokers and probers can still get to wherever they need to delve and you have retained a certain level of modesty. Slip into your pajamas when you stroll, when you see visitors. Short-sleeve sleepwear is preferable, to allow a blood pressure cuff to be slung around your biceps at a moment's notice. Put the gown on again before going to bed for the night, if your regular sleepwear might interfere with necessary access to your body by the staff, or with your comfort in bed.

GETTING AROUND

There are three types of hospital transport: mandatory, voluntary, and hit-and-run. Mandatory has to do with doctor's orders—you have to walk as part of your recovery process. Voluntary means you decide to get up, take a walk, look around. Hit-and-run describes the way attendants foray into your room to announce that you are wanted in X ray or Cardiology or wherever, pack you into a wheelchair, and whisk you off to a rendezvous with technology. Hospitals are the only place where you do not hail public transportation—it hails you.

When a hospital employee comes to shuttle you off to some eagerly waiting machine in another part of the building, hospital policy might require that you use the wheelchair for legal reasons. If you have a choice, walk instead. Activate those muscles. It will help to prevent bedsores and other problems associated with a sedentary life-style. If the attendant insists that you ride—and if his insistence is based more on his own convenience or a desire to speed things up than on what is good for you—ignore him. Walk if you want to.

Take a walk whenever you feel like it (except late at night or at mealtime). That is another reason to bring your slippers along, as well as a robe and pajamas.

Some hospitals have a special lounge area for patients, or a veranda for good-weather days. Go there for a change of scene. Go to these places with your visitors so they don't have to see you in bed. Sit in these havens to think, to knit, to read (the light is probably better there, too), to nap. For an hour or so you can put to one side the fact that you are in a hospital. Then you can walk back.

If your hospital has no sitting areas for patients, get up and walk around anyway. When you get out of bed and step out of your room, strolling not only improves your constitution, but it is a clear declaration of independence.

THE MARKETPLACE

If at all possible, do not buy anything in the hospital or at the hospital gift shop.

Out of toothpaste? Need a comb? Get a friend or relative to buy it for you at a place where they charge prices that are within the range of reality. This applies also to the candy bars and assorted stuffed or stitched doodads and flowers that are the staples of hospital gift shops.

You might think that with all the overcharging going on in other key areas of the hospital, a patient would get a bit of a break on supplies and munchies.

No way.

THE FOOD

So few positive things have ever, in the history of the world, been said about hospital food, it would only be redundant to go into how unappealing, awful-tasting, and unaesthetic these alleged comestibles are. It does make a lot of sense, however, to go to the heart of the real hospital food problem: the poor level of nourishment it provides. Michael A. Weiner precisely explains the situation in his book *The Way of the Skeptical Nutritionist* (New York: Macmillan, 1981):

> The majority of patients who are hospitalized, even if they have not come to the hospital malnourished, develop malnourishment within seven to ten days of hospitalization. . . . Instead of people becoming

revitalized, they become progressively rundown and malnourished; in fact, the malnourishment can extend to the point where they become *more* susceptible to various diseases, especially the highly infectious. . . . a considerable amount of the so-called posthospitalization weakness or asthenia is not only due to bed rest but is a manifestation of malnourishment that occurs within the hospital.

Granted, some people, especially the elderly, arrive at the hospital with an already existent malnutrition problem. Still, hospital food provides few of them with nutritional support for improvement or recovery. They eat more and allegedly "better" food served in the hospital, yet their malnutrition profiles only get worse, until some condition or another, exacerbated by the food situation, does them in.

Here are some other points about hospital-induced malnutrition to keep in mind:

▶ An estimated 50,000 preventable hospital deaths per year in the United States are caused by malnutrition.

▶ Much of the malnutrition may be the result of drug side effects, and many hospital dietitians are ignorant of the interaction between drugs and nutrients. Patients taking some types of blood pressure medication, for example, suffer a depletion of magnesium, which is often not replenished in the food they get on the hospital tray. Cardiac arrhythmias are a classic response to magnesium deficiency.

▶ The ordinary hospital diet appears to be "balanced" and seems to include "the four basic food groups." In reality, the diet is unbalanced and it lags about forty years behind current enlightened thinking on the subject of food.

▶ In *Anatomy of an Illness as Perceived by the Patient* (New York: Norton, 1979), Norman Cousins decried the quality of the food he received in the hospital. "What seemed inexcusable to me was the profusion of processed foods, some of which contained preservatives or harmful dyes," he wrote. "White bread, with its chemical softeners and bleached flour, was offered with every meal. Vegetables were often overcooked and thus deprived of much of their nutritional value."

▶ Disease itself alters the way the body accepts and uses nutrients. A health problem can increase a person's nutritional needs. This is especially so among the elderly, and it continues over the course of the disease. Yet many dietitians are unaware of this added nutritional requirement, or they have never been taught how to adjust patient's diets accordingly.

▶ Hospital kitchens (or the food services and catering businesses that make the meals and ship them to the hospital) create standardized meals. There is the boilerplate diabetic meal, the low-salt meal, the low-fat meal, etc. The problem with this, according to an editorial in the January 14, 1984 issue of the *British Medical Journal* is that "people differ in their nutritional needs. Tables of recommended intakes or nutrients do not apply to individuals, so that it is difficult to be certain that their diet satisfied their requirements."

▶ According to experts, protein-calorie malnutrition in U.S. hospitals is so bad that at least 30 percent of patients in them are malnourished. Among these, so many have lost enough weight that their chance of surviving the operation they need is 5 percent. And if they stay in the hospital long enough, they begin to show the same nutrition-based health deterioration problems as those found in citizens of Third World nations.

▶ Most studies agree that if a patient's malnutrition is alleviated, the length of his hospital stay will decrease, thus saving money for all of us.

Determine who is in charge of your nutritional health when you are at the hospital. Is it the doctor or the dietitian? Sometimes neither takes responsibility—the doctor doesn't know what to do, and the dietitian waits for the doctor's orders—and the patient suffers from the waffling.

It is shocking to learn that many physicians and hospital staffs have little or no knowledge of the important role nutrition and good food play in the recovery scenario of a patient. Even more shocking, as Stanley J. Dudrick, M.D., recalls in a 1984 article in *Forbes,* was an instance when a hospital administrator tried to improve a facility's profit-and-loss margin by cutting down the size of the patients' meals. All the more reason why consumers need to monitor their own nutritional well-being.

Sickly patients rarely get any help with eating their meals. Once most food handlers or nurses' aides deliver the food, they leave. If you don't eat, don't depend on the staff to be alarmed or to alert anyone about it, even if several meals in a row are returned uneaten. (Sometimes, though, nurses don't know that the patient hasn't eaten, because a hungry visitor or the patient in the next bed has helped himself to the contents of the tray. This is a real danger to the patient who isn't eating.)

Self-Defense Measures

What can you do to protect yourself from trouble with hospital food?

Try to Get Yourself Into a Hospital that Serves Good Food. You may end up feeling like a dietary Diogenes, wandering with lantern in hand, looking in vain for an honest meal. If you ask questions, visit kitchens, look at menus, and sample the food, you might come up with something good, or at least something tolerable.

Be Sure You Get the Food You're Supposed to Get. This means discussing your diet and nutritional requirements with somebody who really knows about these things. Don't assume that your doctor is the right person for this. Doctors are notoriously underinformed when it comes to nutrition. Most doctors have never taken a class in nutrition; even now, in the medical schools that offer it, nutrition is an elective course. The hospital dietitian might have more to offer. Perhaps. If there is anybody at the hospital with nutritional experience—a nurse, perhaps—try to arrange for a nutritional counseling session and provide your dietary history, if your doctor hasn't taken one.

Check on the food you are served to be sure it is what you should have or what you have ordered. Mix-ups do occur. And if your meal is supposed to be hot, it should be hot; if it's supposed to be cold, then it ought to be cold. You are paying for these meals. They must be the right food at the right temperature. If they aren't raise a ruckus.

When it comes to eating well enough in a hospital to stay alive and get better, you might have to risk losing your hospital wing's Mr. or Miss Congeniality contest. If the hospital employees aren't willing or able to take responsibility for you and your nutritional concerns, you will have to take that responsibility yourself by asking questions and demanding answers.

Take Appropriate Vitamin and Mineral Supplements in Appropriate Doses. "It may be advisable to consider vitamin supplementation for hospital patients, especially those on restricted diets or with limited appetites, whose needs may not be met with institutional foods." That admonition from the home economics research center of Washington State University at Pullman appeared in the June 1983 issue of the *Journal of the American Dietetic Association.* Many others concur.

Ask your nutritional consultant which vitamins or minerals you should be taking to ward off possible deficiencies. Find out dosage, frequency, and whether to take them with meals or before or after.

Get these supplements from a neighborhood pharmacy, health food store, or some other establishment. Do not let the doctor or anybody else talk you into buying them at the hospital, for you will be vastly overcharged for vitamin and mineral pills or capsules that are no better than those you could buy on your own.

Make sure the doctor marks on your chart that you are to be given your own vitamins, or that the supplements are to stay in your possession so you can take them yourself. Don't let anybody give you anything that isn't yours. Keep track of what you get (in the chart provided at the back of this book) to be sure you aren't charged for what you never received.

Bring Your Own Food. Talk it over with your doctor and your nurses. Tell them that you intend either to replace the meals offered by the hospital or to supplement them. Don't *ask* the doctor or nurse if this is OK to do—*tell* them it is what you intend to do. Ask their advice about which foods to avoid and which to include. Follow their advice when it seems sound; be prepared to reject their advice if it doesn't make sense.

Prepare the meals ahead of your admission to the hospital or, if that's not possible, have your visitors drop by with good food and drink. Have them bring the food in containers labeled with your name for storage in a nearby refrigerator. Arrange with the nursing staff for this food delivery and storage. Be sure a notation is made on your chart and that all of the staff involved in food handling and distribution know about it.

Ask to reserve a regular space in the fridge for your things. Be considerate; don't expect room for mounds of edibles or anything extralarge—no whole watermelons, please—and don't pack anything that needs freezing. Bring a little bit extra of the extraspecial goodies to share with the staff. It is a nice gesture that shows you appreciate the trouble they are going to for you. Also, it's a bit of a bribe and an insurance policy.

Of course, if you are planning to eat only your food, you won't be eating theirs. So why pay for it? Call in the hospital administrator or the patients' representative and see if you can work out some sort of a reduction in your daily room charge. The administrator will resist this agreement as passionately as he would a request that he join you on the operating table. But make your points, press forward with your reasoning. You might get some kind of a discount deal or rebate. If you do, have it put in writing. Every promise of extraordinary service made to you by a hospital employee ought to be put in writing.

While we are discussing food in a hospital setting, take note of this important warning: If you are receiving radiation or drug therapies for cancer, beware of certain foods, especially salads and raw vegetables. Even though these garden items may be washed thoroughly, some strains of bacteria that could endanger you in your immunosuppressed state are still alive and well and hiding in the crevices. According to researchers from the Stanford University and University of Maryland schools of medicine, "nearly 50 percent of infections in cancer patients have been shown to be caused by hospital-acquired organisms which have colonized the patients' digestive tract." And infection in a cancer patient is a major danger.

Choking to death on hospital food is not a frequent occurrence, but it happens often enough to warrant a few warnings—especially since hospital staffs have been known to confuse the symptoms of choking with the symptoms of heart attack and perform the wrong emergency procedures on the distressed individual. To avoid the threat of choking, you should sit up while you are eating (especially if you are elderly, because old age often slows down the reflexes of the throat and larynx). You should also chew the food well (and, if you have no teeth, few teeth, or ill-fitting dentures, make sure there are no large chunks of meat in your meal). Avoid eating if you have just been sedated, because sedatives dull the centers of your brain that control swallowing.

THE VISITING TROOPS

A hospital room is not the den in your private home. Quiet, a certain amount of decorum, consideration for the person in the other bed and *his* or *her* visitors—these are the basics.

▶ Try to stay within the visitation guidelines. True, these rules are often arbitrary, and many of them are designed more for the staff's convenience than for your personal needs. But in most cases it is best to abide by them.

► In most hospitals visiting hours are fairly generous (except in intensive care units, where limits on time and numbers of guests generally make sense). However, if you are scared, lonely, or worried about tomorrow's procedure, then it is your right as a patient and as a fragile human being to have your visitor or visitors stay with you past visiting hours. Perhaps you need your visitor to spend the night nearby. If the nurse tries to send your visitor away, stand your ground. Ask to see the head nurse. If you are not satisfied, demand to see the patients' representative or the hospital administrator, no matter what time it is. If you must, call your doctor at home, and then your lawyer. You can have somebody there with you past hours if you want. The rules be damned.

► Your visitors certainly can pour water into a glass for you or regulate the thermostat. Beyond such favors, it is the staff's job to tend to you. They are paid to do it, and they should do it for many reasons, not the least of which are legal considerations.

► Be sure *you*, not one of your visitors, request or demand service from the nurses or others. Having your visitors do this confuses and infuriates the nurses and is downright dangerous for you. It damages your image as an assertive, knowledgeable medical consumer.

► If you do not want visitors, don't have them. Ask the staff to arrange for this.

4

WHAT
THE WISE
TRAVELER
KNOWS

Seasoned travelers learn to be ready for trouble. They know what to do if luggage gets lost, hotel reservations aren't honored, guides don't deliver as promised, or prepaid meals are inedible. They know how to avoid the common pitfalls and how to get satisfaction when a costly trip doesn't live up to the brochure's promise. Old hands at the hospital tour learn to anticipate trouble, too. They know that one's lab test results can be confused with others, nurses can deliver the wrong medications, infections can be picked up from hospital personnel, and important rights might be relinquished in consent forms.

This chapter will save you from learning the hard way. It will show you how to take care of yourself before your safety or your rights are endangered.

WHERE AND HOW
TO COMPLAIN

When it comes to lodging, hospitals and hotels, as we have seen, are establishments of a different hue. When it comes to complaining, however, a hospital and a restaurant are comparable.

In a restaurant, when you have problems with the food or the seats, you complain to the chef or the waiter or the boss (or to the friend who sent you there by highly recommending the place). When you think there are major sanitation or related problems affecting your health and the well-being of every customer, you get in touch with your city's board of health.

In a hospital, when the food or service or any of various care

functions are bothering you, you talk to the people directly responsible and then go up the chain of command to the hospital administrator, if necessary, until your gripe is satisfactorily laid to rest. (You
may have to bring your doctor into the proceedings and demand
that he use his clout to help resolve the situation.)

But when there are major defects in the way the hospital is run,
you have to go to an outside authority to get things straight. If there
are health hazards, if there are safety code violations, if there are
employees who you believe are dangerous to patients or who have
harmed you—or if there are conditions or policies in the hospital that
you are convinced break the law and/or endanger the lives of the
people in the facility and may have put yours in jeopardy—you need
to make a formal complaint to the appropriate government agency.

Since all hospitals are licensed by the state, complaints about
hospital facilities and upkeep (fire safety, square footage of rooms,
infection control, dirty rooms and halls, and similar conditions)
should be addressed to your state's department of hospital/facilities
licensing.

If your complaint is about the unprofessional behavior or inade-
quacy of doctors, nurses, or medical technicians, contact the appropriate regulatory agency: for doctors, the Board of Medical
Examiners; for nurses, the Board of Nurse Examiners; for technicians, the Office of Occupational or Professional Licensing. The
People's Medical Society will be glad to supply the addresses and
phone numbers for these agencies in your state. Contact: PMS, 462
Walnut Street, Allentown, PA 18102 (Phone: [215] 770-1670).

Should your complaint have to do with billing, you can and
should contact your insurance company. If you suspect that
charges or discrepancies in your bill are no accident but represent
a criminal act on the hospital's part, contact your state attorney
general's office.

Your complaints, addressed to the proper licensing agency (you
might want to call that agency and find out the name of the person
who reviews complaints and address all information to him or her),
should be in writing and include the following:

▶ Name of the institution/individuals you are complaining
   about

▶ Nature of the complaint (describe what happened—include
   important details, but keep the letter to the point)

▶ When it occurred (date and time)

Dear PMS,

In the December issue you gave the telephone number of the Inspector General's Hotline to report incidents of Medicare and Medicaid fraud, abuse, and waste: (800) 368-5779 (in Maryland: [800] 638-3986).

While I think it is a good idea, I think it is better to give the address of the inspector general. Some people could better write their complaints instead of calling.

A. S., Brooklyn, New York

(ED. NOTE: You're absolutely right. Here it is: Office of the Inspector General, 5250 HHS North Building, 330 Independence Avenue SW, Washington, DC 20201.)

▶ Names of witnesses, if any; statements of these witnesses, if possible

▶ Copies of documents, if any, that support your claim.

Your letter might follow this form:

> Dear (Commissioner/Secretary/Director/Chairman),
>   I am writing to file a formal complaint against (name of person or institution or both), arising from an incident in which I believe I was wronged. I am requesting that a full administrative review process be initiated so that I may be given a complete hearing. I can provide documentation to support my complaint. Also, I will cooperate fully with the investigating officer assigned to my case.
>   I will briefly describe what happened and why I believe I am justified in filing this complaint. (Relate here exactly what happened.)
>   I await your reply. I will gladly complete any additional forms, if necessary. Your assistance in this matter is appreciated.
> Your signature
> Name
> Address
> Phone number

Even though you are fired up and want action fast, let us not forget that you are discussing an institution with yet another institution. Such entities do not act quickly. Expect to wait thirty to sixty days before you hear any sort of response to your complaint.

If the licensing board feels there is merit in your charges, they will prepare a full review. If your complaint does not strike them as an extremely serious one, it is possible the board could recommend some action that will be agreeable to you and the party against whom you lodged the complaint. If, however, yours is seen as a more serious matter, the board will appoint a hearing officer who will collect additional materials. A hearing will be scheduled, and you will be called to give your side of the story.

At the hearing, which in some ways is similar to a court proceeding, testimony is taken from all parties. Consider having an attorney present to help you.

When the session is concluded, the hearing officer reviews all testimony, and will issue his findings, usually within a month. These findings could be anything from dismissal of your complaint to a recommendation for disciplinary action against the practitioner or institution. It is also possible that a settlement will be recommended, and the offending party ordered to make good.

But what if you don't get the satisfaction you want from the hearing? Is that all there is?

Not quite. You may decide to pursue your case in court by instituting a malpractice suit. First, consult with a competent attorney who can advise you of your chances for success.

PATIENTS' RIGHTS

This whole book is about your rights as a hospital patient. It would not have been needed if you were receiving the benefits of those rights as a matter of course—or if you even knew what those rights were.

Therefore, the following document ought to be of some interest. It is "A Patient's Bill of Rights," a list thought up by the American Hospital Association in 1973. If your hospital is an AHA member, you should have been handed a brochure with the "Bill of Rights" in it when you were admitted, or before.

As manifestos go, it is not a bad one. The hospitals that hand it out ought to read it occasionally . . . or once.

Though vague and open to interpretation in places, and though not reviewed or updated to reflect possible changes in the hospital world since its adoption, it is still of value as a bargaining tool, and as an implicit contract between the hospital and you.

To obtain these rights, however, may require some action to ensure that they are not honored more in the breach than in the observance. It is important to see these twelve points as a bill of rights for *consumers,* which implies activism, rather than a bill of

A PATIENT'S BILL OF RIGHTS

The American Hospital Association presents "A Patient's Bill of Rights" with the expectation that observance of these rights will contribute to more effective patient care and greater satisfaction for the patient, his physician, and the hospital organization. Further, the association presents these rights in the expectation that they will be supported by the hospital on behalf of its patients as an integral part of the healing process. It is recognized that a personal relationship between the physician and the patient is essential for the provision of proper medical care.

The traditional physician-patient relationship takes on a new dimension when care is rendered within an organizational structure. Legal precedent has established that the institution itself also has a responsibility to the patient. It is in recognition of these factors that these rights are affirmed.

1. The patient has the right to considerate and respectful care.

2. The patient has the right to obtain from his physician complete current information concerning his diagnosis, treatment, and prognosis in terms the patient can be reasonably expected to understand. When it is not medically advisable to give such information to the patient, the information should be made available to an appropriate person in his behalf. He has the right to know, by name, the physician responsible for coordinating his care.

3. The patient has the right to receive from his physician information necessary to give informed consent prior to the start of any procedure and/or treatment. Except in emergencies, such information for informed consent should include, but not necessarily be limited to, the specific procedure and/or treatment, the medically significant risks involved, and the probable duration of incapacitation. Where medically significant alternatives for care or treatment exist, or when the patient requests information concerning medical alternatives, the patient has the right to such information. The patient also has the right to know the name of the person responsible for the procedures and/or treatment.

4. The patient has the right to refuse treatment to the extent permitted by law and to be informed of the medical consequences of his action.

5. The patient has the right to every consideration of his privacy concerning his own medical care program. Case discussion, consultation, examination, and treatment are confidential and should be conducted discreetly. Those not directly involved in his care must have the permission of the patient to be present.

6. The patient has the right to expect that all communications and records pertaining to his care should be treated as confidential.

7. The patient has the right to expect that within its capacity a hospital must make reasonable response to the request of a patient for services. The hospital must provide evaluation, service, and/or referral as indicated by the urgency of the case. When medically permissible, a patient may be transferred to another facility only after he has received complete information and explanation concerning the needs for and alternatives to such a transfer. The institution to which the patient is to be transferred must first have accepted the patient for transfer.

8. The patient has the right to obtain information as to any relationship of his hospital to other health care and educational institutions insofar as his care is concerned. The patient has the right to obtain information as to the existence of any professional relationship among individuals, by name, who are treating him.

9. The patient has the right to be advised if the hospital proposes to engage in or perform human experimentation affecting his care or treatment. The patient has the right to refuse to participate in such research projects.

10. The patient has the right to expect reasonable continuity of care. He has the right to know in advance what appointment times and physicians are available and where. The patient has the right to expect that the hospital will provide a mechanism whereby he is informed by his physician or a delegate of the physician of the patient's continuing health care requirements following discharge.

11. The patient has the right to examine and receive an explanation of his bill, regardless of source of payment.

12. The patient has the right to know what hospital rules and regulations apply to his conduct as a patient.

No catalog of rights can guarantee for the patient the kind of treatment he has a right to expect. A hospital has many functions to perform, including the prevention and treatment of disease, the education of both health professionals and patients, and the conduct of clinical research. All these activities must be conducted with an overriding concern for the patient, and, above all, the recognition of his dignity as a human being. Success in achieving this recognition ensures success in the defense of the rights of the patient.

rights for patients, which implies passivity. For, as Haug and Lavin remind us in their book *Consumerism in Medicine: Challenging Physician Authority* (Beverly Hills, Calif.: Sage Publications, 1983), "Consumerism implies buyer's challenge of seller's claims. It represents an approach of doubt and caution, rather than faith and trust, in any transaction, including the medical."

> Whether you call it assertive, aggressive, nasty, demanding, antsy, or picky, that's what you have to be in a hospital. . . . While it would be nice to leave the hospital with a flock of new friends waving good-bye, put "new friends" at the bottom of your priority list and "improved health" at the top.
>
> Barbara Huttmann, R.N., *The Patient's Advocate*
> (New York: Penguin Books, 1981)

Keep these pages marked and handy. While the hospital experience is not an us-versus-them situation (at least not all the time), this bill of rights is their word given to you, and it's up to you to make certain they keep it.

WHAT IF...?

What Should You Do if: You Believe You Are Being Treated by an Impaired or Incompetent Physician?   If statistics hold true, of every ten doctors you see in the hospital, at least one will be either incompetent or mentally or physically impaired. New York's state health commissioner has called this situation in his jurisdiction a "public peril." The State of New Jersey studied the issue of the impaired physician and found a significant problem. And not much is being done about it.

Drug addiction and alcoholism are the prime "impairers." Medical practitioners performing delicate operations or prescribing potent pharmaceuticals while they are practically "out on their feet" is a horrific thought, but it is widespread enough to raise great concern. Study upon study has shown that physician rates of alcoholism and drug addiction either match or exceed those of the general population.

Incompetence is another matter. It is often difficult for a patient to assess who is an incompetent doctor and who isn't. The doctor may be doing all right as far as you are concerned but may be harming or even killing other patients. You would never know it unless you overheard gossip or read about it in the newspaper. Incompetence is something a physician's peers ought to be able to see. The real scandal is that doctors *do* see the incompetents among

Dear PMS,

On May 7, while at the kitchen sink, I banged the back of my head on the cupboard. This knocked me unconscious. It was about 8 P.M. When I picked myself up off the floor, I could not remember a thing. One of the ladies who lives here in my apartment building drove me to the hospital.

The young doctor who seemed to be in charge in the emergency room said, "Well, we have no beds, so she will have to go home." He was rude, crude, and unthinking about it.

But the SOB went home and another doctor came on and bingo, I was admitted at 3 A.M. to a four-bed ward in which there were two empty beds. Recall, I was told not one bed was available in the whole hospital.

A nurse came in and said, "You won't get much sleep tonight, as I will have to take your blood pressure every half hour." It was taken only twice. Why? Because a man across the hall climbed over the side rails of his bed, tipped over IV bottles, and cut his feet. This nurse was working alone. If I had started to bleed intercranially, I would have been found dead in the bed come morning.

Because I couldn't remember what happened, they rounded up every medical student they could find. I did not have pajamas and robe with me but was in a hospital gown. I was gotten out of bed with my bare ass hanging out and asked to walk a straight line, and bend over, in front of about ten students, mostly male. It was horribly embarrassing.

They did every test that can be done, I do believe. They took my blood by the gallon. I have severe rheumatoid arthritis and told the doctor I needed 600 mg of Motrin three or four times a day. So the dumbhead wrote this as a PRN order, so I had to ask for it. I would ask in the early morning and with luck get one by 3 P.M. I then could ask for more, but it went in one ear and out the other of the evening and night staff. I was in the hospital five days and was crippled with arthritis so bad I could hardly get out of the place.

My bed never got made. I was never given water to wash in. I had to get up and do these things myself. My back was never rubbed even once. There was absolutely no compassion shown by any doctor, nurse, laboratory technician, X-ray technician, food service worker, or cleaning woman, It was such a horrible experience it makes me shudder even now as I write this.

S. B., R.N., Syracuse, New York

them and the impaired and those who are too old or sick to continue practicing or don't keep up with new advances in medicine. But out of some misguided loyalty to one of their own, they do nothing and say nothing. As the New York *Daily News* described the situation in a 1983 editorial, "For years, the medical profession has been dangerously lax about letting incompetent doctors stay in practice. Hospitals might let a bungler go, but it was always hushed up so the guy could go down the street and start fresh at another hospital."

Robert C. Coe, M.D., of the Washington State Medical Disciplinary Board, sees a great danger in the "escapees from medical discipline, those whose licenses have been revoked by various state authorities for unprofessional conduct or behavior." Coe warns that these physicians migrate, that they "carry their disease throughout the country," and that this migration "simply allows them to continue their unprofessional behavior."

"Hospital Politics Won't Let Me Stop a Dangerous Doctor" was the headline of an article in *Medical Economics* magazine. "Why the Conspiracy of Silence Won't Die" was another. Perhaps the medical profession is beginning to address the issue. But perhaps these are merely isolated cries. The statistics show that of 760 physician misconduct cases reported to New York State authorities in one year, only 75—fewer than 10 percent—were reported by doctors or hospitals.

Even more startling is just how few doctors receive any kind of punishment. Again looking at New York State—in 1986 there were 56,000 physicians in the state. There were a total of 198 actions. In other words, 3.4 actions per 1,000 physicians. Of those actions, 64 doctors had their licenses revoked, 20 were suspended for a period of time, and the remainder were either fined or had restrictions placed upon them. Organized medicine's arguments aside, it is hard to believe that any profession is that good. The evidence suggests that none is.

Unless and until the industry starts policing itself, it is up to us to do as much as we can. After all, we are the potential victims.

So if you see or are treated by a doctor who continually has liquor on his breath, has the jitters, seems in a thick haze, is forgetful to the point of causing you physical harm, makes a sexual advance toward you, or in any way seems to be incapable of making a decision or performing his duties (constant covering up for the doctor by other hospital staff is a sure giveaway), then you need to act. Speak to the hospital administrator or patients' representative, explaining the situation and saying that you have been in touch with your attorney. The threat of legal action against the hospital because of the actions of one of its doctors (along with the bad publicity that might accompany such a disclosure) could get the hospital bigwigs to get an investigation going. To be sure things get done, make a formal complaint yourself to the appropriate governmental agency and stick with it.

One important point to remember: If and when you should find yourself in the position of having to blow the whistle on physician misconduct, there's not much point in filing your grievance with the county or state medical association or society. Such groups are doctors' trade organizations and, as such, work to support and defend doctors and their causes. Writing to the American Medical Association or its local equivalent to take a doctor to task is about as effective as writing a note, putting it in a bottle, and tossing it in the ocean—without putting the cork in it first.

Not all doctors brought to face charges will lose their license to practice. Only the irredeemable should. Others with serious problems will benefit by having to face their conditions, and with the help of places like the Ridgeview Institute in Atlanta and other treatment and rehabilitation centers for impaired or addicted physicians, they can return to a better life, helping people heal themselves in a better way.

What Should You Do if: You Think You Are Having Too Many Blood Samples Taken?   This is a serious problem and it could lead to complications. Several times a day a technician might march into your room, declare that another test has been ordered, and soon the popular hospital game "Let's Try to Find a Good Vein" might be in full swing. You are stuck, sucked, and left sitting with your arm bent, a glob of cotton nestled in the crook of it.

Why so many tests? Sometimes they are necessary; but sometimes the sheer number of such syringe raids reflects the hospital staff's indecision, incompetence, or lack of consideration.

When Norman Cousins was in the hospital with the condition that led to his writing *Anatomy of an Illness,* he came up against this problem: four different departments came after him for separate blood extractions on the same day. He wondered why each department couldn't dip into the same single blood specimen. Therefore, he had a sign posted on his hospital room door to inform the blood bandits that he intended to allow just one specimen to be taken from him every third day, and that the various departments could all draw from the same vial.

That's a good, get-tough action. When they come to stick you, ask why and who ordered it. If you are not satisfied with the answer, refuse to let them have their way with you. When the doctor or patients' representative comes to see what's the matter, explain your decision and your determination.

What Should You Do if: Your Hospital Room and Surroundings Are Too Noisy?   Noise is dangerous, and not just to eardrums.

Studies have shown that noise—which is an especially stress-causing form of pollution—can raise your blood pressure to unhealthy levels, among other physiological reactions.

It is bad enough when noise gets to you when you are healthy. But when you are sick, it is really bad news.

Two studies prove it. One, by the UCLA Center for Health Sciences, measured the noise levels in two-, three-, and four-patient rooms in a nearby Veterans Administration hospital. The researchers found that the average noise levels over a twenty-four-hour period for each type of room arrangement exceeded the levels approved and recommended by the Environmental Protection Agency. The peak levels, according to the study, "were equal to or greater than those of a vacuum cleaner." The noise in this hospital (and it is not atypical establishment) interfered with "the rest and sleep needed for the recuperation of the patients."

This last point was underscored by the findings of a second study that observed the effect on patients of noise from the construction of a new University of Minnesota hospital building just outside their windows. Those patients in the opthalmology wing received the brunt of the booming pile drivers and the rattle of tractors and trucks. The researchers compared the length of hospital stay of cataract surgery patients during construction noise with those who had recuperated when there was no such noise. They concluded that "patient stay is significantly increased during a noisy period compared to a quiet one." Interestingly, the researchers thought the reason why this is so could be either or both of two possibilities: that the noise directly affects wound healing, or that it has a detrimental effect on the work efficiency of hospital personnel.

Better acoustics and soundproofing in rooms and halls and quieter hospital machinery—these are effective but long-range measures, and beyond your control. What you can do now is to first ask politely that the noise be lessened or cut out altogether, especially if the source is under human control. If that doesn't work, demand the quiet you need in the form of another room that is away from the noisy nurses' station, the elevator, the lounges, the stairwells, and other disturbances. Don't take "No" or "Not available" for an answer.

If the problem of noisiness is everywhere within the hospital, and it doesn't seem worth changing hospitals over, the solution is a pocket-size radio and tape player with a personal headset. That way you can drown out the offending sounds with pleasant tones of your own, including perhaps instructional or foreign-language-lesson tapes. Using earplugs is another solution.

What Should You Do if: You Are Continually Awakened at All Hours of the Night for This Test or That Sample? A major complaint cited by the vast majority of hospital patients is the irritating custom of being awakened in the middle of the night for something seemingly as minor as a temperature reading. Like the Spanish siesta that implies the need for a nap even if you are not tired, the middle-of-the-night wake-a-thon seems to occur even if the need for the test or sample has long passed.

Obviously, some arousals may be necessary. If you require around-the-clock monitoring due to the severity of your condition or the volatility of the medication you are taking, a grin-and-bear-it attitude is the best to assume.

On the other hand, if you suspect the need for nocturnal awakenings is inappropriate or past the point of being necessary, discuss it with your doctor. Ask why you need to be brought out from restful slumber two or three times a night? Make him justify the need.

Don't be afraid to suggest an alternative. Ask if two awakenings a night could not provide the same information as three. Or maybe he could shift the schedule slightly so that one sample or reading is done just before bed, only one during sleeping hours, and one at dawn.

Don't be shy about discussing this with your doctor. Often in the rush-around world of doctoring, yesterday's orders are no longer valid. Your questions might serve as his reminder that less monitoring is now required.

What Should You Do if: You and Your Nurse(s) Are Not Getting Along? It happens. Angels of mercy are only human and even the most patient of patients can take only so much. Conflicts do arise, especially if the patient involved is a sharp consumer.

The first thing to do is try to talk it over. Bring the tension out in the open with the person you are tense about. Together, try to figure out why things are the way they are, and what can be done to smooth them out. The matter could be settled amicably right then and there without having to bring anyone else into it.

If that approach is unsuccessful, it is time to call in the infantry: your doctor, the nurse's superior, the patients' representative. These peacemaker-mediators can wade into the fray and try to unfray it by various means. These include moving you to a room under another nurse's jurisdiction or transferring the nurse to other duties if he or she seems to be having a problem with others besides you. The nurse's superior can also help to resolve his or her difficulties, personal or professional.

Start with the personal before you go for the institutional. Don't go over anybody's head unless it is absolutely imperative.

What Should You Do if: You Feel Your Doctor Isn't Visiting You in the Hospital Often Enough?   By "often enough" we mean once a day (once every other day, if yours is a lengthy stay for a stable ailment that doesn't require daily visits).

Tell the doctor you are feeling shortchanged. Tell him that the form at the back of this book (that you have been filling in every day) is proof of his absence and/or negligence. Tell him that the charges he levies for hospital visits had better jibe with your records or he isn't going to be paid. It's remarkable how the frequency of doctor visits increases when the purely mercenary aspect is brought into play.

Your doctor might try to explain that you have been asleep when he has visited. That is probably simple excuse-making. The doctor might say that he has only had to check your chart, since you seem to be doing so well. That is probably a limp excuse, too. But it brings up a very good point: If your doctor isn't visiting you regularly, it could be that he isn't all that worried about you. In fact, it could mean that you don't need to be in the hospital anymore. You are just still hanging around there because the doctor has been so busy with his patient load that your release may have slipped his mind. But this reason is not valid for more than a day or two. Past that, greed may be a factor, or the doctor may be hiding something from you, or the doctor may not know what he is doing.

Get to the bottom of things. Get satisfaction and, perhaps, get out. It might be the time to consider finishing recovery at home, in a hotel, or in a nursing home.

What Should You Do if: You Are Given Food Before Surgery?   Don't touch it. It could be a very serious mistake.

In most situations patients aren't supposed to have anything to eat for a certain number of prescribed hours before an operation. If food does enter the stomach too soon before surgery, it could mess up certain important bodily function readings and/or adversely affect the body's reaction to the administered anesthetic. Very dire complications could result.

Moreover, that mediocre meal could end up being your most expensive ever. The surgeon or anesthesiologist might cancel your operation because you have eaten, and the rescheduling could add another costly day or two or more to your hospital stay.

If you are having surgery, ask your nurse or doctor if and for what hours you are NPO—*non per os* (nothing per mouth). Determine with

100 percent certainty what your meal situation is to avoid frustration, or worse.

What Should You Do if: You Don't Want to Take the Sleeping Pills You Are Being Given?   If you are sleeping just fine without a sleeping pill, then don't take one. Don't just nod and accept the pill, even if you plan to get rid of it surreptitiously. It will surely show up on your bill.

Tell your doctor you don't want to have a sleeping pill prescribed for you, or for that matter, any other drug that might knock you out. Make sure he marks your request on your chart. If, despite this, a nurse brings something to make you sleep, refuse it. Direct that person to the note on your chart. If necessary, call your doctor and have him clarify the situation. And make sure you are not charged for your nonmedicinal night's sleep.

What Should You Do if: Your Surgery Is Called Off?   What you should do—what you have to do—when this happens is to get information and keep your spirits up. A called-off operation without information breeds fear. This is especially so if you have already been removed from your room, prepped, and left lying in the operating room's outer hall for a time, only to be wheeled back to your room without surgery and without a clue. What's wrong? you wonder. Did they find something *else* wrong with me? Is my condition more serious than they thought? Is my condition inoperable?

It is usually none of these things, more likely a scheduling mistake or your developing a cold or fever that necessitates a delay. It could be any number of not very serious things. But unless you know, you will tend to imagine the worst.

Talk to your surgeon as soon as you can and find out why the operation was halted. Is it postponed or canceled? If canceled, why? If postponed, what is the new date? Why that date?

If the postponement is only until the next morning, you might as well stay put. If, however, your surgery has been pushed back a few days, look into the possibility of leaving the hospital and waiting at home (a far less costly place to do nothing). Then you can check in the night before, or preferably, the morning of the rescheduled surgery.

You might also want to discuss with the surgeon and somebody from the hospital billing department how this postponement will affect your bill. Why should you have to pay extra if the delay is their doing? Why should you have to pay twice for the presurgery medication and preparation? You shouldn't. Talk it over, be firm. Some accommodation can probably be reached.

What Should You Do if: You Resent the Way Hospital Personnel Refer to and Address You? "I am writing to offer a patient's view of a practice seen increasingly in medical circles: addressing patients by their first names."

So began a letter in the January 27, 1983 issue of the *New England Journal of Medicine* that struck at the heart of an annoying and often demeaning situation: Doctors behaving as though they were your parents and treating you like a child. Means of address is one of the methods used to maintain an unequal "doctor-patient" status, instead of allowing it to become the person-to-person caring relationship it ought to be.

"On occasion, perhaps first names are used to put the patient at ease," wrote Elizabeth Babbott Conant, Ph.D., of Canisius College. "But it is a bogus, unearned familiarity." As it is, she explained, only close family members have ever called her Elizabeth, and so the casual use of it by doctors and nurses "was proof that we were strangers and hence was less reassuring than a more formal address would have been."

To prove a point about status, the next time she made an appointment, Dr. Conant gave her professional title. "The difference (and deference) was notable," she recalled.

"Any procedure that increases confidence and inner energy will be important," the letter went on. "Any procedure that disempowers or diminishes the sense of self may impede the patient's progress. By reinforcing dependency and passivity [by automatic use of the first name], you have stolen power from your potential ally."

Perhaps demanding more formal address will help equalize the relationship. Or, conversely, calling the doctor by his or her first name (as he or she does to you) will get the message across and strip away that practiced facade of professional invulnerability.

What Should You Do if: There Is a Hospital Strike? If you are not yet in the hospital that's being struck, don't go. If not every hospital is affected, and if your doctor has privileges in another equally good hospital that is not being struck, see if you can go there. But don't go to a second-rate place just to be in a hospital.

If you are already in the hospital when nurses, doctors, or support employees take a hike, you might choose to stay, if the strike is a symbolic one with a short-range, prior-announced end time, which should be no longer than twenty-four hours. Otherwise, you ought to leave (why pay for days of sitting on ice?), unless the hospital is running smoothly and things are getting done *by people with qualifications to do them,* despite the walkout.

One thing to remember if you are within hospital walls when the work action occurs and you are in no shape to leave: Don't panic. Emergency services and crucial operations usually go on despite strikes. If you need intensive care or special attention, you will almost surely get it without disruption. The strike will do you no harm.

In fact, for many people a strike could do some good—it could even be a lifesaver. During the 1976 Los Angeles County doctors' strike, for example, physicians withheld nonemergency services for thirty-five days. A study by the UCLA School of Public Health and the California State Department of Health found that "the doctors" withdrawal of services—consisting in large part of elective procedures—appears to have caused relatively slight inconvenience to the people of Los Angeles County."

Moreover, the county's death rate during this time was significantly lower than for that period over the previous five years, but shot up again as soon as the strike was over and elective surgeries resumed. Concluded the researchers: "These findings . . . lend support to the mounting evidence that people might benefit if less elective surgery were performed in the United States."

MALPRACTICE

Miller and Keane's *Encyclopedia and Dictionary of Medicine, Nursing, and Allied Health* (Philadelphia: W. B. Saunders, 1983) describes malpractice as

> any professional misconduct, unreasonable lack of skill or fidelity in professional duties, or illegal or immoral conduct. Malpractice is one form of negligence, which in legal terms can be defined as the omission to do something that a reasonable man, guided by those ordinary considerations which ordinarily regulate human affairs, would do, or the doing of something that a reasonable and prudent man would not do. In medical and nursing practice, malpractice means bad, wrong, or injudicious treatment of a patient professionally; it results in injury, unnecessary suffering, or death to the patient. The court may hold that malpractice has occurred even though the physician or nurse acted in good faith. Also, malpractice and negligence may occur through omission to act as well as commission of an unwise or negligent act.

Pretty straightforward definition for a very complex, very hot issue that is getting more complex and hotter all the time. And the more it heats up, the more defensive everyone involved gets.

"Defensive" is the key word here. Medical malpractice and defensive medicine are related issues. Defensive medicine is the effect on physician practice patterns resulting from the perceived threat of future malpractice litigation. Doctors complain that this relationship—with the threat of a lawsuit dangling by a thread over every physician-patient exchange—forces them to practice this so-called defensive medicine which, they say, adds substantially to the already escalating costs of health care. The doctors remind us that to err is human. They aim the blame for what they see as a malpractice crisis at greedy lawyers.

According to the St. Paul Fire and Marine Insurance Company, the largest medical malpractice insurer, malpractice claims nearly tripled in the first five years of the 1980s and so did the average amount paid out per claim. In turn, malpractice premiums jumped sharply.

For their part, the Association of Trial Lawyers of America make the counterclaim that malpractice premiums account for only 1/3 of 1 percent of the estimated cost of health care in this country.

Further statistics—these from *Medical Economic*'s "Continuing Survey"—bear out the tone of the lawyers' claim. According to the survey, the median outlay for malpractice coverage comes to 4.5 percent of doctors' gross practice income. Interestingly, the figure was 3 percent in the 1970s. If malpractice premiums as a percentage of physicians' incomes are only 1.5 percent higher more than a decade ago, it is clear that doctors in general are suffering little in the pocketbook, despite their cries to the contrary.

If you look at the dollar amounts, you'll see that the median premium paid in 1988 by the typical M.D. was $9,850. In 1981, it was $3,650. Though an increase, it was in line with the inflation rate during that time. Your insurance premiums probably went up, too, during the same period.

Amid the numbers and the angry finger-wagging (and the proposals that consumers be limited to the amounts they can collect for pain and suffering caused by malpractice) lies the reality: The number and dollar amount of claims being paid out by insurers for malpractice acknowledge the fact that there is a good deal of negligent or incompetent medicine being practiced, and that the number-one reason for the higher number of malpractice suits is malpractice, no more, no less. And it is the consumer, not the doctors and not the hospitals, who ultimately pays for the malpractice. He pays in blood and in money, too, because the doctors and hospitals pass the cost of their mistakes on to their patients.

Who Is Held Responsible?

We have presented the general malpractice picture. What bears directly on your hospital experience and you is, first of all, the corporate negligence doctrine and the concept of corporate liability. What this means is that since 1965 the scope of legal responsibility for malpractice has widened. Before that time a hospital was seen as nothing more than a place where doctors from private practice came to play their trades; if those doctors committed acts of malpractice, only they were liable for suits. The hospital was not seen as a party to the misdeeds. The hospital became involved in litigation only when one of its employed staff—nurses, technicians, a very few salaried physicians, and other personnel—caused patients harm.

But *Darling* v. *Charleston Community Memorial Hospital* changed all that. It became, in the words of the American Medical Association's general counsel, "the first case to impose liability on the hospital for deficiencies in the quality of medical care provided to patients by the independent physicians practicing in the hospital." Later cases only strengthened this legal position, extending liability to hospitals for being lax or negligent in the ways they gave privileges to physicians. One recent decision has stated that a hospital is liable for the actions of the emergency room services in that hospital, even if those services are provided by an independent company under contract to the hospital.

But doctors and hospitals don't like to be sued, even if they are wrong. In fact, they would like to make consumers feel it is anti-American to zap a doc who has zapped a patient. Since the mid-1970s, with a big push in the latter half of the 1980s, the American Medical Association and other organized medical entities have been leaders in the fight for tort reform.

The torts they are talking about are not the kind you eat—those tasty delights that add girth to the midriff or clots to the bloodstream. No such medical humanitarianism.

The torts medicine wants to reform are the legal ones. Organized medicine wants to limit the ability of a medical victim from getting into court against a doctor or hospital. And, to some extent they have been successful in protecting bad guys from the results of their mistakes. But all is not lost. Many of the laws medical organizations successfully ushered through state legislatures have been overturned in the courts; many because they violated the fundamental rights of victims to have their day in court.

The battle is not over despite malpractice insurance rates leveling off in 1989 and in some cases dropping by as much as 15 percent in some states. Organized medicine does not want to face the music when it errs.

The upshot of all this is that, should malpractice occur in the hospital, it is probable that both the offending professional and the institution that gave that person the go-ahead to work there are defendants, and both may be sued.

This has had a chilling effect on hospital administrators every-where. It has especially caused them to reconsider or deny privileges to doctors who have ever had or are currently involved in malprac-tice suits, however frivolous. However, it might serve one of con-sumerism's ends by forcing hospitals to weed out the bad practitioners. (To be fair, it is not only bad doctors who get slapped with malpractice suits; some good doctors in high-risk specialty areas, fraught with failure possibilities, are often sued.) Of course, strong vested interest groups are lobbying intensely to get laws passed that would limit liability.

If your doctor has made a mistake in diagnosing your condition and that diagnosis has affected the outcome, if you have been physically or emotionally harmed by his professional treatment, if procedures were performed without your consent, if too much of you was removed during surgery or some of the equipment was left in—all these and other instances are grounds for legal action.

In which area of medical care does most malpractice occur? Here is a list, based on figures supplied by the St. Paul Fire and Marine Insurance Company for 1983:

MALPRACTICE TROUBLE SPOTS

Location	% of Claims
Hospital operating room	32.3
Physician's office	18.0
Hospital emergency room	12.3
Hospital patient care area	11.8
Hospital obstetrics units	8.2
Clinic	7.9
Hospital—other areas	5.3
Hospital outpatient surgery	1.0
Surgicenters	0.8
Other locations	2.4

Even more recently the Minnesota Department of Commerce conducted a study of every individual malpractice claim filed, over

4,700 of them, with the St. Paul Companies and the Minnesota Medical Insurance Exchange in the states of Minnesota, South Dakota, and North Dakota. The years reviewed were from 1982 to 1987. These are the problem areas they noted:

Location	% of Claims
Hospital operating room	34.3
Clinic	23.1
Hospital patient care area	10.5
Hospital obstetrics unit	9.4
Hospital emergency room	9.0
Physician's office	7.6
Hospital—other areas	4.6
Other locations	1.5

It is interesting to note that the two reports are not that much different. The changes between the earlier study and the newer one probably are due to the shift to more outpatient services.

Knowing where malpractice most often occurs can help you to be on guard when you find yourself in any of those departments. If you have information about your condition, your treatment options, your physician's success record in this procedure (the hospital's, too, for that matter), and the risks, you can head off malpractice before it happens. It is especially important to let the physician know that you know a lot, and that you are keeping tabs on things.

Even though you choose the "best" hospital, the "best" doctor, the most appropriate course of treatment, and in all respects pave the smoothest road to success, it is still possible for mistakes, errors, and/or gross negligence to occur. Then you have to decide on your next step.

If You Decide to Sue...

You might want to file a malpractice suit if your injuries are severe and you have a strong desire to get satisfaction from a clearly inadequate doctor or institution. This is a matter for you and a good, qualified malpractice attorney to go over. Be careful to select the right attorney. There are at least as many lawyers who ought to be charged with malpractice as there are doctors who should be.

Your case had better be strong, your evidence solid, and your resolve firm, because a malpractice case can take years from first to last. That is why many cases end in out-of-court settlements.

Perhaps your injuries are not quite so severe, or your attorney doesn't see much optimism for a court ruling in your favor, but you feel things have been botched, and you have been wronged by doctor or hospital. You could meet with the doctor and hospital representatives to air your grievances, explain that you are a reasonable person, but that if things can't be settled satisfactorily and monetarily, you will be obliged to sue their pants off. The threat of a malpractice suit is often as effective as the real thing, and doctors and hospitals will often come across and make amends based on their fear of legal action.

Another option in lieu of a suit is simply to refuse to pay your bill. When they come after you for the money, pull out your malpractice suit trump card. You will be amazed at how quickly the onslaught will recede, especially if your response to their dunning comes on your attorney's stationery.

You must be aware that this is not a game one plays to avoid paying justified billings. Only when real injury or malpractice has occurred should you involve yourself in these actions. Don't file frivolous lawsuits. No one profits except the lawyers.

Finally, there is arbitration. Several states sanction arbitration as an alternative dispute-resolving forum for medical malpractice claims.

A patient who signs an arbitration agreement before treatment gives up his right to a jury trial if there is a later claim of malpractice and a lawsuit. Instead, the case is presented to a theoretically neutral panel consisting of one arbitrator chosen by the patient, one chosen by the doctor, and one disinterested arbitrator. The panel decides all questions of fault and sets an award. This decision generally cannot be appealed in a court of law.

Doctors believe that arbitration benefits them by reducing the time and expense of a court case and avoiding excessive monetary awards to patients by sympathetic juries. Some patients choose arbitration because it can be less costly and speedier than a full-blown trial. Patients seriously injured by their physicians' incompetence may need money for immediate treatment. This may cause them to want their cases to be heard by an arbitration panel rather than wait (perhaps years) until the matter comes before a judge and jury in court.

Although arbitration might ultimately benefit many, you cannot be coerced into signing an arbitration agreement. In no state can a patient be forced to choose between signing the arbitration agreement or forgoing medical care. If you can prove that the contract was unfair or that you were coerced into signing without knowing the risks, alternatives, and disadvantages of arbitration, a court can invalidate the agreement. In some states a patient is allowed to revoke or rescind the agreement within thirty or sixty days after signing.

Arbitration is something to think about and discuss with advisers, legal and otherwise.

CONSENT

Informed consent is, simply, the idea that you have the right to available information about your condition and about the benefits and risks of procedures the doctors want to perform on you. Then you can make an informed decision about what is done to your body and your life before you give the go-ahead or refusal.

Unfortunately, the definition in theory is the only simple thing about informed consent. In practice, it is a complex, controversial boiling pot.

Why? Many physicians and their trade organizations believe that informed consent is an unworkable idea that obstructs quality care. Patients and consumer groups feel that informed consent is an important tool in establishing autonomy and creating a true doctor-patient partnership, one in which physicians are willing to explain and patients are able to understand and decide.

Many doctors say that medicine is too complicated for unschooled nonphysicians to understand. Why should they spend their valuable time when there can be no satisfactory end? To them, informed consent is a charade.

Medical consumers respond by claiming that many doctors do not even try to simplify medical information to make it accessible to the general public, which is a lot smarter than many doctors give it credit for. The consumers also point out that since doctors do not get paid to talk but to perform procedures, they see taking time to discuss potential risks and options as a way of losing time and money. Also, if they explain things accurately, they might actually talk you out of having the test or operation.

Many doctors also say that patients really don't want to know everything about their conditions and upcoming procedures. They say that the fear created in a patient by hearing all the things that could go wrong is detrimental to the patient's well-being. The facts, though, paint a different picture. A survey undertaken by the President's Commission for the Study of Ethical Problems in Medicine and Biomedical and Behavioral Research found that 96 percent of patients said they wanted to know everything. That number included 85 percent who said they would even want to hear the most "dismal facts," even if one of those facts was imminent death.

Furthermore, a goodly number of studies has shown that people who are told all the possible negatives (as well as positives) ahead of time make much better postoperative adjustments to stress and pain. Psychologist Irving Janis calls this phenomenon "emotional inoculation," in which patients can prepare themselves and even rehearse recovery scenarios.

Resentment at having anything impinge on their professional autonomy, and their own uncertainty about the effectiveness and safety of the procedures they are recommending, are two more reasons why doctors don't like informed consent. And they have been successful in lobbying legislators to see their side of things. Less than half the states in this country have informed-consent laws on the books to protect patients.

Let's look at informed consent as it affects you directly during your hospital stay.

The Consent Form at
the Admissions Desk

As a new patient, one of the first papers shoved under your nose by the admissions person is a consent form. It is not exactly an informed-consent situation, because although you are doing a whole load of consenting, they are not doing any informing. This is a "blanket consent form," and by signing it you are in essence saying, "Do with me as you will. I am giving up all rights to make decisions, to say no, or to sue you if you do me harm." In one short form, your rights are negated.

If that is your cup of tea, then sign the thing blindly and be done with it. But if you value your rights, if you don't take losing them lightly, and if you want to let the hospital know they can't toy with you, then hold off on that John Hancock for a moment. It is almost certain that if you refuse to sign this consent form you will not be admitted to the hospital. You can try, but expect a rebuff. Instead, sign the form—but only after you have added to or modified it to your liking. Write on the form that you are signing it only because you would not be admitted otherwise, and that you have no intention of giving up any of the rights the form is forcing you to give up.

If there are any items to which you take specific and strong objection, note them. If the admissions person says you can't add statements to the form, ask to see his superior or a hospital administrator if need be. A hospital bigwig will probably let you do whatever you want with the form, because he will know that such blanket rights-robbers are more than likely indefensible in a court of law. They just use them, it seems, to keep the uninformed and easily intimidated in line.

Once you are admitted to the hospital, it is up to your doctor, surgeon, anesthesiologist, or whomever else will be operating or performing a procedure on you to explain what is going to be done and why. He or she must tell you what you can expect before, during, and after, and about alternative forms of treatment, even ones that are more hazardous than those recommended. You will then be handed a consent form to sign that will give your OK for a specific course of action.

If you have not been informed to your satisfaction and/or are more than a bit unsure about giving your consent to your doctor's game plan, don't sign the form. Ask for more information. Ask about survival rates and statistical proofs of the effectiveness and safety of the procedure. (A lot of this territory should have already been covered during office visits and previous discussions.) If you are really doubtful, ask for printed materials that provide support for the route your doctor wants to take.

Tape-record the conversations with the doctor or doctors, to help you remember and to act as a piece of evidence should that sort of thing be needed later. If your doctor were smart, he would keep a similar record for his own protection.

Consent Form for a Specific Procedure

The consent form reproduced here is similar to the ones used in most hospitals, give or take a few phrases and clauses. A form of this sort is a specific consent form; that is, it indicates that by your signature you have agreed to the performance of a specific procedure in a specific way for which you have received adequate informational background. A different form should be completed before every procedure that you believe requires a consent contract. It might be a bit too picky to ask for risk-versus-benefit statistics and a consent form before having a urinalysis or blood test performed. But exercising your right of informed consent before undergoing a stress test, ultrasound, perhaps even some X rays, or similar "minor" procedures is justified if you want or need such assurances. The doctor may try to smooth-talk you out of it and will probably think you're a real pain in the butt. Never mind. It is your life. A doctor's chagrin is a small price to pay for your protection.

Be sure that all the clauses are true and represent your beliefs before you sign the form. Be careful. The forms are filled with booby traps. If you need to alter, amend, or revise the form to fit your situation, then do so. For example, in the form shown here, you might possibly require more space to set forth your reservations than the extremely generous and expansive two lines afforded you in number 3. Or you might not go along with number 4, which, in effect, makes a mockery of the form and the entire informed-consent process. You might not want your operation to be that day's surgical show, so number 6 would be something you couldn't agree to. Some forms have patients consenting to allow filming and video-taping of their operations. You might not want that. Let them know they are refused permission to do so. Number 7 certainly leaves the door wide open for cover-ups by destroying evidence of botched surgeries. You might not agree to that. Say so, in writing.

And mark down items that aren't on the form that you think must be on it before you will give your consent. For example, an important condition to add is that you will not consent to the operation unless it is performed by *your* surgeon. You do not consent to a colleague, resident, or intern doing the operation for the first time while your surgeon acts as a teacher-observer. If you are paying big money for the Big Guy, then you should have the Big Guy.

Don't be rushed into signing the form. Give it a few good thinks, and certainly enough time to tailor it to your specific situation. Sometimes you can understand your medical condition and treatment options just fine; it is the consent form you can't make heads or tails of. If that is the case, request that somebody from the administrator's office or the hospital's legal department clarify the form or parts of it for you. And also get that explanation down on tape.

Two final points: Everything mentioned in this section applies equally if you are granting consent for procedures to be performed on a child who is too young to understand or give an informed consent, or on an incompetent patient. In an emergency, when there

Consent to Operation or Other Special Procedure

PATIENT _____ AGE _____

DATE _____ TIME _____ A.M. CONSENT
P.M. OBTAINED AT _____
(i.e., physicians office, hospital, etc.)

1. I authorize the performance upon _____ of the following operation or
(Myself or name of patient)

procedure _____
(State nature and extent of operation)

to be performed at The Hospital under the direction of Dr. _____
and/or such associates and assistants as may be selected by him.

2. The nature and purpose of the operation, referred to in Paragraph 1 hereof and the possible alternative
methods of treatment have been explained to me by Dr. _____ and to my complete
satisfaction. No guarantee or assurance has been given by anyone as to the results that may be obtained.

3. I acknowledge that I have been afforded the opportunity to ask any questions with respect to the
operation and any risks or complications thereto and to set forth, in the space provided below, any
limitations or restrictions with respect to this consent:

_____

(If None, write "none") _____

4. I consent to the performance of operations, procedures, and treatment in addition to or different from
those now contemplated as described above, whether or not arising from presently unforeseen conditions,
which the above-named doctor or his associates or assistants may in his or their judgment consider
necessary or advisable in my present illness.

5. I understand that anesthesia shall be administered during this operation under the direction of the
responsible physician.

6. For the purpose of advancing medical education, I consent to the admittance of observers to the
operating room.

7. I consent to the disposal by hospital authorities of any tissues or parts that may be removed.

I CERTIFY THAT I HAVE READ AND FULLY UNDERSTAND THE ABOVE CONSENT, THAT THE EX-
PLANATIONS THEREIN REFERRED TO WERE MADE, THAT ALL BLANKS OR STATEMENTS REQUIR-
ING INSERTION OR COMPLETION WERE FILLED IN, AND THAT INAPPLICABLE PARAGRAPHS, IF
ANY, WERE STRICKEN BEFORE I SIGNED.

Signature of Patient _____

Signature of Witness _____
Witness to signature only

When a patient is a minor or incompetent to give consent:
Signature of person authorized
to consent for patient _____

Relationship to patient _____

The foregoing consent was signed in my presence, and in my opinion the person did so freely with full
knowledge and understanding.

Signature of Physician _____

Signature of Witness _____
Witness to signature only

is no time for lengthy discussion, consent is implied and assumed by doctors and the law as a given.

Informed consent is not and should not be a piece of paper, but an ongoing process, a partnership of information-sharing and trust between doctor and patient.

YOUR CHART AND
MEDICAL RECORD

Except in a very few hospitals, patients' charts (the story in hospitalese of the patient's current stay) don't hang from a hook at the foot of the bed anymore. Only in movies do charts appear to be a bright red line graph running jaggedly like the Himalayas across the front of a single sheet of paper.

In most hospitals a chart is a sheaf of papers grouped together in a sturdy, no-nonsense clipboard and kept in a rack at or near the nurses' station. While there may be a graph or two in the package, the chart is mostly a conglomeration of reports from a multitude of departments: X ray, EKG, respiratory and rehabilitation services, various labs (urinalysis, nuclear medicine, hematology, bacteriology, etc.). Also within this substantial stack are doctors' notes on your progress, your history, and physical exams, plus consultation reports and various consent forms, among others.

Your chart probably has all the information you could want or would need to help you understand your condition, to learn what is being said about you by professionals and the diagnosis and prognosis of your condition. It can be an especially important minivolume of facts and figures for you if your doctor or hospital staff isn't being very clear in explaining your condition, or seems to be reticent in giving you information about yourself.

The chart can be a significant tool. A few studies show that some patients' physical and psychological conditions improve when they read their charts regularly and see things that confirm or dispute their hopes or fears, written in official black and white. A small number of experimental programs in hospitals have allowed patients to mark their own charts and keep them current because of the benefit derived from doing so. It also demystifies the chart, and medical practice in general.

In most hospitals, though, the problem is getting your hands on your chart. It isn't often that patients ask for their charts—they have been conditioned not to. It is almost unheard of for the staff to volunteer them. Your request to see your chart may be the first of its kind that some young staffers have ever received, and they might not know whether they should or shouldn't accommodate you. They usually act on the side of shouldn't, just to be safe. Other personnel consciously keep your chart from you for unfounded reasons that perpetuate the exclusivity of information in the hands of medical professionals. They may think you couldn't possibly understand their complex lingo, or they may be embarrassed to show you things they've written about you (see "The Language" in chapter 3, "When in Rome . . .").

How to Get to See Your Chart

If you want to see your chart, ask your nurse first. He or she is the one who lives with it at hand all day and gets to know you better than nearly anyone else during your hospital stay. Your nurse is less protective than others involved and might be amenable to leaving your chart with you—even on the sly—for a short while, without authorization. The nurse might resent you less than he or she resents the doctor who doesn't tell his patient anything.

If the nurse can't or won't assist you, try the doctor, then the patients' representative, and on up to the hospital administrator. If all else fails and your need to see your chart is strong (perhaps you suspect a cover-up), it is time to call in an attorney to petition for your right to see that chart.

The permanent file of your past and current dealings with the institution—in essence a compilation of your charts kept together in a central filing system—is your medical record. It is often necessary to see your record. For example, you might believe that it contains information that might help you decide whether to pursue a malpractice case or not. You might want to compare your current course of treatments with previous ones. You might just want to see it out of curiosity or to have a copy of it for your own home health files.

In only twenty-five states do you have the legal right to see your medical records on demand. Even then, the right is not absolute. In the law passed in 1984 in California, for instance, physicians have the option of giving you a summary of your record instead of a copy of the real thing. You have to pay copying, clerical, and mailing costs, and perhaps another fee to the doctor for his or her time in preparing the summary.

But don't be totally put off by the statistics. While half the states have some form of statute giving you limited, if not full, access to your records, the others do not prohibit you from getting them. It is just that they have no laws on the books requiring access. This means one hospital may willingly make your records available, while another may treat them as state secrets.

Even in states where access to medical records is legally mandated, those laws are frequently disregarded. It is an affront to all citizens that they have little or no power under the law to see information that is about themselves. Is it not dangerous to be so left out in the informational cold?

The files belong to the hospital. The information belongs to you.

Make formal requests to the hospital for your medical records. If they do not accede to your first request, follow it up with another, this one hinting at legal action. Be prepared to take that legal action, for hospitals and doctors form a very tight circle to protect each other. They know that knowledge is power, and they want the power to be in their hands, not yours.

Suppose you want to or need to see your medical records. You have run up against a bureaucratic brick wall, and you really don't have the heart or resources to enter into a protracted legal squabble. There is another method that might work. It is an end-around maneuver recommended by some medical consumer activists: Find yourself a consumer-oriented physician who is on your side; have him request your records, which he will then pass on to you. It is a good, honest ploy for a truly worthy cause.

NOSOCOMIAL INFECTIONS

A hospital is no place for a sick person. Nosocomial infections are one reason why.

Nosocomial (pronounced nohs-oh-KOH-me-ul) infections are those acquired during hospitalization and produced by microorganisms that dwell with relative impunity in hospitals. Nosocomial infections aren't present in patients on admission. In other words, you didn't have it when you came in, but got it while you were there. It is a souvenir of your visit that doesn't come from the gift shop.

It is a costly souvenir. It is estimated that the recovery time necessary to combat a nosocomial infection is about four extra days of stay at an average additional cost of $800 per day (factoring in both room and ancillary charges). That's $3,200 per infection. Nosocomial infections account for 15 percent of all hospital charges and end up adding, at a minimum, $2.5 billion to America's medical bills. Some say the true figure is double that, especially because about a fourth of all infections acquired in the hospital don't show up until after the patient is discharged. Then work-related expenses and costly readmission to the hospital can be factored in.

Robert Haley, M.D., director of the Division of Epidemiology and Preventive Medicine at the University of Texas Southwestern Medical School, states flatly that nosocomial infections are adding "an unnecessary $4 billion a year to our national medical bill." One group of experts say the figure is much higher. They claim, in the November 1986 edition of the *American Journal of Surgery,* that surgical wound infections alone (of which there are more than a million each year in the United States) "add an average of seven days to the usual hospital stay of surgical patients and cost more than $10 billion in direct and indirect expenses."

And a nosocomial infection can be a most deadly souvenir: Some estimates of infection-related deaths run as high as 100,000 (some even higher, 300,000 or so) a year. Five to 10 percent of hospitalized patients (or about 2 million people) acquire hospital infections annually, and in approximately 3 percent of those cases, the infection is the cause of death.

Nosocomial infection rates are highest in large teaching hospitals and lowest in nonteaching hospitals. Obviously, the large teaching facilities attract the sickest patients, but it also points out the difficulties large facilities have in maintaining necessary sanitary discipline. More people buzzing around the hospital means more chances for the spread of infection.

Here are some more disturbing infection-related facts:

▶ In the United States more than 100,000 hospital patients annually acquire nosocomial bacteremia—the presence of bacteria in the blood, Richard E. Dixon, M.D., says the mortality rates "range from 20 percent for patients who do not develop shock, to greater than 80 percent for those who do."

▶ Infection is the most frequent cause of death in cancer patients.

▶ Pneumonia, now reported as the most common hospital-acquired infection leading to death, occurs in 0.5 to 5 percent of all in-hospital patients and in 12 to 15 percent of patients ill enough to require intensive care. It has a morbidity and mortality rate of 20 to 50 percent and may be responsible for 15 percent of all hospital-associated deaths. It may be introduced into the lungs by way of contaminated respiratory therapy equipment or simply by breathing the air filled with droplets of infection from other patients or medical personnel coughing, especially in the close quarters of intensive care units.

Why is nosocomial infection so widespread, so lethal a problem in modern hospitals? For one thing, hospitals are where the sick people are. Those who are weak when hospitalized and those weakened in the hospital are highly susceptible to infection. These infections come from the microorganisms and pathogens that thrive in the hospital setting or arrive on the coattails of new patients coming in from the community at large.

Add to that the increase in invasive procedures and major surgeries. Consider the increased use of drugs that reduce the body's rejection of implants but at the same time suppress the body's immune system, leaving the door wide open for infections that can kill—for example, nosocomial pneumonia, which develops in approximately 300,000 patients a year. Other frequently seen types of nosocomial infections are those that attack the urinary tract, most usually because of urinary catheters (the cause of approximately 40 percent of all nosocomial infections), surgical wounds (about 25 percent), and the lower respiratory tract (approximately 15 percent).

Another cause of patient susceptibility to hospital infections is, ironically, antibiotics. Typically, when there is a rash of infections, hospitals haul out the antibiotics to do away with the monsters that the antibiotics themselves have nurtured. And it may work for a while—until the aftereffects set in. Not only do patients have bad reactions to the drugs, but there is a rapid development of strains of bacteria resistant to the antibiotics that were once effective against these organisms. The amount of penicillin required to treat an infection today is fifty times greater than it was thirty years ago.

"As many as two-thirds of the hospital patients given antibiotics are receiving them inappropriately," stated an editorial in the May 1, 1983 issue of the *Canadian Medical Association Journal.* Research from the University of California at San Francisco bears this out: 62 percent of patients receiving antibiotics in community

Dear PMS,

I was admitted to the hospital with a gallbladder attack. I had surgery for removal of the gallbladder. The next night I became very ill and was rushed back to surgery. The hole from this surgery was left open for five days, and I was in intensive care. You could have put a pie plate in the hole, it was so large. No one told me or my husband why this was done.

A few days later I was back in surgery and a plastic surgeon had to layer in muscle and adhere it to my ribs and run a new blood supply to feed the right side. I spent thirty-eight days in the hospital. A blood clot went through my heart and lodged in my lung. The incision reopened to about a four-by-five-inch hole as infection was apparent.

I was released from the hospital under the care of a home nurse and remained bedridden for months. During that time I had plastic surgery as an outpatient to close the hole. Several skin grafts were performed.

Finally, I demanded to know what was the reason for all this surgery and why I was so sick. It was supposed to be just a gallbladder surgery. It was then that the original surgeon told me that the circulating nurse in the operating room the day of my first surgery was a carrier of streptococcus and had infected me. The nurse had infected ten people before me and one died. The hospital knew this, and the nurse was on antibiotic injections at the time of my surgery.

I hired a lawyer to sue the hospital and nurse. He claimed he could not get one doctor to testify for me. He warned me if I did file and lost the case, it could cost me $20,000 to $30,000 in lawyer fees. This scared me and I didn't have the money to take the chance. My hospital and doctor bills were over $50,000 as it was.

My whole life was turned upside down. I don't have any nerves left. Why will no doctor testify?

How can a hospital do this and get away scot-free?

M. V. T., Acme, Michigan

---

hospitals "failed to have definite evidence of infection" before the drug regimen was begun. About the same figure applies to university hospitals.

The ways nosocomial infections are spread are numerous. Organisms can be transmitted in food and water, in transfused blood and intravenous fluids, in pharmaceuticals, through the air, by direct human contact, on towels and sheets, and via the housekeeping crew, to name but a few.

Certain places in the hospital must be diligently monitored, for they can be especially hazardous for patients and hospital personnel as well. These include the hemodialysis unit (the equipment can be a source of hepatitis B, a virulent and difficult-to-destroy organism);

intensive care units (occupied by patients who are extremely weak and thus susceptible to infection and operated under emergency measures that often have to forsake pristine sanitary procedures in order to save a life), the infant nursery, and the operating room.

"The outpatient and admitting departments are areas of the hospital not frequently associated with nosocomial infections, but they, too, can be the site of significant problems," write Bennett and Brachman in *Hospital Infections* (Boston: Little, Brown, 1979). "Patients who acquire pathogenic organisms while in the hospital but who do not develop overt infection until after discharge may return later to the outpatient department for therapy," thus infecting many of those simply waiting there.

To these potential sources of infection, add plain old carelessness, if not callousness. The Institute for Child Health reports that many hospital workers who come in direct contact with patients don't take the time, or are not concerned enough, to take the simplest and best known of precautionary measures: washing their hands properly. And doctors are among the worst offenders. No wonder: "Most medical schools don't teach practical prevention, stressing things like washing," explains Timothy R. Franson, M.D., hospital epidemiologist at the Medical College of Wisconsin. Case in point: In two intensive care units studied, hands were washed after patient contact less than half the time. Unwashed hands are prime culprits in the spread of many nosocomial infections.

How to Protect Yourself

What can be done to protect you from nosocomial infections? It is impossible, of course, to surround yourself with an impervious safety shield and keen electric eyes that will detect and rub out errant, nasty microbes. There is no surefire defense for you if the rest of the hospital is a vast and bubbling breeding ground. So the first step in infection protection is to try to gain admission to a hospital that has a good nosocomial record. Ask your doctor about it. Contact your local department of health. Ask the hospital directly. Be on your guard if they paint too rosy a picture, warn Bennett and Brachman: "If a hospital indicates that it has no problem, it is almost a certainty that the staff is not conducting a surveillance, and thus they do not have an appreciation of their own nosocomial infection situation."

An active infection control committee is a good sign that the hospital is concerned about infections and is trying to monitor and control them. Ask if that is the case. Another good sign is if someone on the staff is a member of the infection watchdog organization, the Association for Practitioners in Infection Control. Hospitals with a greater than average concern for the nosocomial infection danger will have at least one nurse-epidemiologist on staff to maintain surveillance. Find out if there's one in your hospital.

Some things you can do personally and actively while in the hospital:

▶ Try to make sure that all hospital personnel who come in contact with you have washed their hands. If you so desire, ask them to do so, in your room, in your presence.

▶ If a roommate becomes infected, or if you are concerned that what he or she has could possibly be transmitted to you via the air or through use of a common bathroom, ask your doctor or the staff nurse-epidemiologist about your risks. Change your room at once if there is any chance that you might become infected, because once you are infected, it is too late. You may have to be put in isolation along with your roommate.

▶ If you are undergoing surgery or a procedure that requires the removal of hair, refuse to be shaven the night before surgery. One study indicates that among people shaved the day prior to their operations, the nosocomial infection rate was 5.6 percent. Chemical depilatories reduce that rate to just 0.6 percent. Using barber clippers to remove hair the morning of surgery yields a low infection rate, too.

    Of course, there is a good question you might ask: Is shaving or clipping or any other form of hair removal necessary at all? Maybe not—and especially when it comes to obstetrical-gynecological situations. Removing hair before vaginal delivery or surgery in that area is probably uncalled for, because the old idea that hair creates a climate for infection is unsubstantiated by clinical studies.

▶ Have nurses regularly check the drainage of urinary catheters to help you maintain cleanliness.

While it is true that one-third of all infections treated in hospitals are nosocomial infections, it is also estimated that as many as half of all such infections are preventable. With luck, information, and diligence, you might be able to prevent your own.

IATROGENIC DISEASE

Iatrogenic disease may be considered a nosocomial problem, in a general sense, because it takes place most often in a hospital. Its origin, though, is with the doctor, hence "iatrogenic": from the Greek, meaning "doctor-caused" or "doctor-produced." Iatrogenic disease is just what the doctor ordered.

Iatrogenic disease is no small problem. In one major study conducted at a teaching hospital, researchers from Boston University Medical Center found that of 815 consecutive admissions, 36 percent were there because of an iatrogenic problem, and in 2 percent of the patients, iatrogenesis was a contributing factor in the patients' deaths. If one were able to generalize from this study, one would arrive at the conclusion that iatrogenic mishaps kill nearly half a million people a year and add at least a billion dollars to America's medical bill.

Iatrogenesis comes in all shapes and sizes and types. There is the iatrogenesis that occurs when a doctor performs a procedure that has greater risks than benefits, and the gamble is lost. There is the iatrogenesis that occurs when the doctor hasn't prepared himself for the unexpected complication, although it was always a possibility. There is the iatrogenesis that occurs when a doctor makes a mistake, in judgment or in handiwork. He might go ahead and do something without having adequate knowledge of or skills for the procedure but compensates for this by having more than adequate misguided confidence and false pride.

Many iatrogenic occurrences are isolated events, a doctor creating a medical condition in a patient who didn't have it to begin with. One person doing something wrong to another. An unintentional, personal act. A mishap. But there are also what Eugene D. Robin, M.D., in *Matters of Life and Death* (New York: W. H. Freeman, 1984), calls "iatroepidemics": epidemics or plagues caused by doctors. They are "systematic errors incorporated into medical practice." That is, all doctors agree on a procedure or series of steps, which they all use to treat problems in the course of their practice. These become the accepted ways. The problem is that these procedures and steps, though officially sanctioned, kill or harm patients. They are very often crackpot schemes dressed up in pseudoscientific robes, or insufficiently tested operations and drugs that are used anyway because word gets around that they might be valuable. A jump-on-the-bandwagon mentality.

Among iatroepidemics, Robin includes mastectomies, the prescribing of DES (diethylstilbestrol) to prevent spontaneous abortions (but which led to genital cancers in some of the children of mothers who took it), tonsillectomies, brain surgeries for schizophrenia, the prescribing of thalidomide, radiation for acne, and others. The list is long. And it is getting longer all the time.

High-Risk Areas for Iatrogenesis

There are several areas of medical practice in which iatrogenesis is most prevalent. You need to know the dangers that could lie in these areas. Alertness, awareness, and a healthy dose of suspicion are essential to avoid becoming an iatrogenic victim.

Diagnosis. Diagnosing illnesses is the keystone of medicine, its very foundation. Without an accurate diagnosis, medical practice has no purpose, and patients are treated in ways that are ineffective or worse—a lot worse. Unfortunately, "a lot worse" is happening more often than anybody (especially the patients) would like.

Some very good studies in some very important journals are making it clear that faulty diagnosis is becoming a major iatrogenic problem. For example, a study by researchers from Baptist Memorial Hospital and the University of Tennessee College of Medicine in Memphis revealed that heart attacks were misdiagnosed 47 percent of the time. From the Baylor College of Medicine in Houston came the report that medical residents made diagnostic errors— incorrect findings and oversights—13.1 percent of the time, interns 15.6 percent of the time, and that at least one error occurred during the examination of two-thirds of all patients seen. Both of these studies appeared in the *Journal of the American Medical Association.*

The *New England Journal of Medicine* reported a Harvard hospital study showing that 10 percent of all patients who had died *might have lived* if they had received the correct diagnosis. In some categories of disease the misdiagnosis figures were as high as 24 percent.

What in the world is going on? The researchers point the finger at too great a reliance on technology and statistics and lab results, and not enough use of human skills and common sense and brain work. Doctors may be believing the machines and mistrusting their

own eyes. Whatever the reasons, the results are that people die or
get hurt, iatrogenically, because doctors aren't doing their jobs well
or properly in these situations.

Furthermore, when it comes to diagnostic testing, a patient can
become ill because of those very tests. "Enough tests," says Charles
Ford, M.D., of the Vanderbilt University School of Medicine, "and,
sooner or later, the patient will have a real disease caused by the
process of diagnosing and treating." In other words, iatrogenesis.

Surgery. Heart specialist Robert G. Schneider, M.D., in *When to
Say No to Surgery* (Englewood Cliffs, N.J.: Prentice-Hall, 1982), has
come up with this apt, knowing concoction that he calls "A Recipe
for Surgery":

> Take one part of an overhead technology.
> Enhance with researchers anxious to publish.
> Blend in premature media reports tainted with melodrama.
> Stir well.
>
> Pepper with statistical bias.
> Flavor with funds from insurance and government.
> Heat to boiling.
>
> Sprinkle liberally with surgeons in search of operations, fame and
> fortune.
> Spice with empty hospital beds and idle operating room suites.
> Mix with a pinch of instrument sales and a drop in drug company
> profits.
> Simmer over low heat.
>
> Add in haste: Patients seeking miracles, fast cures and simple solutions
> (such patients are easy to find).
>
> Serve with Hope and Expectation.
>
> Blame fate and poor protoplasm when something goes sour.

Those are the ingredients for the potluck casserole known as
unnecessary surgery, an iatrogenic nightmare that some claim com-
prises somewhere between 10 and 20 percent of all surgery.
Schneider puts the unnecessary surgery figure at 15 to 25 percent
as an average, multiplies it by the number of operations performed
each year, and comes up with a total of somewhere between 3
million and 6.25 million annual unnecessary operations, leading to
a ballpark figure of 40,000 to 80,000 unnecessary surgery deaths in
America every year.

The operations mentioned most often as probably unnecessary
are many that are elective, many that are female-oriented (mastectomies, hysterectomies, cesarean sections), tonsillectomies, knee
operations, back operations. Most recently, vascular surgery has

come under attack. It is meant to unblock clogged blood pathways in the extremities, but physician critics claim that these operations are performed without statistical proof of their effectiveness. They say that the operations are ultimately useless, because when one obstruction is removed, another pops up, leading to more and more high-cost surgery.

Both critics and surgeons have to agree on one fact: Statistics show that the number of operations each year increases, not in proportion to the rise in population but rather in proportion to the rise in the number of surgeons. The more surgeons in the market-place looking to make a living, the more operations there are. Could the population, rising at only about 5 percent a year really need about 35 percent more operations a year? Or is it just that surgeons need business, and so create it?

A few years ago *R.N. Magazine* took a national opinion poll of more than 12,000 nurses. They were asked about surgery. To the surprise of many, 46 percent of those responding put the amount of unnecessary surgery at 30 percent or more. Another 20 percent of nurses said the unnecessary surgery figure was more like 50 percent.

Asked the magazine's editors: "Are they right? Aside from M.D.'s

---

DRUGS, THE ELDERLY, AND THE "ZEALOUS PROFESSION"

"Having more illnesses [as older folks do] means having to see doctors more often and, worse, having to see more different kinds of doctors," explains Harvey N. Mandell, M.D., writing in a 1984 issue of *Postgraduate Medicine.* "When patients are seen more often by more doctors and more different kinds of doctors, they will, as sure as night follows day, get more medications more often for more things."

A snowball effect on the prescribing of medications occurs, according to Mandell, and pretty soon not only has an elderly patient become a victim of "polypharmacy," but that person may also begin to suffer mental distur-bances, "exchanging serenity for suspicion and hallucination.

"So it goes on and on with nobody to protect elderly patients from our zealous profession."

Mandell's solution to this problem is a good one: "Maybe a law should be passed wherein every time we start a new medication in an elderly patient we are legally bound to stop a previous one. Under this law, no one could get more than four medications at a time, including laxatives. And unless the blood pressure in a patient over 80 years of age were at least 150 mm Hg. diastolic, we would not be permitted to prescribe antihyper-tensives."

who often won't give an estimate (in public), who's better qualified to say?"

Drugs. As an area of iatrogenic abuse, drugs are probably in the lead. Doctors aren't as well educated in dosages and side effects as they might be. That is why they are so easily influenced, duped, or co-opted by pharmaceutical company salespersons who have commissions and promotions on their minds. There is a great deal of sloppy prescribing—overprescribing, mostly. There is also unwise, uncertain, and sometimes unethical prescribing.

More has been written about drugs as iatrogenic sources than about any other iatrogenic source. That is because abuse is easier to spot and may be the only one of the iatrogenic problems that has a chance of being cleaned up anytime soon. Diagnosis and surgery are direct activities of doctors, so there is a lot of defensiveness, few voices among the ranks speaking out, few studies undertaken to dig into those aspects. The iatrogenic drug problem, on the other hand, doesn't have this good ol' boy network veil of secrecy. The blame for the drug situation can be sloughed off on the pharmaceutical companies or nurses or others. This makes it seem less of a doctor-oriented scandal. At least the doctors think so.

Here are some facts and results from studies of just the past few years:

▶ "Various estimates place the incidence of adverse drug reactions in hospitalized patients at 18 percent or higher." (*Postgraduate Medicine,* January 1980)

▶ According to Kenneth Barker, a pharmacist at Auburn University, hospitals with the best drug-problem records make mistakes 2 to 3 percent of the time. In an average 300-bed hospital, that comes to somewhere between 60 and 90 drug errors every day. In some small hospitals medication errors run as high as 11 percent. Those errors include giving a patient too much medication, too little, or none at all when required, as well as administering the drugs improperly.

▶ Vaginal yeast infection is being seen now as an iatrogenic disease brought on, according to researchers, by the overprescribing by doctors of antibiotics.

▶ When researchers at the Yale School of Medicine studied six hospital emergency rooms and 620 cases where tetanus shots needed to be given, they discovered that 23 percent

of the patients were treated incorrectly (6 percent were
untreated, 17 percent were overtreated), and that "patients
at highest risk for tetanus . . . had the lowest likelihood (27
percent) of receiving correct antitetanus treatment."

▶ Some drugs designed to stop irregular heartbeats ironically
end up causing heart attacks. Anesthesia is responsible for
more than a thousand deaths every year.

How can these iatrogenic mishaps and epidemics be stopped?
It isn't easy. The solution has to start in the medical schools, with
better physician training, especially in pharmaceutical prescribing.
It has to be carried through into the hospitals, which need to have
stricter regulations and strong utilization review committees looking hard at doctors overprescribing, overdiagnosing and testing, and
overoperating. Hospitals need to institute tougher privilege policies
and disciplinary panels.
How can you as a patient protect yourself from doctor-produced
problems?
So long as medical care is provided by humans, there will be error
and greed and iatrogenesis. But it can be held within acceptable
limits, a point it hasn't reached yet. That is why you have to maintain an attitude of wariness. If you are not yet in a hospital, be wary
of going into one. If you are in one, be wary of everything scheduled
to be done to you. Get as much information as you can about what
is to be done to you, what drug is being prescribed for you. Learn
the names of the drugs you need to take, their doses and sizes and
even their colors, so that you will be able to spot a mistake or
question a change. Before you give the green light for anything, be
sure the benefits outweigh the risks. Don't be talked into "fad"
operations. Get second opinions and third opinions. When in
doubt—and especially if that doubt has to do with elective surgery—don't. Take nothing for granted. And question, question,
question.

UNDERTREATMENT OF
PAIN

Relief of pain and suffering should be the fundamental goal of every
physician, yet the latest research indicates that physicians chroni-
cally underprescribe medications, thereby causing patients needless
suffering. According to a survey undertaken at Chicago's Rush-

Presbyterian–St. Luke's Medical Center and published in the journal *Pain,* 65 percent of hospitalized patients reported experiencing unbearable pain at some point.

Why are doctors reluctant to give adequate doses of painkilling drugs? After all, isn't the ancient medical dictum "to cure sometimes, to comfort always"?

Doctors underprescribe largely because they fear that heavy doses of drugs will create addicts. They hold back even when their patients have only weeks or months to live. Dr. Russell Portnoy, director of analgesic studies at New York's Memorial Sloan-Kettering Cancer Center calls this a practice based on "a medical myth."

Unfortunately, this misconception persists despite an important study published a decade ago in the *New England Journal of Medicine.* Out of 11,882 hospital patients treated with painkilling drugs, only four were found to have become addicted.

Still, the myth survives, and not only among prescribing physicians but caregiving nurses as well. The Rush-Presbyterian–St. Luke's survey found that, on the average, nurses gave their patients only one-fourth of the doses of painkillers allowed by the physicians. From this and other studies it's clear that misinformation—concerning effective doses, duration of effects, and dangers of addiction—is rampant and, according to Portnoy, persists in part because of gaps in medical education. Currently, the typical four-year medical curriculum devotes four hours or less to pain, and most experts agree that is not enough. This appalling state of affairs is echoed in a 1987 report by the Hastings Center, an eminent think tank specializing in medical ethics. "Guidelines on the Termination of Life-Sustaining Treatment and the Care of the Dying" concluded that "many health care professionals have inadequate knowledge about the pharmacology of pain relief and the appropriate use of narcotics and similar agents for dying patients."

So much for the problem. Now, what can you do if you are in pain and relief is not forthcoming?

If you find yourself in this situation, realize that you (or a family member or friend) must play the major role.

▶ Discuss with your doctor your fear of or concern about pain and your desire for adequate medication for control of pain. Pain is a complex symptom, and not all of it is physical in origin; much derives from anxiety, a sense of hopelessness, family stress, fear, spiritual concerns—and all can lower your threshold for pain, thereby creating the perception of more and more pain. *Together,* discover the cause of your pain.

▶ Be sure to ask what the adverse side effects of the painkilling drugs are. A June 1988 article in *Postgraduate Medicine* points out that pain control measures often fail because the patient could not anticipate the adverse side effects.

▶ Communicate as honestly as you can the extent of your pain. Some experts recommend that doctors ask two key questions: Does the medicine ever take the pain away completely? Does the pain return before the next dose of medicine? According to Robert G. Twycross and Sylvia A. Lack in *Symptom Control in Far Advanced Cancer: Pain Relief,* if the first answer is no, then the dose should be increased. If the second answer is yes, then the dose should also be increased. But don't wait for your doctor to ask the questions. Give him or her the answers right away.

▶ Discuss with your physician the alternative therapies for pain relief—for example, biofeedback, hypnosis, relaxation techniques, and acupuncture. While they may not work in your case, they have in many others.

▶ And don't forget to include the matter of pain in your living will, if you have one. (See "Planning Your Departure" later in this chapter.) Specify in your living will that you wish medication to keep you as pain-free as possible.

Pain is a point of dignity. It's an inhumane medical system that sits back and allows a person to die in pain when there are means available to control it.

For more information on the treatment of pain, contact: International Pain Foundation, 909 N.E. 43rd Street, Suite 306, Seattle, WA 98105-6020.

WOMEN AND HOSPITALS

Women use the medical system more than men do. In return, they are used by the system, if not abused by it, more than men are.

When the American College of Surgeons (ACS) listed the ten most-often-performed surgeries in the United States, five of them—

dilation and curettage, hysterectomy, ligation and division of fallopian tubes, cesarean section, and oophorectomy, in that order—involved only women. Of every ten patients who undergo surgery, six are women.

The 1986 figures (reported to the world in 1989) of in-hospital performed surgeries shows that four of the top ten are exclusive to women. The hit parade includes cervical cesarean sections in the number-one position (820,960 performed), abdominal hysterectomy at number three (468,022), repair of obstetric laceration at number seven (266,211), and forceps delivery with episiotomy in the number-ten spot (231,015). The list is a bit technical in how the procedures are broken down. For example, vaginal hysterectomies came in at the fifteenth position, but if added to abdominal hysterectomies the category would move into the number-two position with a combined 622,972 surgeries performed.

These figures are also a bit deceiving. With the great move toward outpatient and same-day surgeries, many previously done surgeries are now being done in physicians' offices or at other outpatient centers.

Women have come to (or have been led to) believe that they are walking medical disaster areas. Many of them expect to break out at any moment in some mental or physical weakness or to discover a cancer that is bound to leave them ill or mutilated or at a loss of personal empowerment.

"Why have women as patients been so totally at the mercy of doctors and of the health care system?" asks Cynthia Carver, M.D., in her book *Patient Beware* (Scarborough, Ontario, Canada: Prentice-Hall, 1984). The answer: "Women often get the worst health care because of their upbringing and conditioning. They learn to seek and follow advice from doctors in a docile and unquestioning way."

But it takes two to tango. Explains Carver: "Male doctors have been conditioned in the same system. The women in their lives, as mothers, wives or nurses, have served as adjuncts to men. These doctors will naturally tend to take a dominant role in the relationship with their patients, and in their attitudes towards their patients' rights and responsibilities, they can only reflect their own upbringing and societal biases."

Doctors and hospitals are quick to treat women patients and take their money, although studies and reports show that doctors tend to take men's complaints more seriously than women's and ascribe women's complaints to something emotional or psychogenic—all in their heads. Silly women. The weaker sex.

Of course, this doesn't stop doctors from operating on them. It certainly increases the number of prescriptions for sedatives and psychotropic drugs by doctors for female patients. This is in addition to the scores of other pharmaceuticals designed by men to artificially turn on or shut off some female biological function. The thalidomide and DES controversies and tragedies are among the consequences.

It is very clear that women have to be concerned, careful, and diligent when it comes to dealings with the medical profession. And especially so in these areas:

Hysterectomies. The American Medical Association once put this, the surgical removal of the uterus, second on the list of operations often performed unnecessarily. There are some doctors who are constant offenders and some hospitals that are hotbeds of abuse when it comes to hysterectomies, urging women to have surgery for a prolapsed (or sagging) uterus when the operation is not even indicated, but is profitable.

Equally appalling is the large number of women who make the decision—most often with a physician's urging—to have their perfectly healthy uterus removed. These women have an inexplicable desire to be rid of a cancer that doesn't even exist (but that could *possibly* develop sometime, they have been convinced) or to find a permanent and foolproof contraceptive method. So they follow the rather drastic course of having an elective hysterectomy.

After quite a bit of this, the American College of Obstetricians and Gynecologists' committee on gynecological practice finally went on record calling elective hysterectomies unjustified. "Despite advances in surgical techniques, this operation still carries a substantial risk of morbidity," the committee said. More than eight hundred women a year die from hysterectomies or from preexisting conditions worsened by the operation.

Women should reject the idea of elective hysterectomies, dissuade friends and relatives from having them, and put pressure on local surgeons and hospitals to stop performing this senseless, misogynistic, but lucrative surgery.

Cesarean Sections. In many cases cesareans, or C-sections, are necessary to save the life of the fetus or that of the mother. This is true in spite of critics who hold that fetal monitoring is overused and can be blamed for the increase in marginally necessary C-sections.

However, a mother-to-be must find out about a doctor's or hospital's policy and proclivity toward C-sections, because it is an operation ripe for abuse. Many cesareans are performed simply because the doctor doesn't want to wait around for things to move along at their natural speed, and so alters nature's time clock to accommodate his own. Also, doctors make more money on C-section deliveries than on vaginal deliveries. Some doctors and some hospitals have a good money-making thing going with cesareans. Ask friends who have used your obstetrician or delivered in your hospital about their experiences. Find out what they know about the doctor's attitude toward surgical deliveries and the hospital's record on C-sections. Call the local government health agency to see if it has any cesarean statistics for the hospital. Ask your doctor directly how he decides on cesareans, or ask another doctor you can trust to tell you the truth.

One of the reasons that the C-section rate is about 25 percent of all births is repeat births. Physicians have long held the belief that after a cesarean, all subsequent births have to be cesareans, too. It was thought that a vaginal delivery might rupture the place in the uterus where the incision had previously been made, thus leading to serious hemorrhaging. A reevaluation of this old saw has finally taken place.

In 1989 the American College of Obstetricians and Gynecologists (ACOG) issued strong guidelines stating that repeat cesarean deliveries should no longer be routine. According to ACOG, 50 to 80 percent of women who have had one or more low transverse cesareans should, as a matter of course, deliver vaginally unless specific complications arise. (The ACOG still recommends against vaginal birth for women with a "classical" cesarean scar—a high, vertical incision rarely used these days.)

How many women will be affected by this change in policy? Somewhere around 150,000 to 200,000 annually. Of all the cesareans performed, one in three are repeat cesarean customers. When you consider that England has a total cesarean rate of 11.3 percent, compared with our 25 percent rate, it is clear why the subject has been a topic of great controversy.

Unnecessary cesareans are costly—and they can be deadly. They expose mother and child to dangers of infection, complication, and error that are attendant with any form of surgery. Maternal mortality for cesarean deliveries is about 1 in 2,500 according to statistics quoted in a *New York Times* article. That is four times higher than the mortality rate for vaginal deliveries, which is 1 in 10,000.

Doctors are not the only ones to have leaned too heavily toward cesarean births. C-sections have flourished because many hospitals have refused to allow women to progress through labor after a previous cesarean. The ACOG guidelines call for all hospitals to develop procedures that encourage vaginal birth.

Unfortunately, the new standards do not address the issue of unnecessary first-time cesareans. But help may be coming here from the insurance industry, which is striving to curb the C-section rate by hitting doctors where it hurts—in the pocketbook. Blue Cross and Blue Shield plans in several states have begun to reduce payment for cesareans to discourage scalpel-toting doctors. The Rhode Island Blue Cross/Blue Shield plan pays physicians the same fee for either type of delivery.

Now doctors and hospitals have no more excuses for perpetuating the old saw "Once a cesarean, always a cesarean."

Childbirth. "Men have rewritten the drama of obstetrics to make them the stars instead of women," says Marsden G. Wagner, M.D., of the World Health Organization (WHO). Wagner also tells of a WHO study showing that "the majority of routine procedures carried out during pregnancy and delivery have never been proved to be of value and some are positively harmful."

The area of childbirth is one in which women have been able to assert some influence and have things go more their way. As a result, there has been a rise in birthing centers, a reintroduction of midwives, an increased belief in the importance of mother-infant bonding, the rejection of standard operating-procedure episiotomies, the similar rejection of many drugs, a new wave of natural childbirth methods, and a widespread renewed interest in breast-feeding. The hospitals were quick to see where new profit and public relations opportunities lay. And if that meant catering to women and treating them better, then so be it. The hospitals co-opted these concepts and created versions and interpretations of their own.

A birthing room in a hospital wasn't quite the same as an independent birthing center, in atmosphere or in looks. The work of midwives in hospitals, when they were allowed to be there at all, was constrained by doctors. The midwives practiced only on the advice and consent of those medical professionals who let the midwives do the work but took a chunk of the fee. In hospital maternity wards there is still the strong atmosphere of men dominating women. But some changes have taken place and women have benefited.

Renewed interest by women in home births is, however, a concept most doctors just can't abide. They say it is dangerous, backward, and old-fashioned. And they have influence enough to have the law on their side, in many cases. Marsden Wagner has a different view of things. "Doctors, to remain in control, must work within their territory, which may be why so many oppose home birth," he says. "The one country in Europe with over one-third of all births taking place at home (Holland) is also the country with the lowest or near-lowest mortality figures." Infant mortality figures in the United States are hardly enviable.

Hospital versus home could be the next childbirth combat arena. But you can be sure, one way or another, that hospitals will find a way to make money out of it.

Breast Cancer. States are passing laws making it mandatory for physicians to inform breast cancer patients of all treatment options. This is especially important in light of test results showing that lumpectomies (removal of the tumor only) are as effective as mastectomies (total breast removal) in cases where the cancer is localized and has not spread (which is the fact in about 60 percent of the cases). Lumpectomies are quicker and cheaper and less dangerous than mastectomies; and they do not disfigure a woman.

It is not uncommon for surgeons to perform one-step breast cancer surgery. This means that when a patient is on the operating table to have a biopsy done to see if cancer is present, a frozen section is examined and if malignant, the doctor then and there, while the patient is still under anesthesia, goes ahead and performs a mastectomy. What a surprise for the patient on awakening. This one-step method does not allow the patient to get a second opinions or seek alternative therapies, including lumpectomy, with or without radiation.

Women with suspected breast cancer should avoid giving surgeons such carte blanche with their bodies. Consent forms should indicate specific procedures only. The patient's desires must be known and acted on.

Much of the gap between the medical profession and women is a result of the failure to communicate. A bridge can be and must be constructed. Women hold up half the sky, as the saying goes; they are doing more than their share in supporting medicine and must be heard. Michelle Harrison, M.D., put it this way: "I have this fantasy of this big room with doctors and women being locked in with each other and just doctors having to listen, having to hear what women are saying. Because I don't think most doctors hear what women are saying."

CHILDREN AND
HOSPITALS

A child patient has every right that an adult patient has. That includes everything from bringing food from home (especially if the child has never eaten meat or sugar or other foodstuffs for health or religious reasons) to demanding informed consent and disclosure of information.

In terms of nearly everything else, though, a child is most definitely a child. Despite the care of specialty trained pediatrics professionals (if you are lucky enough to be in a hospital that has them), a little boy or girl is going to be frightened and even traumatized just by being in a strange place with strange people and without Mommy and Daddy.

That is why Mommy and Daddy have to be there as much as possible. "Parents must not only be allowed to visit, live in, or participate, they must be encouraged, supported, and educated to be of the greatest possible help to the hospitalized child," wrote Barbara M. Kursch, M.D., in a 1978 issue of the *American Journal of Public Health.* She noted further: "It has been largely pressure from parents, not action from the medical profession or associated professionals,

---

A MORATORIUM ON TONSILLECTOMIES?

Many medical professionals are beginning to 'fess up publicly to the pointlessness of performing tonsil-removing surgery. But none have put the case better than Harvey N. Mandell, M.D., who writes regularly for *Postgraduate Medicine.*

He gives these as sound reasons for tonsillectomy: (1) if the tonsils have grown large enough to obstruct airflow or cause sleep disorders, and (2) if the tonsil is abscessed ("although agreement on this is not unanimous," Mandell adds). A tumor of the tonsil (extremely rare) would also call for excision.

Notice that frequent sore throat is not among the reasons. "Pharyngitis [sore throat] is caused by lots of different microorganisms, and why tonsillectomy should be expected to reduce the incidence of viral pharyngitis is unexplained."

Mandell objects to the casual attitude toward this seemingly unnecessary surgery since "every operation and every anesthesia has potential for complications up to and including death."

"Ask the doctors around your hospital if their children have had their tonsils removed," says Mandell. "If your medical staff is like ours, you will find that *most doctor's kids still have their tonsils."* Why? The answer seems obvious.

Mandell's recommendation: "I suggest a moratorium on tonsillectomies in the United States and Canada [except for the conditions listed above]. . . . I predict that this moratorium will injure the public health in no way. . . ."

that has resulted in improved practices for child care in hospitals."

Despite visitation rules and limited hours, if you feel that your child needs you to be there, then be there as long as is necessary. Stay all day. Spend the night. Some hospitals provide sleeping accommodations for parents in the same room with or near the child. If nurses or other personnel ask you to leave because visiting hours are over, politely refuse. Get an OK from the child's doctor or go to the hospital administrator (or beyond if necessary) to confirm your right to stay.

Parents, especially of young children, should prepare the child for the hospital stay, as long before admission as they can. They should also be active participants in the child's care, if the child's condition allows. Some hospitals (the Children's Health Center of the University of Texas Medical Branch, to name a prominent one) have instituted care-by-parent units. In these the parents tend to all nonemergency, routine needs of the child. There are no nurses. Measurements, such as blood pressure and temperature, are read by the parents. The chart is kept current by them. It is a situation that is good for the child, good for the parent, and good for the pocketbook. It is one-third cheaper than the normal charge for pediatric unit care.

Some doctors and nurses see parents who get involved with their kids' hospital care as meddlers and obstructions. That is their ego problem, not yours. Do what you think you need to do to soothe, comfort, and care for this child you know far better than they do.

If the rules restrict children under a certain age from visiting hospital patients, and if that rule means your child's friends can't visit, break it. A kid needs his pals, for any number of good reasons. It is your job to make sure they get together, even if you have to confront the hospital, or sue.

DYING, DEATH,
AND BEYOND

It is possible that the condition that brought you to the hospital will be the cause of your death. Perhaps you are in the last stage of an incurable disease; maybe the severe weakening of your heart, or of some other organ or body system, is irreversible.

Death in the hospital can also be sudden, surprising, unexpected.

Natural, iatrogenic, or thoroughly inexplicable causes may be at the root of such deaths.

Patients and doctors see death differently, of course. To the patient it may be the welcome end to a harsh struggle, or the undesired cessation of a life hardly lived. It may represent peace, fear, the most awesome of personal involvements. To the doctor, death is an affront. Death is seen by many doctors not as the natural event it is but as a slap in the face, a professional failure.

That is why doctors fight hard—sometimes too hard and senselessly—to keep some patients alive who have a right to die in peace, with dignity. Many hopelessly ill and dying patients are vehemently opposed to leaving this life as victims of doctors' heroics. Life at what price? That is the question. What further pain of survival is desired, what further financial burden to the survivors is fair? The quality of life, and of death, are the central issues. What good are additional days of life if they are merely days of excruciating pain or of drug-dreamy existence or of mere survival by being plugged into machines that sustain life but undercut its sanctity—and operate against the wishes of the dying?

There is often a gap in communication between doctors and patients when it comes to sustaining life. A study published in the April 26, 1984 issue of the *New England Journal of Medicine* showed that of all patients who received lifesaving cardiopulmonary resuscitation at Boston's Beth Israel Hospital, one-third said they hadn't wanted to be resuscitated and would not want to be should the occasion arise again. Even patients designated DNR (do not resuscitate) at their and their families' request, find themselves being brought back to tenuous life again and again by doctors who believe they can fix them up and get them walking out the hospital front door.

Nurses, in general, are more in touch with the needs, desires, and feelings of the dying. Approximately 10 percent of them, in a 1983 survey in *Nursing Life* magazine, admitted having given patients drug overdoses to hasten their deaths. In other situations nurses will, despite doctors orders, refuse or "neglect" to resuscitate patients who want to die. They will take the risk and responsibility of pulling the plug or will look away when someone else on staff—or the patient's family—does it.

The Beth Israel study showed that doctors often didn't speak to their patients. They didn't ask what the patient wanted. Instead, the doctors relied on impressions and suppositions. They guessed wrong one out of every three times. A statement by the hospital suggested that "physicians and their hospitalized patients should routinely and openly discuss [resuscitation] . . . to ensure that each is aware of the other's attitude toward the procedure and the quality-of-life issues associated with it."

You and your doctor should do so, too. He or she should be made to know how you stand on the matter, as should your family. An agreement in principle can be reached, and your attitudes toward artificial life support may win you your desired end. If your doctor won't agree to your desires or won't even enter into the discussion, find a doctor who will. You can also ask to speak with members of the hospital's Ethics Committee, if there is one, about your wishes in the matter.

New Definitions of Death

In their book *Playing God,* Thomas and Celia Scully say, "For the first time in history, physicians have the ability, know-how, and sophisticated technology to sustain the physical life of patients beyond any reasonable quality of life they may want to endure." And with these great medical "advancements" has come a major complication; nobody can agree on just what death is!

It used to be simple. You stopped breathing, your heart stopped, your pupils dilated—you were dead. Not so today. No longer is the old-fashioned heart-and-lung concept of death applicable.

So to be in control of your own death, it is important that you understand how the medical and legal worlds are redefining what once used to be as certain as taxes.

The changes in the definition of death have come about thanks to what the *Medico-Legal Journal* calls the "revolution in intensive-care technology, which now enables artificial ventilation and circulation, feeding by the intravenous route, and the elimination of waste products of metabolism by dialysis machines to be resorted to on bodies whose brains have been irreversibly destroyed." In other words, today modern medicine can keep dead people alive.

As a result, the definition of death has been broadened to include the irreversible loss of all brain function—brain death. In a landmark 1968 report, the Ad Hoc Committee of the Harvard Medical School to Examine the Definition of Brain Death laid down four characteristics of a permanently nonfunctioning brain:

1. Unreceptivity and unresponsivity—total unawareness to externally applied stimuli.

2. No movement or breathing—one hour's observation of spontaneous muscular movements, breathing or response to stimuli. (If the person is on a respirator, absence of breathing must be established by three minutes off the machine.)

3. No reflexes present—fixed and dilated pupils, no eye movement or blinking, no contraction of muscles due to stimulation.

4. Flat electroencephalogram (EEG)—after ten minutes of recording.

These tests, according to the report, are to be done twice, twenty-four hours apart.

By either laws or court decisions, most states recognize the concept of brain death, but have left the final determination to the doctors. And most statutes conform to what is called the Uniform Determination of Death Act: "An individual who has sustained either (1) irreversible cessation of circulatory and respiratory functions, or (2) irreversible cessation of all functions of the entire brain, including the brain stem, is dead. A determination must be made in accordance with accepted medical standards."

But some states have no legislation. In those, according to Derek Humphry and Ann Wickett in their book *The Right to Die,* decisions on what constitutes death are left to physicians' own definitions. Check with your state bar association to find out what applies in your state.

Even a legal definition of brain death does not completely eliminate the uncertainty surrounding the issue. A 1985 report in the *Washington Post*'s "Health" section noted that the criteria for determining brain death vary slightly from hospital to hospital. So check with your hospital to see what "standards" they use to determine brain death. And make sure that the criteria include total lack of movement, inability to breathe without a respirator, total unresponsiveness to stimuli, and total absence of reflexes.

But that's not the end of it. Even with recognized and legislated definitions of brain death and established criteria for determining it, there is uncertainty among some physicians who question whether brain death refers to the entire brain, including the brain stem, or just cerebral death, which is partial death of the brain. There is now a growing movement to modify the concept of brain death to include people in what is called a persistent vegetative state. The medicos even abbreviate it for you—PVS. There are an estimated 10,000 PVSers in the United States.

To qualify for PVS status, only part of the brain need be destroyed; the main stem is intact, so the person is capable of reflex functions such as breathing and sleeping, but incapable of thought or even awareness of his or her environment. Often labeled cognitive death, PVS can last for years, with absolutely no hope for improvement.

Even cognitive death sparks debate. One side asks "Where will it all end . . . in experiments on these people?" Others believe the long-term unconscious may someday "wake up." Obviously, the debate will go on for years. The important thing is to know where you stand, how you would like to be treated, and what to do to make your choice the one followed.

Planning Your Departure

When you consider today's "what is death?" atmosphere, planning one's demise, or at least the circumstances around it, may be a necessity.

Basically, there are two legal routes available to help assure that your death occurs on your terms: living wills and durable power of attorney.

A living will is a written statement that you do not want life-prolonging medical procedures to be performed when your condition is hopeless and there is no chance of regaining a meaningful life. They have been around for a while. In 1976 California became the first state to pass what is called the Natural Death Act.

Although called a "will," it has nothing to do with property, but rather with one's self. It is also intended to take effect while you are living. It is an advance directive, operative only at the time you are terminally ill and unconscious, or otherwise incompetent to discuss and decide with your physician what treatment you wish.

Not only a tool to control the extent and type of medical care you receive at the end of your life, a living will can also help reduce the emotional stresses and strains felt by both your family and your doctor, who must make decisions whether to withhold, withdraw, or continue medical treatment that cannot cure or reverse your terminal condition.

As of 1990, thirty-nine states and the District of Columbia have some form of living will laws. They go by various titles: "natural death acts," "death-with-dignity acts," "medical treatment decision acts," "right-to-die acts," etc.

Along with the variation in titles, they also vary in provisions from state to state. Here are some things you should check on:

▶ Are more than the two standard witnesses required, and is notarization mandatory?

▶ Is implementation of the living will prohibited if you are pregnant?

▶ Does the withdrawal of life-sustaining treatment include artificial feeding and hydration? An issue fraught with controversy, many states' living will laws specifically prohibit the withdrawal of food and water, others allow it, and some sidestep the issue entirely.

▶ Must you follow a particular form or are you permitted to add personalized instructions?

▶ Is your state's living will valid in another state?

And remember that even if your state does not have a living will statute there are some steps you can take to exercise some control over your passing. Alice Mehling of the Society for the Right to Die says, "Even without a living will law, everyone has the common law right to refuse treatment." She recommends executing a general living will form as clear and convincing evidence of what you want.

The big question, though, is, must your hospital or doctor accept your advance directive? Mehling says yes, pointing out that the "growing body of legal opinion is that [failure to comply with a valid living will] is grounds for battery action."

The other, legal way, to attempt to die with dignity at the hospital is through the "durable power of attorney for health care." This is an alternative form of advance directive, a written document, that allows you to name someone as agent (also called proxy or "attorney-in-fact") with authority to make medical decisions for you (according to previously expressed wishes) in the event you become incompetent and are unable to make those decisions for yourself.

In nonmedical matters, the durable power of attorney is used to authorize another person to make decisions or take actions on your behalf in financial or property transactions. Every state, and the District of Columbia, have durable-power-of-attorney laws, and these laws have been used as the basis for health care directives.

But some states have gone a step further and passed legislation creating a durable power of attorney specifically for health care decisions. This is to distinguish your health wishes from other legal matters. Yet even those states without specific durable-power-of-attorney-for-health laws have generally recognized such documents. (Check with your state bar association for more information on the law.)

The best strategy is to have both a living will and a durable power of attorney. Remember, a living will is only about the final moments of life. Considered more flexible than a living will, a durable power of attorney can be written to include the authority to make decisions about several areas of medical treatment, not just the termination of life support, on behalf of people incapable of making their own decisions, such as after a serious accident, a permanent loss of consciousness, or an incapacitating illness.

Last Gasps

When we mentioned DNR (do not resuscitate) earlier in this section, you may not have been aware just how controversial and confusing the issue can be. A DNR order means that should respiration or heartbeat fail, cardiopulmonary resuscitative measures (CPR) will not be started or carried out. A DNR order means that the patient will not be given brief emergency CPR, nor will the patient be placed on long-term mechanical life support equipment.

Before there were laws and guidelines, decisions about when to turn on the technology or when to let nature run its course were left to the medical team. Back in those olden days, not much more than a decade or two ago, only medical and nursing personnel knew whether a person was designated DNR. It was the prevailing medical opinion that it was "inappropriate" to discuss the matter with the patient.

An outcome of such secrecy was that there was a tacit agreement among hospital staff to engage in "slow codes" (have the resuscitation team purposely move slowly) or "show codes" (have the team feign a resuscitation effort, for the family's sake). No matter what it was called, everyone on the health care team knew what to do and not do.

A nationwide survey of DNR orders in intensive care units, reported in the *Journal of the American Medical Association,* January 17, 1986, found that 75 percent of the time ICU or attending physicians initiated the DNR orders, and only 8 percent of the time did the family do so. The thirteen-hospital study of more than 7,000 admissions found that only one patient gave the word, and only one patient had a living will that stipulated no resuscitation.

But this scenario is changing. One of the primary reasons is the movement—led by organizations like the People's Medical Society—for more patient autonomy. For example, as of January 1, 1988, all hospitals seeking accreditation by the Joint Commission on Accreditation of Healthcare Organizations had to have a policy in place concerning the withholding of resuscitation services to patients.

The message is clear: Find out what your hospital's specific DNR policy consists of.

Here are some specific points you should keep in mind about DNR orders:

▶ Plan ahead. Timing is essential. A study reported in the *Journal of the American Medical Association,* July 11, 1986, noted that DNR orders are written at the time when most patients are not capable of participating in the decision, although the majority of people in the survey were considered competent when they were admitted.

▶ Don't be afraid to talk to your doctor about it in advance of hospitalization. The chances are the doctor will not bring the issue up to you. It is really something you must initiate.

▶ Make sure your family knows your wishes so that they may act with confidence if they are put into a decision-making position.

▶ Document your wishes concerning emergency resuscitation, and have your physician make it part of your record.

Most important, remember that a DNR order is not an irrevocable decision. You can always change your mind, for whatever reason. All you need to do is speak up.

Let Me Go

Of all the life-sustaining treatments in a hospital, the most controversial is the withholding or withdrawing of artificial feeding.

Many authorities, however, see an emerging legal trend concerning the issue. Courts in at least fifteen states have ruled that patients have the same right to refuse feeding tubes as to refuse other medical treatment. Even the American Medical Association supports the notion.

In a 1987 precedent-setting ruling, the New Jersey Supreme Court affirmed a lower-court decision that had been the first ruling to support removal of life-extending, artificial feeding and hydration from a patient diagnosed as terminally ill.

For the most part, competent patients have the right to refuse artificial feeding; the right is not limited to comatose or terminally ill patients. For competent patients artificial feeding, as with other treatments, can be stopped in accordance with the patient's previously expressed wishes.

So here are some pointers to help you to keep control:

▶ Document your wishes about artificial feeding and be as specific as you can.

▶ Know your state's living will law (if it has one) and what it says about artificial feeding. Some laws don't even mention it.

▶ Know the common feeding and hydration treatments available should you not be able to eat in the usual way. Discuss them with your physician and what purpose they will serve. The decision should be based on whether the burden is worth the benefit—to you—not the medical team.

▶ Be sure you know your physician's feelings about withholding or withdrawing artificial feeding. This is one decision where a conflict between you and your physician should not exist.

For more information on right-to-die laws and living wills, write Concern for Dying and/or Society for the Right to Die, both at 250 West 57th Street, New York, NY 10107; Elisabeth Kübler-Ross Center, South Route 616, Head Waters, VA 24442; or the National Hemlock Society, P.O. Box 11830, Eugene, OR 97440.

The Hospice Option

A person does not have to spend his or her last days in a hospital. There is, for example, the option of a hospice.

A hospice, in its truest sense, is a place of shelter for travelers. In its relationship to death and dying, a hospice is a comforting place where a terminal patient becomes a person, surrounded by loved ones and caring professionals, all of whom work to make this last stage of life as meaningful and comfortable as any other. Even if the hospice is in or associated with a hospital (it may also be, and usually is, a separate entity, in the city or in a pleasant country setting), the surroundings are not cold or sterile; there are no million-dollar life-support machines. There is only an atmosphere conducive to making the ill person's "journey" as easy as possible, and to helping his or her family adjust to a life without this person. Psychologists, social workers, medical professionals, and religious or spiritual advisers are at hand to help in achieving this goal.

The hospice is still viewed askance by many doctors. Some do not believe in the concept and suggest that hospital care is no worse than hospice care and is probably better. Others are not quite sure where hospices fit in the schedule of a dying patient, and in the framework of patient care. Other doctors (and patients, too) reject hospices because they refuse to admit that death is imminent, or even a real possibility. To them, hospices represent a defeatist attitude, a sign of surrender.

Hospices are not necessarily cheap; some may be as expensive as a hospital. Quality certainly may vary from place to place. And now that there is money to be made from the concept, people who are less dedicated to the hospice movement than to the profit motive are entering the field. They open up a house somewhere and christen it a hospice.

There are qualities and resources a hospice ought to have, and there are things it ought to do and be. To find out what a good hospice should be, where to find one in your area, and whether you should be considering one at all, contact the National Hospice Organization, 1901 North Fort Myer Drive, Suite 307, Arlington, VA 22209. The telephone number is (703) 243–5900.

Beyond the hospital and the hospice, there is home. Dying at home has been a long-standing tradition, more so than dying in a hospital. But with the rise of medical science and the modern medical care institution, this tradition has lost favor. In our society today, dying at home is considered something backward, alien, unseemly, and traumatic, if not downright horrifying. According to statistics, 80 percent of Americans who die this year will die in a medical facility; forty years ago, a majority died at home. Yet, if a family can handle the psychological, emotional, and physical burdens of home care for a dying relative—along with the financial burden if professional nursing care is opted for—then there may be no better place for the dying person. It is comforting to be in familiar surroundings, at peace with the soothing atmosphere of home, looking up from a comfortable bed into the faces of a lifetime.

A final word about the possibility of and preparation for death: Even if your condition is not terminal, not even serious, nor the procedure risky, it might cross your mind that anything can happen. Not a morbid thought, just a practical one. The kind of thought that has made insurance companies multibillion-dollar concerns.

In thinking about this personal unthinkable, you might want to give a thought to afterward, to the disposal of your remains. Donating your organs for transplantation or giving your body to a medical school for the education of students are two options to consider. Talk to your family first, then to the person at Admissions, if you decide that you want your death to help save the life of another.

ANDAS THE SUN SINKS SLOWLY IN THE WEST...

5

Parting is such sweet sorrow, hospitalwise. It is sweet because you will be leaving behind an Alice in Hospital Land universe where catch-22 is the preamble, articles, and all amendments to the constitution. It is sorrow because, like everything else associated with hospitals, leaving is no simple matter.

TWO STYLES OF LEAVE-TAKING

There are a couple of what might be called "styles" of leaving. The first is standard. Your doctor gives word to the hospital, preferably at least twenty-four hours in advance, that you no longer need to be taking up a bed there. You are discharged, take your things, see the cashier, and breathe the fresh air of freedom.

Leaving A.M.A. (Against Medical Advice)

The second "style" is definitely not standard, but one born of personal conviction or necessity: leaving "A.M.A." (against medical advice). This means that you discharge yourself, despite warnings from the doctor in charge and the hospital's medical staff. Sometimes patients leave hospitals A.M.A. unwisely. They think they have recovered completely when they haven't. They want to get back to work sooner than is desirable because they worry that they will be replaced, or for any of a dozen other reasons.

But sometimes the need to get out of a hospital's clutches is real. There might be a staff member who is making life hell for you. Your doctor may be conspiring with the hospital (he or she might even own an interest in it) to keep you there longer than you know you need to be. You know you are not getting the vitamins and minerals you brought; your food from home is "misplaced" on a constant, seemingly malicious basis. The care and medical treatment simply may be below par or worse.

You have discussed your displeasure or concern with your family, the hospital's administrator or patients' representative, or the people involved. The problem remains unchanged and unimproved, or it actually deteriorates. Then it is your right to check yourself out of that hospital and take yourself to another hospital or care facility, or home.

The authorities at the hospital will shove a piece of paper, an against-medical-advice release form (sometimes called an unauthorized-departure form), under your nose and hand you a pen for signing. That form will say that you are leaving their hospital despite doctors' admonitions and that by doing so you are losing all rights to bring suit against them should your condition worsen.

Don't sign it. You don't have to. You are not legally obligated to sign anything in order to leave the hospital. The staff or administration can't keep you there if you don't sign. If they try to restrain you from leaving, contact your lawyer at once.

If you are advised by legal counsel that in refusing to sign the A.M.A. release form you run the risk of being dropped by your insurance company or that you might run into other major problems, then sign the form *only if you amend it.* That is, don't just put your signature to the document. Write at the bottom of it, or in the margins, and explain why you are leaving. (Don't use a separate sheet. It could get "lost.") Explain why it is harmful to your health to stay in this hospital. Explain that you are signing the form under duress, and that you are by no means giving up your right to sue for complications that may occur after your self-discharge, but which resulted from the hospital's misdeeds.

Don't pay your bill. Let them mail it to you or, better yet, to your attorney, who should also get in touch with your insurance company to explain what is going on. Write letters to the doctors, staff, and/or hospital administrators involved, explaining in more detail your complaints, your charges, and your reasons for leaving A.M.A. Before sending these letters by registered mail, discuss their contents with your lawyer. (You wouldn't want to say something in them that could hurt your case.) Then leave any future legal gives-and-takes to him or her.

Tips on a Traditional Departure

You will probably have a more traditional, far less dramatic, and less traumatic departure than the A.M.A. checkout. Still, "traditional" doesn't mean "uncomplicated." There are lots of things to remember to do and to ask before you leave, and leave satisfied.

▶ Just as you did when you checked into the hospital, you should time your exit to save yourself some money. If the new-day room rates begin at noon, leave before noon. Why leave at 10 A.M. if it's cheaper to leave at 9, and you have been ready to go since 8 the night before? When you get the good news that you can leave, plan for an early, economical discharge.

▶ Ask about the posthospital continuation of your care when your doctor comes around to discharge you. (If the doctor isn't there when you are ready to leave, or didn't let you know in person that you could go home, refuse to pay his discharge fee. He didn't earn it.) Ask when you should see him back in the office for a checkup. (And is this covered by the fee already charged you or is it extra?) When can you resume a regular diet, exercise regimen, sex life? When can you go back to work? What should you do to speed your recovery and forestall a relapse or infections? What signs should you watch for that could indicate trouble?

Take notes of what the doctor tells you. Better yet, tape-record the doctor's comments. This is an excellent record for future reference. If you have taken written notes, have the doctor read them over and sign them to indicate they accurately reflect his orders and suggestions to you.

▶ If you haven't already discussed the need for further care—in a nursing home, by a visiting nurse, or any other continued treatment—discuss it now with the appropriate hospital staff person. It is something that should have been gone over during your stay, to give you time to make a wise, informed decision, not one pushed and rushed through by medical professionals.

▶ Have the hospital or your doctor provide for you a list of mutual aid groups in your area. These are national and/or local organizations designed to help you overcome the fears or physical setbacks caused by your operation or condition. They are often composed of people just like you, dealing with similar health problems, talking about them and assisting each other.

   Here are some national clearinghouses that can direct you toward mutual aid groups in your locality, as well as provide you with other information about self-help. If after calling them you are still unsatisfied, contact us at the People's Medical Society. We'll try to steer you in the right direction.

Self-Help Clearinghouse
St. Clare's–Riverside
   Medical Center
Denville, NJ 07834
In N.J. only: (800)
   FOR-MASH
Outside N.J.: (201) 625-7101

National Health Information
   Clearinghouse
P.O. Box 1133
Washington, DC 20013-1133
(800) 336-4797
In Md.: (301) 565-4167

Illinois Self-Help Center
Suite S-122
1600 Dodge Avenue
Evanston, IL 60201
(800) 322-MASH
(312) 328-0470

National Self-Help
   Clearinghouse
City University of New
   York
Graduate Center
33 West 42nd Street
   New York, NY 10036
(212) 840-1259

▶ Be sure to take home everything that's yours, particularly those items the hospital provided and for which you overpaid plenty. Talk to your favorite nurse or the patients' representative to find out what is yours for keeps. (Don't ask the doctor; he or she probably won't have the fuzziest idea what you paid for.) If you don't take your paid-for items home with you, they will either be tossed out or used on another patient, who will also pay for them.

▶ What you *shouldn't* take home from the hospital is hospital-dispensed pharmaceuticals. Don't accept any drugs, prescription or otherwise, that the kind nurse or the good doctor might hand you, unless they are free of charge. They probably won't be. Hospital drugs are grossly overpriced. That goes for drugs sold in pharmacies on hospital premises, too. It is best to have any prescription filled at a less expensive discount drug chain or at the neighborhood pharmacy.

▶ It is not necessary to tip the nursing staff or other hospital employees. You could go broke (if you haven't already) slipping a bill of even small denomination to everybody who crossed your path and did you no harm.

Most hospitals will recommend that if you want to show appreciation tangibly, you do it with something that all the nurses and staff can enjoy; flowers, candy, a fruit basket, something like that sent to the nurses' station. Donate a book to the medical library. Better yet, donate a book (a copy of this book!) or magazine subscription to the patients' library, if there is one.

GOING THROUGH CUSTOMS

Once you have cleared out the closet, looked through drawers, collected together everything that has been stored for you, you are almost ready to go home. First, though, you will have to walk or be wheeled to the cashier to settle your account.

This is a bit easier said than done. Oh sure, some people will just give a cursory glance at the papers before them and blithely sign on the dotted lines, assuming that the hospital wouldn't make a mis-

YOU DESERVE AN HONORABLE DISCHARGE

"It is my opinion that a patient must never leave the hospital without a copy of his or her discharge," writes one of our New York City members.

Three years after having undergone a lung cancer operation in one of New York's premier university medical centers, our member had occasion to see the discharge sheet from that previous stay.

What caught her eye—much to her absolute outrage—was an entry in the "Diagnosis" section of the sheet. There, along with the notations for "adenocarcinoma of right lower lobe" and "basal cell cancer skin of face" was this: "Paranoid schizophrenia."

Our member demanded an explanation of this altogether erroneous blot on her medical record from her surgeon. The response? A very quick apology.

The diagnosis of paranoid schizophrenia, the letter read, had never been made by any specialist who had the ability to do so. "The resident who was on and who filled out the records at that time apparently misinterpreted [some] notes and put down that diagnosis," the apology said by way of explanation . . . or cover-up. The doctor also asserted that he had personally corrected the sheet, and all was now well.

By getting a copy of your discharge, explains our Manhattan member, you will have, in writing, "diagnoses which your surgeon may not have mentioned because he was sure the cardiologist did, and the cardiologist was sure the doctor of record did, ad infinitum."

More to the point, though, is that by letting doctors and hospitals know that you'll be wanting a copy of that discharge sheet "doctors will not feel free to enter undisclosed, damaging psychiatric pronouncements"—casual notations or offhand medical guesses that could damage a person's chances of getting insurance or employment or a good credit rating.

Dear PMS,

Recently, I had cataract surgery and, since I have a health insurance plan, I was not told the hospital fee ahead of time. I did know what the surgical fee would be.

I was in the hospital less than three hours, and for my taking up "space" in the operating and recovery rooms the bill came to $1,500.

I have been told by the doctor's office this is the standard fee charged by the hospital. Another hospital "clammed up" when I asked their charge.

Is this outrageous or not?

M. S. G., Kintnersville, Pennsylvania

take of any great magnitude. What does it matter anyway, their insurance will cover it. This attitude is one of the major reasons why America's annual medical bill is so staggeringly high and why some of America's hospitals are so rich.

In 1983–84 Atlanta-based Equifax Services, Inc., conducted a forty-one-state audit of 3,850 hospital bills and found errors in 98.1 percent of them. Not just little errors either. The average reduction, after the overcharges were eliminated and the bills retallied, was a whopping $1,254. That's almost the average per capita medical expenditure of a U.S. citizen for one year. Most of the errors involved pharmacy and drug charges. However, 96.9 percent of the bills also contained charges for services that were never performed. Equifax blames most of the problem on human error, both in ordering and then canceling tests and in entering charges into computers and data-processing machines.

DEALING WITH THE BILL

You have to review your bill with some care to pick out any overcharges and dispute them. Use the forms at the back of this book as a guide and as evidence. This is important if you have health insurance. You are working to keep your bill down, and if everybody did that, the rates wouldn't go up as much or as fast as they do.

Of course, if you don't have health insurance, or if you have only minimal insurance, it is vital to your financial interest that you pore over your bill with an eye out for any charge that seems irregular. This is especially so if you had to pay for your stay up front. You could be due a refund, and that refund could be larger than what the incorrect bill indicates.

Translating the cuneiform carvings on the Rosetta stone was a lot easier than deciphering a hospital bill. Some hospital bills are yards long; they are usually hard to read and difficult to understand. Most of the bills are full of abbreviations and shorthand entries, and lots of charges for items and services are crammed into that catchall category "Miscellaneous." Sometimes compiling the charges is so tedious and time-consuming that the bill won't be ready for you to examine on the day of your discharge. It will be sent to you instead. Whether you get the bill at the hospital or at home, be certain to get a fully itemized version.

NO SALE

It is amazing. The same people who will take the time and trouble to look for a 50-cent error at the supermarket checkout counter won't even review the bill they get from a hospital. Do a careful review. You might well find charges on the bill for services never received.

In January 1982 my wife gave birth to our daughter. Prior to entering the hospital, we arranged with the doctor for a number of things not to be done while we were in the facility. For example, my wife asked that she not be given an IV unless it was an emergency. We asked that the child not be delivered in the delivery room, but rather in the birthing room, if it was available, or in the labor room. She asked that no medication be given during the labor, unless at the time both of us agreed it might be necessary. In addition, we brought our own vitamins to the hospital, ones the doctor had recommended.

Everything about the delivery went without a hitch. Everything we asked for was done as agreed.

About a week after my wife was discharged, I received a copy of the bill sent to my insurer. On it were charges for vitamins we never ordered or received. There was a charge for the delivery room, which was not used. There were charges for predelivery and postdelivery IVs, none of which was ever used. There were charges for medications that we did not use. There were even pediatrician charges for "well baby" care that never took place, in that the pediatrician to whom this charge was credited was not even at the hospital those three days.

I called the hospital to tell them they had made a mistake. They said not to worry, it had already been paid. I called the insurance company, and after being referred to three or four different persons, was gently told they would look into it. But they gave me the feeling that I was bothering them more than helping them.

I persisted between the hospital and the insurer for a few weeks and eventually was told by the insurer that they had received the money back from the hospital. The hospital told me (or at least a candid representative said) that this billing for services not rendered is quite common practice. Charges such as those I objected to are automatically put on the bill regardless of whether the services are provided or not, because normally these services are used in a delivery. Unless the doctor specifically notes services not used, you get charged for them. In my case they almost got nearly $1,000 for things they never did.

Charles B. Inlander

Don't sign anything and don't give your approval to anything until you are satisfied that your bill is entirely correct. Don't be rushed; don't allow the cashier or billing department employee to pressure you. Go over the bill item by item, no matter how long it takes. Ask questions about anything that isn't clear or seems odd to you. Put a check mark next to those items, and if they can't be justified, have them eliminated. If the hospital won't eliminate them, refuse to pay those portions of the bill.

If the bill is riddled with inaccuracies, errors, and overcharges, to the point where you question the entire bill, don't pay it. Talk to the head of the department, the head of the hospital if you have to. If the bill is too long to examine right then and there in the cashier's office, take it home with you. Go over it at your own pace, then bring it back to the hospital and settle things.

If there are major problems that nobody at the hospital seems able or willing to resolve, or if they refuse to clear an error or explain a muddled entry, simply leave. Call your attorney if you need help or guidance. Have him or her call your insurance company (or make the call yourself) to instruct them not to pay your bill when the

---

Dear PMS,

My mother was admitted to a hospital on a Saturday because she had choked eating lunch at the nursing home. I was called and arrived at the hospital immediately after she was admitted to a room. The choking had been a strain on her heart, but she was sitting up and saying she was hungry and hadn't had her lunch. This was at 12:30 P.M. I stayed with her until 4 P.M.

A resident doctor came and said my mother's physician was out of town and would be back Monday. They were not going to do anything now; they would let her doctor handle it as he was more familiar with her condition.

So, there was nothing done for Mother other than her being given a bed in a semiprivate room. I left Mother sitting up at 4 P.M. At 8 P.M. a nurse called to tell me Mother had just died.

A few months later I received a statement from the hospital for over $2,000 worth of tests and services. I called them and told them there had to be a mistake. I was there from the time Mother was admitted until 4 P.M. She died at 8 P.M., and I had been advised nothing was to be done until the return of her doctor. It was absolutely impossible for any hospital, between 4 P.M. and 8 P.M., to run up $2,000 worth of charges.

I never heard from them again. It was only because I was *there* that I could deny these charges. How many others pay them because they have no way of knowing?

D. M., Ottawa, Kansas

Dear PMS,

It took nine weeks for the hospital I went to to send me an itemized bill of services rendered. The struggle I had to get the bill, even in that prolonged period of time, was extensive. Since I have no insurance, I needed the bill to compare against the first bill for the same procedure I had undergone ten weeks previous.

The first thing I found was that the prices of all the tests had risen. Nothing I could do about that, said both the hospital and the New York State Health Department representative.

However I did notice five items labeled "special handling" under the lab work done. I called the hospital to inquire about this and was told very patronizingly that this meant that lab tests had to be done "stat" (immediately) because surgery was scheduled for the next day and that they had to determine if I was "sick." I pointed out that this had not been on my first bill, that they had my records from ten weeks previous, and that I am a very healthy woman. The hospital representative said she would have someone review my chart.

When she called back, she allowed as to how I was correct, and the powers that be determined there really wasn't any need for all that stat lab work. So I certainly was entitled to a refund!

What happens to people who aren't educated health care consumers? I think you and I both know the answer to that one.

N. T., New York, New York

hospital submits it. The insurance company may hop right in on your side when the situation is explained. Your employer, who may be paying a good chunk of your insurance, should be informed about what you are doing, why you are refusing to pay the bill. You will gain your employer's respect and gratitude, and the company may go to bat for you.

Assert your rights, including your right to refuse to pay a bill that is questionable. The hospital, of course, has a right to send collection agencies after you or to sue you for your actions, if you and the hospital don't come to an agreement. But it might cost them more money to do that than it would to adjust the bill to your satisfaction. If the hospital sees that you have an attorney representing you, and an insurance company and an employer backing you, and that you are firm in your resolve, the hospital might be more inclined to review your bill and settle things.

We truly hope that you have no troubles, finding no billing errors, and leave the hospital happy with your entire experience. If that is not the case, however, and you are determined not to pay your bill, the hospital cannot stop you from leaving the premises. They might try. They might tell you that you can't leave; they

Dear PMS,

My only son, forty-seven years old, died of a massive cerebral hemor-
rhage on November 13. He had not been ill, but simply fell on the floor
unconscious and was gone in less than six hours.

Would you believe a charge of $1,890.85 for a hospitalization of five
hours and forty minutes—no surgery involved! That does not include the
ambulance charge of $190.50—I understand their charges have now dou-
bled since they put a paramedic aboard. I also paid the radiologist $118 to
read the scan taken by a hospital technician.

I asked for an itemization of charges; they are required by law to item-
ize when requested to do so. You have never seen such a ridiculous itemization. It was as though they had pulled a blanket charge out of thin air in the
first place and then reached far and wide for itemizations to add up to that
figure. Eight IVs, six catheter suctions—plus charges for fitting and assem-
bling them—all in two hours' time! These are the lesser charges, but they
demonstrate their contempt for the public, apparently thinking we are too
dumb to question whatever they say or do.

On March 17, I received a mailing addressed to my son. It reminded him
that he had made arrangements to pay the balance due. It said they would
honor any previous payment arrangements agreed to but "perhaps you
will be in a position to pay the balance due or agree to larger monthly
payments."

I've heard nothing further from them since I fired off a letter telling
them that my son is deceased and that he was unconscious and dying when
admitted to the hospital, and that I refuse to pay their preposterous billing.
Further, it appeared they had little or no knowledge whatever about the
case.

Mrs. C. L. P., Hot Springs, Arkansas

might even enlist a security guard to keep you in the hospital until
you sign the proper documents or hand over the cash. This is illegal.
You can bring criminal charges against the hospital, including kid-
napping, for such an action.

HOME SWEET HOME

Now that you are away from the hospital, you can think more
clearly about your experience there. Jot down all the good things
and all the bad, and all the suggestions you might have for improving hospital services and the patients' lot. Use your diary, if you
kept one, to jog your memory.

Then write letters to the people who played key roles in your

Dear PMS,

After challenging the excessive charges made for recent hernia repair, I obtained from both medical men involved their gracious adjustment of the bill in question. Since my insurance would cover only the actual hernia repair and not the necessary incision and closure (because the latter constituted "cosmetic surgery" in their eyes), the surgeon was willing to entirely deduct the cost of the "tummy tuck" from his bill. Not having formerly represented any part of the surgery as "cosmetic," he evidently felt obligated to make adjustment.

The physician assisting at the operation also adjusted his bill accordingly, since he worked on a percentage basis of what the surgeon charged.

These results to my letters, stating all the facts involved and sent to both men at their own office nurse's suggestion, were a good example of what the layperson can do to control the runaway medical costs we are now experiencing. The individual owes it to himself to become more familiar with his own body's requirements so he can knowledgeably challenge exorbitant costs and/or unnecessary surgery.

J. S. S., Federal Way, Washington

Dear PMS,

I went to the hospital for a biopsy to find the cause of a bad laryngitis. I got there at 8 A.M. I was out before noon. I received a bill for this and did not like the items marked "Misc." or other items I did not quite understand. So I asked for explanations.

One Valium pill: $4.15. (I don't remember them giving me a single pill.)

Recovery room: $100. (I just went there to undress and to dress up again.) I was in the operating room a very short while. The price: $375.

I am eighty-six years old, living on my Social Security. I am sure they could have dispensed with a number of "Misc.'s."

While in the recovery room I had to go to the toilet. I am surprised they did not slap me with another $75 for "Latrine, misc." After all, I did flush.

L. C. S., Woonsocket, Rhode Island

hospitalization: your doctors, surgeons, nurses, patients' representatives, hospital administrators, and whoever else had an effect on your stay. Make copies for yourself. These letters—thoughtful, reasoned, restrained, to the point—will help those people understand how you felt as a patient. Let them know what they did right and what they did wrong, and why you are either happy or incensed. Give dates and particulars.

These letters might elicit some thoughtful responses, even some action. If you get only a form letter in return, you know how much your opinions and feelings matter. You have learned something about that person or that institution and know how to deal with them (or not deal with them) in the future. In any case, this correspondence (even if it is one-sided) provides a written record of your hospitalization for your files, just in case you need it for legal reasons later on.

Keeping a posthospitalization diary or journal is a good idea. It can serve as an outlet for your emotions as you come to terms with what has happened to you and within you. A diary can help you gauge the pace and completeness of your recovery. It can help you to collect your thoughts and to frame questions for your medical professionals, your friends, and your family.

The diary can also be a secret friend you can confide in during what can sometimes be a difficult period of adjustment. Don't exclude real flesh-and-blood friends or relatives or mutual aid groups from your life, though. All of these channels can be terrifically important in the process of coming to terms with your continuing condition, your impaired physical abilities, or any disfigurement, real or imagined.

These outlets, and others, might be needed to help you regain your social equilibrium, especially at your place of work. Coworkers might treat you differently when you return to the job after a long convalescence. This awkwardness is usually short-lived, but while it lasts, it can hurt and be very discouraging.

Sometimes the reason for the hospitalization, especially if it was cancer or some contagious disease, can distance fellow employees and even lead to various forms of job discrimination on the part of employers. A study by the University of Southern California showed that as many as one-third or more of workers returning to their jobs after cancer treatment had their salary cut, insurance benefits decreased, and job status lowered, among other negative actions.

This is where friends, family, mutual aid groups, government agencies designated to combat job discrimination, and, if necessary, attorneys may all come into play. They offer faith, confidence, security, hope, and the fighting spirit you might need to make it over the hump of the hospital experience and its aftermath.

Pursuing Legitimate Tax Deductions

During the first days and weeks after your hospital discharge, collect all the bills, receipts, and personal records you accumulated throughout the course of your hospitalization and start working on—or at least thinking about—your medical tax deductions. There are scores of ways to shave dollars off your federal and/or state tax bills without going beyond the law. You were assertive in demanding and gaining what was yours all during the hospitalization process. Why stop now? Pursue these accepted deduction avenues, with or without the aid of an accountant or tax expert. Your deductions cover the money you paid to the hospital, doctors (including M.D.'s, D.O.'s, psychiatrists, and others), dentists, nurses, and nonphysician practitioners (such as chiropractors, optometrists, and in some cases even acupuncturists and masseurs). Don't forget lab fees, prescription pharmaceuticals, tests (including X rays), and a wide scope of medical-related items, products, and equipment prescribed or recommended by your health care professional.

If you traveled to get medical care, either at a hospital or a clinic, as an inpatient or an outpatient, you almost certainly can deduct the cost of travel, some room-and-board living expenses, possibly car rental charges, as well as the treatment itself. A person traveling and staying with you could also take a deduction. Almost any travel for medical purposes, even to and from the drugstore, is deductible.

The tax laws are twisty, murky, and difficult to understand, but one rule of thumb for medical expense deductions is this: If your doctor advised you to do it for your health, it is probably deductible, at least in part. Be sure you have the documentation to prove it. The IRS is sure to be interested in any large or extraordinary medical deductions.

FUTURE VOYAGES

It is unseemly, we know, to talk about your next trip to the hospital already. After all, you just got home. But chances are good that sometime in your life you will be back for another tour of Hospital Land. That journey will be different. You won't be a stranger anymore. You will have a greater feel for the lingo and the life-style. You will know how far you can and should go to get the best care available.

You will have changed, but they will have changed, too. Hospitals and the entire medical delivery system are transforming, not beyond recognition, but beyond the probabilities of even a decade ago. The American Hospital Association predicts that by 1994 hospitals will have fewer doctors and a greater percentage of nonphysicians on staff. There will be an all-out battle among physicians for admitting privileges, says the AHA, because of hospital competition and doctor oversupply. Doctors who today have privileges at a few hospitals may find themselves down to one.

For-profit, chain-owned hospitals will proliferate. Because of this, and because academic medical centers will have to slash their budgets to stay alive, the poor of this country will find themselves shut out from many of the present-day care programs. (Though only approximately 6 percent of hospitals are medical centers, they provide nearly 50 percent of the charity care in this country.) Further cuts in medical center budgets would see the scaling down or elimination of burn care units, neonatal intensive care units, and outpatient departments that serve the immediate and often poverty-level community. To make money, medical centers will need to promote high-cost, high-profit technology and procedures, and will diversify into other related or nonrelated business areas. The seeds have already been planted.

Among all hospitals, there will probably be a growing trend toward specialization.

Medical costs will go up, despite cost-containment efforts. They may not rise as fast as they have recently, but up is definitely the direction. Meanwhile, ethical questions having to do with the dollar value of life and the possibility of having to ration health care will swirl all around us. Expect the moral dilemmas of applying skills and technology in the pursuit of rescuing and prolonging life to intensify as well. And who would dare to predict anything about the future of Medicare?

What does all this mean to you? Where do you fit in? Because the future of health care and its administration will affect you and your loved ones directly, you should be involved in shaping that future.

That could mean getting involved in civic organizations or even hospital committees. When hospitals conduct public meetings to discuss new construction or plans that involve the community at large, attend those meetings. Let your voice be heard. If your hospital has boards that include citizen members, try to get on them. Work from the outside or from the inside to make changes.

Urge politicians to concern themselves with the health and medical interests of their constituents. Get involved in local politics yourself, if that is your style. Bring attention to unsatisfactory situations or conditions. Write letters to the editor, call television and radio stations. If so moved, organize and lead protests against offending institutions.

Join national activists associations and medical consumer groups and bring their message and their clout to your town. The People's Medical Society is one of these groups and is eager to work with you in your community to provide information, heighten consumer awareness, and help you fight the good fight.

"The passive individual patient . . . will not bring about fundamental change while he still remains politically passive and powerless vis-à-vis the medical profession," says Jean Robinson, a medical consumer activist from Great Britain. "Fundamental change can only come about if laypeople have more say in lawmaking, in institutions and quasigovernmental organizations, in resource allocations and in medical training."

It is time for all of us to get involved, to learn, not just for our next "trip," but for everybody's.

Take that spirit to the hospital with you.

NO SENIOR DISCOUNTS

Everywhere you turn nowadays senior citizen discounts abound. From movie houses to cruises, the senior discount has become an institution. But with the exception of a few pharmacies, who discount already jacked-up drug prices, Medical Land is a holdout. For the older American the trip to the hospital is full-fare.

But senior citizens have some assistance on their medical travels: Medicare.

Medicare is the largest entitlement program in the world. Thirty-two million Americans are Medicare-eligible and over 98 percent are beneficiaries. The Medicare program is federally mandated and administered by the Health Care Financing Administration, which is part of the United States Department of Health and Human Services.

But Medicare is not a simple program to understand. Most senior citizens do not know the full range of benefits available, nor do most doctors. People under the age of sixty-five, or otherwise ineligible for the program, think Medicare is simple. They think you turn sixty-five, head to the Social Security Office to register, and the rest is medical heaven. Little do they know.

One People's Medical Society member, a ninety-two-year-old woman, once told us how she was waiting with glee until the next year. She reported that her sixty-four-year-old son would be going on Medicare at that time and she couldn't wait to laugh in his face.

It seems the "youngster" thought his mother was senile because she could not figure out the Medicare forms.

Because the program is so complicated, misconceptions and misinformation concerning it are widespread. This certainly doesn't help the senior citizen who is ill, needs care, or may already be hospitalized.

So, understanding and knowing how to make Medicare work for you, or a family member who is a beneficiary, is not only important, but necessary for a smooth medical landing.

We should begin by noting that we cannot cover everything you need to know about Medicare in this section. It would take an entire book to go over it all. And in fact there is such a book and it happens to be another People's Medical Society book titled *Medicare Made Easy* (Reading, MA.: Addison-Wesley, 1989). We recommend it for every Medicare beneficiary and his or her family.

Let's assume you meet the Medicare eligibility requirements, have signed up for the program, and are now an official card carrier. The first thing you need to know is what Medicare covers.

A common misconception is that Medicare has a wide scope of coverage. In reality, it doesn't. If you compared it to the best private insurance plans using a cost-benefit rating scale, not many people would buy it.

By "covered" we mean that Medicare is willing to pay something for the service. And coverage is limited in a number of ways. One limit is that for many services Medicare pays only part of the bill. Another limit is simply that not every practitioner or facility accepts Medicare, and still another limit is that you will probably have to pay out of pocket or from some other source to supplement what Medicare pays. So the odds are that Medicare will only pay a portion of your medical bill. The rest is your responsibility.

Despite its limitations, Medicare does cover a lot under its two parts: Medicare Part A (Hospital Insurance) and Medicare Part B (Medical Insurance). Here is what Medicare covers for inpatient hospital care (as of January 1990):

▶ Semiprivate room (no more than two beds to a room)

▶ All meals, including any special diets that are needed, plus hyperalimentation (total nutrition via a tube placed in a vein)

▶ Nursing services regularly provided by the unit you are in (Medicare pays for nursing services in the intensive care unit, even though they are more expensive than those on the general medical-surgical floors)

▶ Intensive care, intensive care units, and care in other special care units (for example, a brain surgery unit)

▶ Drugs furnished in the hospital, unless they are excluded because the Food and Drug Administration has not found them "safe and effective"

▶ Blood transfusions, except for the cost of the first three pints of blood

▶ Hospital charges for lab tests

▶ Hospital charges for X rays and radiotherapy

▶ Medical supplies, such as dressings, casts, splints, catheters, and intravenous (IV) lines

▶ Use of durable medical equipment, such as wheelchairs and crutches, while in the hospital

▶ All hospital operating room and recovery room charges

▶ Rehabilitation services, such as physical therapy, speech pathology, and the like, provided during the inpatient stay

It is important to note that the charges of hospital-based physicians, such as pathologists, radiologists, physiatrists, and nuclear medicine and pulmonary specialists, to name a few, are not covered under the hospital insurance portion of Medicare but are paid by Part B, the doctor insurance section. This is often confusing to beneficiaries.

Effective January 1, 1990, Medicare took a step backward with the repeal of catastrophic coverage. Medicare once again pays for a limited number of hospital days (150: 90 regular, 60 lifetime reserve) and reimposed the spell-of-illness deductible ($592 in 1990) and the coinsurance days.

Here's a synopsis of what Medicare pays and what you pay for services under Part A and Part B. These do not include your monthly Medicare premium. (They are also subject to change and revision, so check with your Social Security Office for updated numbers):

Medicare Part A: Hospital Insurance

HOSPITAL DEDUCTIBLE AND COINSURANCE DAYS

$592 deductible first 60 days of each benefit period. $148 per day coinsurance on days 61 through 90. $296 per day coinsurance on days 91 through 150 (lifetime reserve).

SKILLED NURSING FACILITY

100 days per year. $74 per day copayment on days 21 through 100. Three-day prior hospitalization required.

HOSPICE

Up to 210 days as medically necessary.

BLOOD

As needed. Beneficiary pays a deductible equal to the cost of the first 3 pints of blood.

HOME HEALTH SERVICES

7 days per week up to 21 consecutive days. May under certain conditions be extended.

RESPITE CARE

Covered under hospice benefit. Short-term inpatient stay not to exceed 5 consecutive days.

Medicare Part B:
Medical Insurance

PART B DEDUCTIBLE AND COPAYMENT

Beneficiary pays deductible of $75 per year after which Medicare pays 80 percent of all approved charges.

HOME HEALTH CARE

7 days per week up to 21 consecutive days. May under certain conditions be extended.

IMMUNOSUPPRESSIVE DRUGS

Medicare pays 80 percent of the cost of these drugs for one year after the Part B deductible of $75 is met.

NOTE: At the time of this writing, Congress is considering restoring the mammography screening and in-home respite care and expanding home health care and hospice benefits. You will be notified in writing when, and if, this happens.

There are some important steps you should take to maximize your Medicare benefits. One of them is to acquire supplemental Medicare insurance. Often termed "medigap insurance" because it is designed to fill in the gaps in Medicare, it is the single most important purchase a Medicare beneficiary can make, if he or she can afford it.

Approximately 70 percent of Medicare beneficiaries own medigap policies. And well they should. Over the course of a senior citizen's life, from the time they start on Medicare, less than 50 percent of their medical bills are paid by Medicare. Thus, supplemental coverage, while not picking up all the difference, can certainly help maintain a senior citizen's bank account.

Medicare supplemental insurance is sold by private companies and in order to legally call itself a "medigap" or "Medicare supplemental" policy it must meet certain minimum restrictions. In order to be "certified" by the federal government (which is not required, so be careful), the following restrictions apply:

▶ You must be given a free-look period of at least thirty days, during which you can decide to cancel a policy and receive a refund of all premiums paid.

▶ Expected payout of benefits must equal 60 percent of premiums for individual policies and 75 percent of group policies.

Certified insurers are required to follow ethical practices, including submitting advertising to the state insurance commissioner for review.

All of these safeguards are designed to protect senior citizens from insurance hucksters who prey on unsuspecting older Americans.

So be sure to look into supplemental insurance. But, look carefully and compare policies with an eagle's eye. Remember, high premiums do not necessarily mean good policies.

Another important way you can maximize your Medicare benefits is to negotiate with your doctor. That's right—negotiate! You don't need to be a labor leader to conduct doctor-patient negotiations. But negotiate you should—on a number of issues and for a variety of reasons.

Here are some things you can and should negotiate:

Assignment. "Assignment" is a term meaning the doctor will accept what Medicare pays, along with your Medicare-required copayment, as full payment for services. Simply put, if your doctor accepts Medicare assignment, you will never get another bill after the service is delivered. Only 40 percent of the doctors in the United States accept assignment for all services for all their Medicare customers. But yours should be one of them! And your chances of winning this one are excellent if you negotiate.

Tell the doctor that you do not intend to pay anything more than what Medicare pays, plus your mandated copayment. Tell him that if Medicare is not giving him enough, he should take it up with them, not slap it on you. Tell him that you will consider finding another doctor who will accept assignment before you would come back for his services.

The experience of People's Medical Society members who have negotiated assignment is that the majority win. In fact, even the doctor wins because he not only gets his fee, but he also keeps you as a customer. And like any business, keeping customers is the name of the game.

Treatment. Money is not the only thing you can negotiate. Treatment is negotiable as well. One of the reasons Medicare premiums and costs have skyrocketed in recent years is the fact that Medicare is like a blank check for hospitals and doctors. While federal authorities have taken measures to try to stem this outflow of your taxes, there are many steps *you* can take to assure a reasonable bill.

All of the items we talked about in the earlier chapters of this book are negotiable. In fact, the tactics and ideas we gave in those sections are really negotiation techniques.

Utilize them. Don't think that because Medicare pays it's OK to let the doctor go ahead and do anything. What may ultimately line his pocket may ultimately bankrupt you financially and harm you physically.

Here are some other things you should keep in mind about Medicare:

▶ Medicare is not a charity program. Do not hesitate to use it and use it to the maximum benefit. Not only did your tax dollars pay into the program, you are now paying monthly premiums to keep it.

▶ There are numerous situations in which Medicare decides not to pay a provider, or to pay less than the provider wanted. It's important to understand when you don't have to pay for something that Medicare has refused to pay a provider for: You are never obligated to pay for a service unless you can reasonably have been expected to know that the service was not covered, or was not (medically) reasonable and necessary. You are never obligated to pay more than Medicare has decided to pay the provider if the provider has agreed to accept assignment.

▶ Any denial of payment for services made by Medicare is appealable. You should always exercise your right to appeal.

▶ Review your hospital bill carefully and review what Medicare has paid. If you suspect that Medicare has overpaid, been billed for services you did not receive, or has been billed more than once for services rendered, contact Medicare immediately.

► Medicare cannot discharge you from the hospital. Only a doctor can discharge you. Many senior citizens have been told by hospital personnel, including doctors, that their Medicare benefits have run out and that they must leave the hospital. That is an outright lie. Any doctor or hospital representative who said such a thing should be immediately reported to Medicare. In fact, there is even a form that every hospital is required to give each Medicare beneficiary every time they are admitted to the hospital that explains their discharge rights and the Medicare beneficiary's right to appeal any discharge. Make sure you are given such a form when you enter the hospital.

► When in doubt, ask for help. Medicare is complicated, with a language of its own. If you do not understand everything or anything, do not be afraid to get assistance. You can find assistance in a variety of places. One source is your local Social Security Office. They have many brochures and booklets about Medicare. Senior centers and senior organizations often have special assistance programs. Don't forget the People's Medical Society. We are at 462 Walnut Street, Allentown, PA 18102 (Phone: [215] 770-1670) and are here to assist you.

Finally, don't hesitate to call your federal congressman or senators. In reality, they are your Medicare insurance agents. Utilize their staffs and services to help clarify a Medicare matter or assist in getting answers to your questions.

YOUR MEDICAL RIGHTS: DO YOU REALLY KNOW THEM?

We're always talking about demanding our rights—but do we really know what our rights are? Do you know for sure which legal actions are under your control and which are beyond it? Do you have a true handle on what kinds of actions you are empowered to take when it comes to your medical care, and especially the care when you are critically ill and perhaps even too ill to make decisions?

Test your knowledge of such things by taking this quiz, and see what your R.Q.—your Rights Quotient—really is. It could mean the difference between first-class and low-class treatment, and it could help avoid family disruptions and heartbreak.

The questions and answers are based on current law, People's Medical Society's legal advisers, and in part on information from two sources provided by the American Civil Liberties Union: *The Rights of the Critically Ill* by John A. Robertson (New York: Bantam Books, 1983) and *The Rights of Hospital Patients* by George J. Annas (Carbondale: Southern Illinois University Press, 1989).

1. There is a legal right to health care in the United States. *True or False?*

2. A doctor can lie to a patient about the seriousness of an illness if the doctor thinks it will spare the patient anxiety and grief. *True or False?*

3. A patient can override objections by the family and demand to be told the nature of his illness. *True or False?*

4. A patient has the legal right to keep his illness a secret from the family. *True or False?*

5. The family has the legal right to stop treatment of a competent, critically ill family member, even if the patient wants it continued. *True or False?*

6. A cancer patient has a right to have his doctor prescribe or administer laetrile. *True or False?*

7. A competent adult can refuse medical care that could keep him alive. *True or False?*

8. A patient can sue a doctor who treats him against his will in order to keep him alive. *True or False?*

9. A patient can be thrown out of a hospital if he can't pay. *True or False?*

10. A doctor can (a) refuse to treat a patient who can't pay; (b) stop treating a patient who can't pay. *True or False?*

11. If, in an emergency situation, a person is brought to a hospital that does not have an emergency room, the hospital has the obligation to take in and care for the person anyway. *True or False?*

12. A hospital can prevent a patient from leaving. *True or False?*

13. A doctor must refer a patient to a specialist or seek a consultation if the patient requests it. *True or False?*

14. A doctor can refuse to continue to see a patient without first obtaining the services of another doctor for the patient. *True or False?*

15. A hospital patient has the right to refuse to be examined by medical students, interns, or residents. *True or False?*

Check your answers against the ones below:

1. *False.* Neither the Constitution nor the Declaration of Independence guarantees this right. There is no legal right to demand medical care.

2. *False.* A doctor is obligated, under all circumstances, to tell a patient his diagnosis and prognosis. If the doctor fails to do so, he can be sued for malpractice. If the patient has specifically expressed a desire to know his diagnosis and prognosis, and the doctor does not tell him, it can be construed as a breach of contract. And if the doctor keeps back information that ultimately obstructs crucial medical, financial, or personal decisions on the part of the patient, then the doctor could be held liable for the damages that result.

   There are two instances when the doctor is off the legal hook: when the patient has specifically expressed a desire not to know, and when the doctor reasonably believes that bad news could do real harm to the patient (known as "therapeutic privilege").

3. *True.* If the patient is competent, the family has no right to have information relevant to the person's medical condition withheld from him.

4. *True.* A patient can ask that his condition be kept secret, and the doctor has to go along.

5. *False.* If the ill person is (and this is important) competent and also has the money to pay for treatment, the family has no legal power to stop it. The doctor's duty is to the ill person, not to family members. In terminal cases the law is fuzzier. The patient has the right to treatment that will prolong life even a few days, but this right might not include continued maximum treatment if he is in a comatose or unconscious state.

6. *False.* Even in states where laetrile is legal, doctors aren't obligated to use it. Writes John Robertson: "Since laetrile has not

been shown to be effective, a doctor who refuses to prescribe it would not be violating his duty to provide the patient with effective medical care. If the patient objects, [he or she] is free to terminate the relationship and seek care elsewhere."

7. *True.* According to some rulings, rejection of lifesaving treatment is protected by the constitutional guarantee of right of privacy. There would have to be some pretty good reason for interfering with this right.

8. *True.* Despite a doctor's seeming good intentions or ethical concerns, he can be sued for battery, false imprisonment, or lack of informed consent. The doctor could even end up being responsible for the cost of the care. A patient can also get a court order, if necessary, to force a doctor to stop treatment on penalty of contempt of court.

9. *False.* Once a person has been admitted and needs continued care, the hospital probably can't discharge him. The hospital could have the person transferred to another hospital, but only if the patient were in stable enough condition to be moved. If the patient is discharged because he can't pay, and then gets worse or incurs further damage, he could sue, claiming abandonment.

10. (a) *True.* (b) *False.* Writes Robertson: "Although not obligated to begin treatment, once this is undertaken, [the doctor] is obligated to continue as long as the patient will benefit or [until] the patient withdraws." Otherwise, abandonment can be claimed, and a civil suit could follow. However, if the doctor has made it clear at the start of treatment that ability to pay is a condition of continuing care, he can cut off treatment.

11. *False.* In most states there is no legal obligation to do so, and a severely injured person could, within the law, be turned away. Some states have laws requiring hospitals to have emergency rooms. In these places, and in all situations where a hospital has an emergency room, that emergency room cannot turn away a person brought to it in an emergency state.

12. *False.* If the person is of sound mind, he can leave at any time, and the hospital can't do a thing about it—unless it wants to risk a suit for false imprisonment. And this applies even if the person hasn't paid his bill, or the bill of his child. A person may be asked to sign an against-medical-advice release form, but there is no legal obligation for the person to do so in order to leave the hospital.

13. *True.* This is not a law, but good practice. It is also a portion of the American Medical Association's Principles of Medical Ethics. And, if the doctor refuses a patient's request for a referral or consultation, and it turns out that the doctor's reassurance of proper treatment was wrong, a negligence suit is probably the patient's next step, one likely to be successful.

14. *False.* The only way a doctor-patient relationship ends is if (a) both parties agree to its end, (b) if it is ended by the patient, (c) if the doctor is no longer needed, or (d) if the doctor withdraws from the case after having given reasonable notice. Otherwise, a case for abandonment can be made by the patient.

15. *True.* Writes George Annas: "All patients have a right to refuse to be examined by anyone in the hospital setting." In addition, fraud can be claimed if consent for an examination was given when a medical student was introduced as "Doctor" to the patient, and the patient believed him to be a doctor.

6 Be sure to write

YOUR HOSPITAL RIGHTS WORKBOOK

Personnel List
Telephone Log
Receipt for Personal Items
Daily Log—Who Did What
Daily Log—Who Did What
  When
Tests Record

Dispensed Items Log
Your Personal Clinical Chart
Medication Record
Pain Chart
Hospital Service Opinion
  Form
People's Medical Society
  Hospital Evaluation Form

Space does not permit us to reproduce enough copies of every form to cover each day of even a short hospital stay. Therefore, we invite you to make photocopies of these forms in numbers to fit your needs.

PERSONNEL LIST

Many doctors, nurses, and other hospital employees will be coming and going in and out of your room throughout your stay. This list can help you keep track of the comers and goers.

The "Comments" column is there for descriptive information—"tall," "brown short hair," "has a limp," and other kinds of memory joggers—so that when you need to remember who did what or who said what (or who *didn't* do or *didn't* say), you will be able to distinguish between Drs. Briscom and Griscom or tell Nurse Masters from Nurse Blasters or sort out the three interns named Smith.

Keeping track of people in this way will help you to fill out a few of the other forms in this section, too.

Name of Employee	Title	Job	Comments

TELEPHONE LOG

Charging you for items and services you never received is something that hospitals are really good at. The telephone bill is a prime error area. Who can remember if it was three calls to Aunt Sadie or four . . . one or two to home or the office? Here is a form to help you keep unmade and/or unauthorized phone calls from turning up on your bill.

Date	Time	Party You Called	Party Who Called You	Length of Call

RECEIPT FOR PERSONAL ITEMS

Usually, personal items you bring to the hospital with you are put in a closet or in some place of relative safekeeping, and a receipt is issued. Problem is, sometimes the receipt disappears.

This is your very own receipt for items stashed away for you by an attendant. It will help you to convince skeptical hospital employees that you do indeed have such and such stored away somewhere on the premises. It also lists items not stored away, in case they somehow disappear. The personnel's knowledge that you have a form such as this might act as a kind of insurance—it could reduce the chance of anything of yours getting "lost."

Items Stored	Description	Value
1.		
2.		
3.		
4.		
5.		
6.		
7.		
8.		

Items Removed and Stored by: _____

Signature of Hospital Representative: _____

RECEIPT FOR PERSONAL ITEMS –CONTINUED

Items Kept at Bedside	Description	Value
1.		
2.		
3.		
4.		
5.		
6.		
7.		
8.		

Items' Presence at Bedside Noted by: _____

Witness Signature: _____

Additional Notes _____

DAILY LOG—WHO DID WHAT

People don't always do what they say they are going to do, or they might even do something and then say they didn't. It happens all the time in the real world, and it happens in hospitals, too. In hospitals, the gulf between what is reportedly done and what is actually done is sometimes a wide one. Frequently the discrepancy is grounds for complaint and action, sometimes escalating to a malpractice suit or other litigation.

Documentation is what you need in such situations. Using this form you can keep a daily record of visits to your room by your medical professionals and the vast array of hospital personnel. With this log you will be able to see—and to demonstrate at the cashier's office or in the courtroom—whether the anesthesiologist really did drop by to chat about your complaints, or how often your doctor stopped in to see how you were doing. You will also be able to determine who really provided care and concern and rank that all on a "Satisfaction Scale" of 1 to 10, with 10 a perfect experience.

Make sure this log is accurate. It may come in very handy somewhere up the road.

Name/ Job Title	Date	What Was Done/Said	Comments	Satisfaction Scale (1–10)

Additional Notes

DAILY LOG—WHO DID WHAT WHEN

This is the flip side of the previous form. In this one, time is of the essence. In the "Daily Log—Who Did What," you were recording who in fact showed up. In this log, the major concern is how much time they spent with you, at what time of day, and what they did.

This form is important for keeping track of quantity (and, perhaps, quality) of care. How much time does it take for the new nurse to take blood from you? Is it a painful eternity or a quick stick? When your doctor comes to check on your progress, does he just pop his head in the door for 10 mechanically cheery seconds or does he spend a reasonable amount of time with you? And is he charging you the same visitation fee for 10 worthless seconds as for 10 valuable minutes?

Personnel	Date	Time	Length of Visit	What Did/Said	How You Felt Afterward	Satisfaction Scale (1–10)

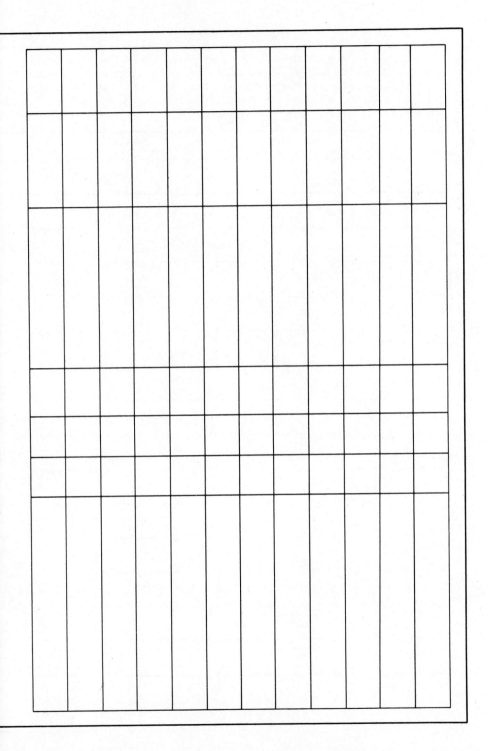

TESTS RECORD

This form records the types of tests you are getting and what you are getting out of them. Hospital lab tests—blood, urine, and other specimens—as well as X rays, ought to be listed here. Keep good notes. This is a prime overuse/overcharge area, and a few tests that you never actually suffered through could show up on your bill.

Date	Time	Name of Test/ Procedure	Who Gave It/ Where	

Additional Notes _____

_____

_____

	Reason Given for Having Test	Cost	Results (Doctor's Interpretation)	Side Effects (If Any)

DISPENSED ITEMS LOG

For everything from the oxygen tank next to your bed, to the cotton swabs dispensed for a nonemergency ear waxectomy, you will be getting the bill. "Free," in the hospital lexicon, only describes the sensation experienced by patients upon leaving. Everything costs—plenty and often.

Frequently, lots of little items are lumped together in so-called itemized bills under large categories labeled "Misc." Missed "Misc.'s" are probably *the* major overcharge and false charge culprits.

Why pay for stuff you don't need or never saw? Keep track of it all on this form.

Date	Item/ Product Given	Who Gave It	

Additional Notes _____

_____

_____

_____

_____

	Reason for Giving	Cost of Item	If Item Refused, Check Here and Get Nurse's Signature

YOUR PERSONAL CLINICAL CHART

There are all types of vital signs that get measured during your hospital stay and are recorded on your chart. This form, based on a clinical chart used by many hospitals, gives you the opportunity to monitor your own condition and, perhaps, your progress, in two areas: temperature (important to keep track of if you are suffering a viral or bacterial illness) and blood pressure.

If this form does nothing else, it will allow you to participate in segments of your care that you normally surrender unthinkingly.

Doctors and nurses are not used to being asked for exact temperature and blood pressure numbers by their patients. When questioned about what they have seen on the thermometer or the sphygmomanometer (the blood-pressure-measuring machine), the medical professionals usually respond with vague mutterings—"It's good," "It's normal," "It's better"—that cover their speedy retreat from your room without giving any valuable information to you about *you*. By asking them what your exact temperature is, or what the systolic and diastolic blood pressure readings are—and insisting that they tell you—you will be letting them know they are dealing with an involved, concerned, knowledgeable and active patient. Besides, aren't you just the least bit curious to know the details of what's going on inside you?

For the blood pressure portion, mark two dots for each of the daily readings: one on the line alongside the high-number reading (or systolic) and one below alongside the low-number reading (or diastolic). Connect these two dots, and you will have a vertical visualization of your blood pressure readings every four hours for a week.

When you find out what your temperature is, place a dot on the appropriate line under the column for the time (or closest time) and day it was measured. Then, over the course of your hospital stay, simply connect the dots to get a clearer picture of your thermal hills and valleys.

If you would like to keep track of your pulse rate, use the blood pressure section of the chart. Take a different color pencil or pen and put a dot on the line alongside the number that represents beats per minute.

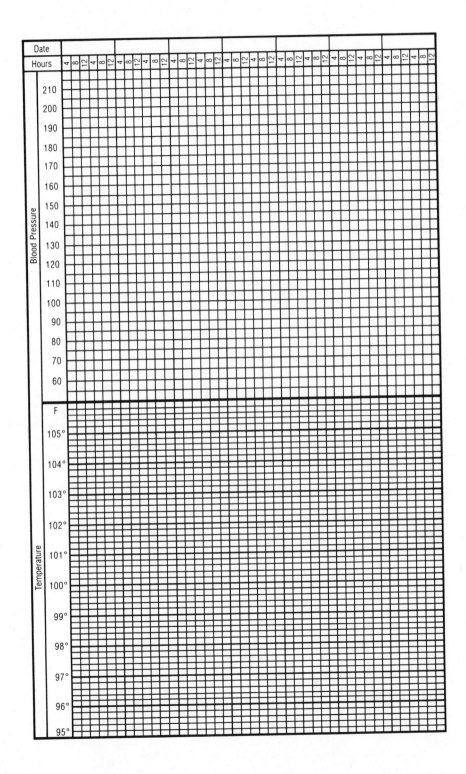

MEDICATION RECORD

In the hospital world nothing is certain. Except medication.

Drugs can be miraculous lifesavers. But if these powerful drugs are given in the wrong dose or given too often or mistakenly given to a patient, the effects can be devastating. Be on guard.

This chart will help you double-check your medications. Mistakes happen; charts and prescription orders may not be accurate. One good way to avoid becoming a victim is to keep your own complete record of what you are taking. Who will be more concerned about you than you?

If what you are being given doesn't jibe with what was prescribed, point it out in no uncertain terms. And *don't take the medication* until you have personally double-checked with your doctor, your nurse, or the hospital pharmacist. And mark it all down on this record form.

Date/Time	Drug	Dosage	

Additional Notes _____

_____

_____

_____

_____

	Dispensed by	Form (Pill, Liquid, Injection)	Side Effects (If Any)	Reason Given for Taking Drug

PAIN CHART

Peanut butter and jelly, Abbott and Costello, hospitals and pain—think of one, naturally you think of the other. They go together.

This form will help you keep a record of your pain, when it happens and why, and what is done about it. If you don't think you're getting the pain relief you should get—or if you think you are being drugged silly and have asked for less of the pain killers—this chart can be your record of how the hospital did or did not meet your needs.

Date/Time	Pain (Type: Dull, Sharp, Etc.) Location of Pain	Length of Pain Period	How Treated	Drugs Used/Dosage	

Additional Notes _____

_____

_____

_____

_____

	Dispensed by	Form (Pill, Liquid, Injection)	Side Effects (If Any)	Treatment Given for Side Effects	Type of Treatment

Hospital Service Opinion Form

Hospitals get your funds, whether directly or through a third-party payer, but they rarely get your feedback. Some people send thank-you notes and flowers. Others send drop-dead notes and weeds. But both groups are in the minority. Most folks just keep their good or bad times to themselves. Most hospitals, of course, presume that no news is good news.

Maybe the hospital you are in would like to know what and who you liked and disliked and why. What, if any, improvements would you recommend? In these highly competitive times, the hospital administrators, or perhaps the hospital public relations people, might be concerned about image and performance, and whether they can expect your business again.

Since hospitals don't leave a "How Did We Do?" card at your bedside the way hotels do, we have provided one here for you. Just pull it out of the book (or photocopy it) and hand it to the patient representative or some other appropriate hospital employee when you leave. If you are shy, mail it in after you get home. If you want to remain anonymous, then, by all means, remain anonymous.

Type or print clearly. Be honest. Nobody is served if you beat around the bush.

To Whom It May Concern:

I have just completed a stay at your hospital, and I thought you ought to know my feelings about my time there, both good and bad. Perhaps this information can be used constructively in dealing with other patients who will use your facility.

I hope you accept this form in the spirit in which it is offered: seriously, good-naturedly, and optimistically.

1. My length of stay was _____ days.

2. During that time I used:

_____ X-Ray facilities   _____ Emergency Room

_____ Intensive Care Unit   _____ Operating Room

_____ Coronary Care Unit   _____ Nuclear Medicine facilities

_____ Maternity Ward   _____ Other _____

3. On a scale of 1 (poor) to 5 (excellent), I feel the care and treatment I received and the professional behavior in each department was as follows:

_____ X-Ray   _____ Emergency Room

_____ Intensive Care Unit   _____ Operating Room

_____ Coronary Care Unit   _____ Nuclear Medicine

_____ Maternity Ward   _____ Other _____

4. My primary care nurse was: _____

I found his/her care:

_____ Excellent _____ Good _____ Fair _____ Poor

Reason(s) I (circle one) liked/disliked this nurse:

_____

_____

_____

5. My room was:

_____ clean   _____ dirty   _____ comfortable

_____ hot   _____ cold   _____ quiet

_____ noisy   _____ bright   _____ dark

How my room could be improved: _____

_____

6. The food was:

_____ Excellent _____ Good _____ Fair _____ Poor

It was usually served:

_____ at a good time   _____ at a bad time

_____ at the proper temperature   _____ at the wrong temperature

I (circle one) liked/disliked the food because:

_____

7. Other opinions about the care I received:

_____

_____

8. I (circle one) will/will not use this hospital again.

9. I (circle one) will/will not recommend that friends and relatives use this hospital.

10. I (circle one) will/will not ask my doctor to admit me to this hospital again.

Name _____

Address _____

City _____ State _____ Zip _____

I (circle one) would/would not like a response to this form.

This form was provided to this patient by the People's Medical Society,
462 Walnut Street, Allentown, PA 18102; © 1985 People's Medical Society.

People's Medical Society Hospital
Evaluation Form

This form is a bit different from the rest. Filling it out will not only help you, but will help many other people as well.

Here is what it is all about. A while back the People's Medical Society put together something called the Physician Evaluation Form. It looked a little like this form—asking questions about cost and efficiency and disclosure of information, among other things—except it was geared toward analyzing doctors. We sent a form to all PMS members, asking every one of them to fill in the form after the next visit to the doctor, then mail it to us, and we would then send them back a blank one to fill in after their next visit—and so on for as long as we both shall live.

The response was enormous. Thousands upon thousands of Physician Evaluation Forms were returned to us (and continue to be returned to us), and every one was entered into a computer. From all the information we received and plugged into the machine, we were able to generate not only broad, basic national statistics—average length of waiting time, general satisfaction with care, and so forth—but also specific facts about individual doctors all across the country. This information was then made available to People's Medical Society members as a help in choosing a good physician or nonphysician practitioner.

Same idea here. By sending this form to the People's Medical Society, you will be helping us accumulate lots of general statistics and specific data about hospitals nationwide. And ultimately you will be helping yourself, your family, your friends—and that poor scared guy out there, listening to his doctor tell him he has to go into the hospital. With the kind of information the People's Medical Society can make available to that guy—information that comes from hospital evaluation forms—he needn't be scared. He can make knowledgeable decisions.

Knowledge is power. That is what this form, this book, and the medical consumers' movement—of which the People's Medical Society is a part—is all about.

People's Medical Society Hospital Evaluation Form

Hospital's Name _____

Hospital's Address _____

_____

Type of hospital: _____ Community _____ University Medical Center
_____ Specialized (what specialty?) _____
_____ Other _____
Doctor who admitted you: _____
Were you admitted through an HMO (health maintenance organization)?

_____ Yes _____ No

Background

1. Reason for this stay?

   _____ Medical treatment _____ Surgery _____ Emergency
   _____ Observation _____ Other (please explain)_____

2. Has the condition that prompted *this* hospital stay been treated previously at *this* hospital? _____ Yes _____ No

3. How many previous times have you been admitted to a hospital? ____
How many times in the last year? _____

4. How many previous times have you been admitted to *this* hospital? __
How many times in the last year? _____

5. If you have entered different hospitals at different times during the past year, why did you change hospitals?

_____

_____

_____

Emergency Room

If your hospital visit took place entirely or began in the emergency room, please answer the following questions:

1. How were you brought to the emergency room?

   _____ ambulance _____ cab _____ walked
   _____ someone drove you _____ drove yourself

2. Did you feel the length of time spent in the waiting room before treatment was fair and reasonable? _____ Yes _____ No

If not, why not? _____

_____

_____

3. Were you treated courteously by the emergency room staff?

_____ Yes _____ No

If not, please describe: _____

_____

_____

4. Do you feel the doctor spent enough time with you?

_____ Yes _____ No

5. How much did this visit cost? $_____

Your Hospital Room

1. What type of room did you have? _____ Private _____ Semiprivate
2. How much was your daily room charge? $_____
3. Was the room kept clean? _____ Yes _____ No
4. The room temperature?

_____ too hot _____ too cold _____ satisfactory

5. Did you have sufficient privacy when you needed it?

_____ Yes _____ No

6. Did you have a window? _____ Yes _____ No

Did it provide a satisfactory view of the outside?

_____ Yes _____ No

Did you receive light from outside? _____ Yes _____ No

7. Were the bathroom facilities adequate and clean?

_____ Yes _____ No

8. Did you have your own television? _____ Yes _____ No

Did it work properly? _____ Yes _____ No

9. Overall, how would you rate your hospital room? (circle one)

    1 completely unsatisfactory   4 good
    2 poor   5 excellent
    3 adequate

People's Medical Society Hospital Evaluation Form
(continued)

The Food

1. Were your meals served on time? ____ Yes ____ No

2. Were hot meals served hot? ____ Yes ____ No

Were cold meals served cold? ____ Yes ____ No

3. Were you on a special diet? ____ Yes ____ No

Explain _____

Did your meals meet your dietary requirements? ____ Yes ____ No

4. Did you get enough to eat? ____ Yes ____ No

5. Was the food generally tasty? ____ Yes ____ No

6. Overall, how would you rate the hospital food? (circle one)

     1 completely unsatisfactory   4 good
     2 poor   5 excellent
     3 adequate

Nursing Care

1. Did you feel the nurses were:

a. considerate? ____ Yes ____ No

b. friendly? ____ Yes ____ No

c. informative? ____ Yes ____ No

d. responsive to your needs? ____ Yes ____ No

e. good at their jobs? ____ Yes ____ No

2. Overall, how would you rate your nurses' performance? (circle one)

     1 completely unsatisfactory   4 good
     2 poor   5 excellent
     3 adequate

Doctor Performance

1. Did your doctor/surgeon provide you with understandable explanations for any tests, treatments, and/or medications you may have received? ____ Yes ____ No

2. Did your doctor/surgeon discuss any possible negative side effects of the tests, treatments, and/or medications you received?
____ Yes ____ No

3. Did your doctor/surgeon discuss his qualifications to perform any of the tests or treatments you received? _____ Yes _____ No

4. Did your doctor/surgeon provide you with an accurate statement of the possible pain that could be expected from any of the tests, treatments, and/or medications you received? _____ Yes _____ No

5. Did your doctor/surgeon discuss possible alternatives to the tests, treatments, and/or medications you received? _____ Yes _____ No

6. Did your doctor/surgeon provide you with any information about the prevention of this condition's recurrence in the future?
_____ Yes _____ No

7. Overall, how would you rate this doctor's/surgeon's performance? (circle one)

      1 completely unsatisfactory   4 good
      2 poor   5 excellent
      3 adequate

Overall Evaluation

1. Would you use this hospital again? _____ Yes _____ No

2. Would you recommend this hospital to a friend or family member? _____ Yes _____ No

3. Overall, how would you rate this hospital's performance? (circle one)

      1 completely unsatisfactory   4 good
      2 poor   5 excellent
      3 adequate

Your Name _____

Your Address _____

City _____ State _____ Zip _____

Please return this form to: Hospital Evaluation, People's Medical Society, 462 Walnut Street, Allentown, PA 18102.

_____ Check here if you would like us to send you another hospital evaluation form, for the next time.

THE KEY TO TRANSLATING MEDICAL TERMS

You need a tool to take all the pieces—the prefixes, roots, and suffixes that compose so many medical terms—and weld them into understandable words and sentences. The following lists will help you to do that. They include the bits and pieces, roots and modifiers, most commonly used by the medical profession to produce terminology guaranteed to mystify.

First the *prefixes,* the short bits that are attached to the front of words to indicate the wheres, ifs, and how muches:

a, an = not, without
ab = away from
acid = sour
ad = near (*d* changes to *c, f, g, p, s,* or *t* when it precedes roots that begin with those letters)
alb = white
amph(i) = both, twice as much
ante = before
anti = against

ap(o) = detached
brady = slow
contra = against, counter to
cry = cold
dia = through or passing through, going apart, between, across
dys = painful, difficult
e = out from
ecto = outside, outer, exterior
endo = within

epi = upon, on, over
erythr = red
eso = inside
exo = outside
hemi = half
hyper = increased, excessive, above
hypo = under, below, deficient
in = not (*n* changes to *l, m,* or *r* when it precedes roots that begin with those letters)
infra = below
inter = between
intra = within
leuco, leuko = white
macro = large
mal = bad, ill, wrongful, disordered

meta = after, beyond, changing
micro = small
para = beyond, beside
peri = around
poly = many, multiple
post = after
pre = before, in front of
pseud(o) = false
re = again
retro = backward, behind
sub = under, below
super = above, beyond, over
supra = above
syn (also sy, syl, sym) = with, together
tachy = fast

The next group, which might be called the *roots* or *combining forms,* are at the center of the words. They usually indicate the body parts affected by a condition:

abdomin = abdomen, stomach
adeno = gland
adip = fat
angi(o) = vessel (blood, lymph)
aph = sense of touch
arteri(o) = artery
arthr(o) = joint
aur = ear
blephar = eyelid
brachi = arm
bronch = windpipe
cardi(o) = heart
cephal = head
cervic = neck
chole, cholo = bile, gall
cholecyst = gallbladder
chondr = cartilage
col(o) = colon

colpo = vagina
crani(o) = skull
cut = skin
cystido, cysto = bladder, sac, cyst
cyto = cell
dent = tooth
enter = intestine
fasci = face
gastr(o) = stomach
glyco = sugar
gnath = jaw
hema, hemato, hemo = blood
hepat(o) = liver
hyster(o) = uterus
ile, ili = intestines, lower abdomen
labi = lip
lact = milk
lapar = loin, flank, abdomen

laryng = windpipe
lipo = fat
lumbar = loin
mast = breast
meno = menstruation
ment = mind
myel = marrow
myelo = spinal cord
myo = muscle
nephr(o) = kidney
neur(o) = nerve
ocul = eye
odont = teeth
oophor = ovary
ophthalm = eye
orchii(o) = testicle
os = mouth, opening
oss, oste(o) = bone
ot(o) = ear
ov = egg
pharyng = throat
phleb = vein
pleur = rib
pneuma, pneumato, pneumo
   = air, gas, lung

pod = foot
procto = anus, rectum
pulmo = lung
ren = kidney
rhino = nose
salping = fallopian tube
sperm, spermato = semen
splen = spleen
staphyl = uvula
stear = fat
tact = touch
teno = tendon
thorac(o) = chest
thromb = clot, lump
tracheo = windpipe
ur = urine
ureter(o) = tube from kidney
   to bladder, carrying urine
urethra = tube from bladder
   to the exterior
vas = vessel, duct
veno = vein
vesic = bladder

Finally, there are the *suffixes,* the linguistic cabooses with the rather unpleasant job here of specifying what has gone wrong with the part designated by your prefix and combining form or root:

algia = pain
blast = a growth in its early
   stages
cele = tumor, hernia
cente = puncture
desis = fusion
dynia = pain
ectomy = excision of, surgical removal
hydr = water
itis = inflammation
lysis = freeing of
megaly = very large
oma = tumor, swelling
oscopy = looking at an organ
   or internal part

osis = disease, abnormal
   condition or process
ostomy = creation of an
   artificial opening
otomy = incision, cutting
   into
pathy = disease of, abnormality
pexy = fix, sew
plasty = reconstruct, formation of
pnea = breathing
ptosis = falling, drooping
rhage, rhagia, rrhage, rrhagia
   = bursting forth, bleeding
rhea, rrhea = flow, discharge

scler(osis) = hard, hardening   uria = urine (condition of, presence in)

Put them all together, they spell "Oh brother." But really, it isn't all that complicated. For example, say your friendly white-coated confusion-spieler strolls in to report that you are suffering from endocarditis. Just consult the lists: prefix "endo" means within; "cardo" has to do with the heart; and "itis" means inflammation. Endocarditis: inflammation of the inside of the heart (more or less). Certainly not a cheery diagnosis, but at least you have the information you need to ask more intelligent questions about what is going to happen to you next.

Glossary

Abdomen. The part of the body between the chest and the pelvis; the belly. The abdominal cavity contains most of the body's digestive organs, among them the stomach and intestines. Also in this cavity, which is separated from the chest by the diaphragm, are among others the liver, gallbladder, spleen, appendix, kidneys, and pancreas.

Abscess. A collection of pus in the body's tissues, most often caused by bacteria entering through the skin to break down tissue. Swelling and redness usually accompany an abscess, which is a way that the body fights infection.

Ace bandage. An elastic bandage used for support or sprains; Ace is a trade name.

Acetaminophen. An aspirin substitute for people allergic to, or whose stomach cannot tolerate, aspirin. While it reduces pain and fever, it does not reduce the swelling and inflammation of arthritis, as aspirin does.

Acetylsalicylic acid. Aspirin.

Acupuncture. The Chinese medical practice of restoring balance to the body's energy flow (or *c'hi*) by inserting needles into the skin at certain points along the paths this energy takes throughout the body. Its proponents and some scientific studies indicate that this procedure can reduce pain and perhaps act as a therapy in certain physical conditions.

Acute. A term used to describe a condition with symptoms that are severe, develop quickly, and do not last a long time, as opposed to chronic conditions.

Afterbirth. The placenta and the umbilical cord, when expelled from the mother's body after childbirth.

Amniocentesis. The sampling of fluid from the amniotic sac, which contains the fetus, in order to determine if any genetic or other fetal abnormalities are present. Infection and miscarriage, though infrequent, are among the risks involved in this procedure.

Analgesic. A pain-relieving drug.

Anemia. A condition resulting from too few red blood cells or two little hemoglobin in the blood, causing a lack of oxygen to reach body tissues, which in turn manifests itself as fatigue, shortness of breath, and heart problems. Anemia is a symptom of a disease, not a disease itself.

Angina pectoris. A suffocating, often disabling chest pain related to the heart muscle's receiving an insufficient amount of blood, often due to atherosclerosis.

Angiogram. An X-ray picture of a blood vessel.

Angioplasty (percutaneous transluminal angioplasty—PCTA). The insertion and inflation of a tiny balloon in a blood vessel narrowed and clogged by arteriosclerotic plaque, thus pressing the plaque against the vessel walls and widening a pathway for increased blood flow. Increasingly used as a less costly, less risky alternative to cardiac bypass surgery.

Arteriosclerosis. Commonly known as "hardening of the arteries," this is a degenerative condition caused by accumulation of minerals and fatty deposits in the arteries, causing a rigidity and inflexibility that affects the flow of blood through the body. In arteriosclerosis these deposits accumulate in the middle layer of the wall of the artery. Possible causes of arteriosclerosis are high cholesterol levels in the blood, high blood pressure, heredity, and stress, among others.

Atherosclerosis. The most prevalent form of arteriosclerosis, in which the mineral and fatty deposits accumulate in the inner lining of the walls of the arteries. Atherosclerosis is the major cause of stroke and heart attack in the United States.

Audiologist. A health professional who tests hearing and who pinpoints causes of hearing loss, which may then be treated by a medical practitioner.

Autopsy. Inspection and examination of a body after death, ordered by a coroner or medical examiner to determine what caused death; also known as a postmortem examination.

Barbiturate. Sleeping pill. One of the most common of barbiturates is phenobarbital.

Barium enema. A procedure wherein the element barium (in the form of barium sulfate) is injected rectally and fills the colon. Then X-ray pictures are taken of the colon, as a way of discovering abnormalities. The barium sulfate creates a contrast in X-ray pictures, and in this test makes the colon clearly visible.

Barium meal. Commonly referred to as an "upper GI (gastrointestinal) series," this is a procedure wherein a patient, after fasting, swallows barium sulfate. Then X-ray pictures are taken of the stomach, duodenum, and small intestine for examination of possible physical problems or abnormalities. The barium sulfate creates a contrast in X-ray pictures, and in this test makes the upper GI parts clearly visible.

Biopsy. The removal of a portion of body tissue to examine microscopically and make a diagnosis. It is widely used to determine the status of growths that might be cancerous.

Blood pressure. The force of the blood expelled from the heart against the walls of the blood vessels it passes through.

Blood pressure cuff. The apparatus involved in taking a blood pressure measurement. See Sphygmomanometer.

Brain death. A condition in which no brain activity can be determined, and the patient is in a coma from which he or she will not recover. This is fast becoming the legal definition of death across the United States, allowing life support to be discontinued lawfully.

Bypass, coronary or cardiac. A major operation in which a vein, usually from the patient's leg, is removed and reconnected between the aorta and a coronary artery, thus resuming blood flow that had stopped or diminished due to an atherosclerotic obstruction in that artery. The blood flow is literally detoured and bypasses the blocked portion of the artery.

Carcinoma. An extremely malignant form of cancer, wherein the cancerous cells take over healthy tissue cells, and may metastasize, or spread, throughout the body. Stomach, skin, and breast cancers are all of this type.

Cardiac catheterization. A cardiological procedure during which a thin, hollow tube is sent through a vein or artery into the heart to help provide information about the heart's structure and the volume of blood expelled by the heart.

Cerebral vascular accident (CVA). Also known as a stroke, it is a situation in which a ruptured or blocked blood vessel prevents blood from reaching important portions of the brain. This leads to brain damage and subsequent debilitating conditions including paralysis and often death. High blood pressure plays a role in weakening the blood vessels, as does arteriosclerosis.

Cesarean section. A birth delivery made not through the vagina, as is normally the case, but through an incision made through the stomach and uterus. It is performed when there are signs that the fetus is in danger, and that a prolonged labor could be disastrous for both mother and child.

Chemotherapy. The use of medication and chemicals that have toxic effects on specific organisms or selectively attack certain types of cancer. Chemotherapy is used instead of or in conjunction with other treatments, for instance, radiation.

Cholecystectomy. Surgical removal of the gallbladder.

Colostomy. The surgical creation of an opening from the body surface into the colon. This opening acts as an artificial anus in conditions involving cancer and intestinal obstructions where the colon and anus may be diseased and/or removed. Colostomies may be permanent or temporary. Colostomy bags collect the waste issued through the colostomy opening, which is usually on the abdomen.

Coma. A state of deep, long-term unconsciousness—as a result of injury, drug overdose, heart attack, diabetes, among others—that does not respond to treatment, and may or may not lead to death without regaining consciousness. An irreversible coma is also known as brain death.

Computerized axial tomography (CAT). The radiological technique that produces CAT scans, which are internal views of body parts imaged in the form of thin slices.

Defibrillation. The use of electrical shock in an emergency to stabilize and normalize a life-threatening irregular heartbeat. Metal paddles are placed on the chest to transmit the electricity to the heart.

Delirium tremens. Commonly known as the d.t.'s, this is a condition in which violent behavior, trembling, and hallucinations result from the heavy consumption of alcohol.

Dementia praecox. Schizophrenia.

Depilatory. A liquid or cream that, when applied to the skin, removes or destroys hair. It is used as an alternative to shaving.

Dialysis. A mechanical technique used in patients with kidney disease to remove waste products from the blood that are usually eliminated in the urine; also referred to as hemodialysis.

Diastolic. That measurement of blood pressure when the heart is in its resting or relaxation phase, just before the next heartbeat. It is the lower number in a blood pressure reading; that is, in a reading of 120/80, for example, the diastolic pressure is indicated by the 80.

Diethylstilbestrol (DES). A drug used by many women to prevent miscarriages and premature labor, but which has been implicated in causing vaginal and cervical cancers in the female children of those who took it. An iatrogenic drug scandal.

Dilation and curettage (D&C). The scraping of the walls of the uterus as a form of abortion.

Echocardiogram. The result of bouncing ultrasound waves, aimed through the chest, off the heart's internal structures to check for problems with heart valves and possible deformities. It is a noninvasive alternative to cardiac catheterization.

Ectopic pregnancy. A condition in which the fertilized egg lodges not in the uterus but outside it, usually in one of the two fallopian tubes. If a natural abortion does not occur, the misplaced embryo or fetus will grow large enough to rupture the fallopian tube. Emergency surgery is required to remove the tube and the fetus.

Electrocardiogram (EKG or ECG). A record of the heart muscle's activity, collected by electrodes placed on the body that amplify the heart's electrical currents. EKG's are used to detect heart damage, as after a heart attack. They are also often a part of a routine physical examination.

Electroencephalogram (EEG). A record of brain patterns collected by placing electrodes on the scalp. EEG's are often used to detect brain damage, diagnose epilepsy, or confirm brain death.

Embryo. The earliest stages of life's development within the uterus. A fetus is what a human embryo is called from its third month until birth.

Emphysema. A chronic breathing difficulty caused by a structural changes in the lungs and accompanied by persistent coughing, possibly heart disease, and a host of other physical complications. Male smokers are the primary victims of this incurable condition, one of modern society's leading causes of death. There are various treatments to help emphysema sufferers breathe, but good health cannot be restored.

Episiotomy. an incision made in the vagina and pelvic floor just before delivery during childbirth to prevent a damaging tear, and the stitching up of this incision afterward. Not every woman requires an episiotomy, but many obstetricians perform them as a matter of course.

Estrogen. The female sex hormones, often prescribed for use by postmenopausal women, and present in oral contraceptives. Estrogen use has been linked to cancer in some studies.

Fibrillation. A cardiac arrhythmia, or irregular heartbeat, that can lead to cardiac arrest.

Fistula. A passage or tunnel formed in the body by disease, injury, congenital abnormalities or, occasionally, surgery, leading from one internal organ to another or from an internal organ to the body's exterior. Anal fistula is the most common.

Fluoroscope. An X-ray machine that allows direct observation of the body's organs and skeletal structures, instead of utilizing film. Motion can be observed also.

Glands. A group of cells that produce a secretion. There are two types: those that secrete hormones directly into the bloodstream (endocrine glands, such as the thyroid, adrenal, gonads, and islands of Langerhans in the pancreas), and those that send their secretions through ducts (exocrine glands, such as salivary, tear, and sweat glands).

Health maintenance organization (HMO). A new and increasingly popular form of medical care delivery. HMO subscribers pay a flat fee, and after that are entitled to access to the HMOs corps of group practice (usually salaried) physicians and to other services, at no extra cost or for a minimal fee. The goal of an HMO is economical care, created by eliminating the costly fee-for-service form of medicine and stressing preventive medicine.

Heart attack. A popular term for a destructive, often fatal seizure involving the heart. See Myocardial infarction.

Heart-lung machine. A device that "replaces" the heart and its functions while the heart is being operated on. It reroutes the blood outside the body and pumps it with sufficient oxygen.

Hemodialysis. See Dialysis.

Hemoglobin. The protein in red blood cells that carries oxygen to the body tissues.

Hypothermia. A reduction of the body's temperature, either naturally (through exposure to cold or malfunction of the body's "thermostat") or induced. Hypothermia is induced to aid certain surgical procedures, including heart surgery, and can be used as a form of local anesthesia.

Hysterectomy. Removal by surgery of the uterus, through the vagina or abdomen; the surgery may also include removal of the cervix (total hysterectomy), and upper vagina (radical hysterectomy). A cesarean hysterectomy is one in which a cesarean delivery is followed by removal of the uterus.

Iatrogenic. Doctor-caused; used to describe an illness or condition produced in a patient by the actions of a physician.

Ileostomy. A surgically produced opening from the body's abdominal surface into the ileum (small intestine). The purpose is to allow for the removal of feces when a disease or defect requires that the colon be bypassed. It can be either temporary, until the condition is cured, or it can be permanent, as when the colon is removed.

Infarct. An area of tissue that is dead or dying, having been deprived of oxygen by a clot that blocked blood flow. The most common infarctions are cerebral, myocardial or cardiac, and pulmonary.

Inoperable. A situation in which surgery cannot be performed, or if performed, would not successfully treat the problem.

Invasive. Description of a procedure that involves cutting through the skin or inserting an object into the body for diagnostic or therapeutic purposes.

Iron lung. A large metal tank, enclosing the entire body except the head, that assists a person's breathing when paralysis prevents that person from doing so naturally.

Ischemia. A localized deficiency in blood flow, due to an obstruction in the blood vessel.

Keloid. A growth—actually a benign tumor—produced by abnormal tissue repair during the formation of a scar. It is not cancerous, not dangerous, but can be unsightly and annoying. There are treatments to reduce the keloid. Some people are more prone to develop keloids than others.

Laceration. A ragged tear of body tissue, either external or internal; in contrast to a cut or an incision, which are smooth slices. A laceration, though often not as bloody as a cut, is more prone to infection because more surface is exposed.

La Leche League. A group formed to provide information to and support for women who want to breast-feed their babies. The address is: La Leche League International, 9616 Minneapolis Avenue, Franklin Park, IL 60131.

Lymph Glands. Not glands, really, but nodes of tissue that provide a system of protection against bacteria and other attacks against the body's immune system. Lymphadenopathy is abnormal enlargement of the lymph nodes. Lymphoma is a cancer of lymphoid tissue; Hodgkin's disease is one type of lymphoma.

Mammogram. A record of a procedure in which the breast is X-rayed to diagnose certain conditions, including breast cancer.

Matching. The act of comparing one person's blood type with another's, to see if the first may be a blood donor to the second.

Melanoma. A malignant tumor that develops from a mole and spreads rapidly.

Meningitis. Inflammation of the thin layers of tissue around the brain and the spinal cord. It is caused by many agents, including viruses, bacteria, and lead and arsenic poisoning.

Metacarpals. The five bones in the hand between the wrist and the fingers.

Metastasis. The spread of disease-producing organisms or cells, especially cancerous cells, from one part of the body to one that is remote from the original diseased site. The route is most often through the blood or lymph systems. These displaced cells or organisms set up new diseased sites, thus decentralizing the condition and making it more difficult, if not impossible, to treat.

Metatarsals. The five bones in the foot between the ankle and the toes.

Microsurgery. The use of a powerful microscope and specially designed small medical instruments to perform delicate operations, most spectacularly the reattachment of severed body parts.

Myocardial infarction. The death of heart muscle (myocardium) cells after being deprived of oxygen, due usually to a clot or obstruction (occlusion) of blood flow. Commonly known as a heart attack.

Neoplasm. A tumor or a new growth of abnormal tissue that has much uncontrolled cell multiplication.

Nosocomial infection. An infection acquired during hospitalization, produced by microorganisms in the hospital itself. Nosocomial infections are among the leading causes of death in hospitals, being responsible for the deaths of a minimum of 100,000 people annually.

Orthosis. A device used to correct alignment and deformities, provide physical support, and improve the functional use of movable parts of the body. Back braces and leg braces are two types of orthotic appliances.

Osteoporosis. A condition in which the bones become thin and brittle, leading to unexpected fractures. Lack of certain nutrients (especially calcium), insufficient exercise, and advanced age are a few of the causes. Postmenopausal women are at risk because of the cessation of production of estrogen, a protective hormone.

Oxygen tent. A canopy placed over and around a person that delivers and maintains a steady flow of oxygen to prevent tissue damage due to oxygen deficiency.

Pacemaker (electronic cardiac pacemaker). An electrical device that takes over the task of keeping the heartbeat regular when the heart's own natural pacemaker (called the sinoatrial node) is not functioning properly. It works by sending electrical impulses to the heart muscle, to which it is connected. Pacemakers may be temporary or permanent, external or implantable, fixed-rate or on-demand.

Paramedic. A technician trained and skilled in the delivery of medical care in emergency situations.

Pathogen. A disease-producing organism.

Pathology. The science or study of the nature of disease, its origins and the course it takes, and how it affects body tissues and organs.

Peptic ulcer. An erosion of the mucous membrane of the esophagus, stomach (gastric ulcers) or duodenum (the part of the small intestine nearest the stomach), caused by the corrosive properties of gastric juice. A perforated ulcer is one in which the ulceration works its way through the entire thickness of the organ, allowing gastric juice and the contents of the intestine to spill, causing a sometimes fatal infection (peritonitis). Immediate surgery is required.

Physical therapy (PT). The therapeutic technique that uses exercise, hydrotherapy, massage, and other procedures to treat and alleviate pain in weak, injured, or diseased muscles, joints, nerves, and bones. Physical therapists not only examine patients and treat them, but instruct them on how to perform certain corrective, strengthening, and even preventive exercises and activities. Also known as physiotherapy.

Physician assistant. A health-care professional who can legally assume many of the duties of a physician, either in the office or in the operating room.

Placebo. A substance that has no value in a real therapeutic pharmacological sense, but which actually helps a patient who believes that it will work. Placebos are often given to patients who psychologically require a pill (and sometimes do quite well after taking it) or as part of clinical trials to test the effectiveness of new drugs. The placebo effect is a classic example of the mind-body relationship.

Plasma. The liquid part of blood, which makes up 55 percent of the total blood volume.

Prosthesis. An artificial part used to replace a missing body part. Artificial limbs and dentures are both examples of prosthetic devices.

Psychotropic. A type of drug that influences the way the mind works and alters a person's mental state, by relieving anxiety (Valium is an antianxiety drug) and combating depression, psychotic disorders, and other mental problems.

Renal. Having to do with the kidneys.

Resection. Surgical removal of a section of an organ or body tissue.

Sarcoma. A highly malignant tumor, attacking the connective tissues and bones, and which metastasizes through the lymphatic system.

Sepsis. A bacterial invasion of the body or part of the body, in which the microorganisms enter the bloodstream or body tissues. A large-scale, serious bacterial invasion of this sort throughout the entire system is called septicemia, or blood poisoning.

Shock. A sudden, acute failure of the body's circulatory function, it can be caused by injury, disease, allergic reaction, or blood loss. Weak but rapid pulse, low blood pressure, and cold and clammy skin are signs of shock, which can be fatal if untreated.

Sigmoidoscopy. A diagnostic procedure in which a long tubelike device is inserted nonsurgically through the rectum into the colon to examine it directly.

Skin graft. A procedure in which skin from one part of the body is removed and implanted in another part of the body to replace a skin loss.

Sphygmomanometer. The device most commonly used to measure systolic and diastolic blood pressure. Also known as the blood pressure cuff, it allows notation and comparison of blood pressure levels by giving those levels values on a scale measured in millimeters (mm.) of mercury (Hg.).

Spinal tap. A procedure used in helping to diagnose diseases of and injuries to the brain and spinal cord, especially in suspected cases of meningitis and stroke. In a tap the cerebrospinal fluid to be evaluated is removed from the spinal canal through a long, thin needle.

Stenosis. A narrowing of a vessel or passage.

Suture. The closing of a wound by stitching together the opposite edges of the cut or incision.

Syncope. Fainting, as a result of insufficient blood flow to the brain.

Systolic. That measurement of blood pressure taken when the left ventricle contracts and the blood's force against the vessel walls is at its greatest strength. It is the higher number in a blood pressure reading; that is, in a reading of 120/80, for example, the systolic pressure is indicated by the 120.

Thalidomide. A drug used as a sedative, but which, when taken by women in the early stages of pregnancy, causes birth defects and physical deformities in their children.

Toxemia. A condition that results when toxins are spread throughout the body via the bloodstream.

Tracheostomy. A procedure in which an incision is made in the throat and into the trachea (windpipe), thus creating an opening into which a tube is inserted, usually to assist in breathing or to help remove secretions.

Tumor. See Neoplasm.

Typing. The method used to determine a person's blood type.

Ulcer. See Peptic ulcer.

Ultrasound (ultrasonography). A method, using ultrasonic radiation, to create pictures of body structures deep below the surface. While used to get readings on organs, it is traditionally used on pregnant women to gain information about the fetus, despite continuing controversy over its possible long-term negative effects on the unborn child.

Vaccination. A preventive inoculation in which a modified virus (a vaccine) is introduced into the body to provide immunity to a disease.

Vital signs. The basic signs of life: temperature, pulse, and respiration rate.

Workup. All of the standardized steps—lab tests, history, and physical, etc.—taken to establish a diagnosis.

X ray. Electromagnetic radiation used to create pictures of the body's internal structures.

SUGGESTED READING

Any public, private, or People's Medical library would do well to include these volumes in their collection.

If you would like to help your community, neighborhood, town, city, or state develop a library dedicated to making health care information available to every citizen, write to the People's Medical Society for information about its publication *How to Start a People's Medical Library.* The address is: 462 Walnut Street, Allentown, PA 18102.

American Medical Directory, 30th ed. Chicago: American Medical Association, 1988.

Annas, George J. **The Rights of Patients.** Carbondale: Southern Illinois University Press, 1989.

Bennett, John V., and Brachman, Philip S., eds. **Hospital Infections,** 2nd ed. Boston: Little, Brown, 1979.

Berkow, Robert, ed. **The Merck Manual,** 15th ed. Rahway, N.J.: Merck & Co., 1987.

Carver, Cynthia. **Patient Beware.** Scarborough, Ontario: Prentice-Hall, 1984.

Cornacchia, Harold J., and Barrett, Stephen. **Shopping for Health Care.** New York: New American Library, 1982.

Cousins, Norman. **Anatomy of an Illness as Perceived by the Patient.** New York: Norton, 1979.

Dorland's Illustrated Medical Dictionary, 26th ed. Philadelphia: W. B. Saunders, 1985.

Fisher, George Ross. **The Hospital That Ate Chicago.** Philadelphia: W. B. Saunders, 1980.

Gots, Ronald, and Kaufman, Arthur. **The People's Hospital Book.** New York: Avon, 1978.

Haug, Marie, and Lavin, Bebe. **Consumerism in Medicine: Challenging Physician Authority.** Beverly Hills, Calif.: Sage Publications, 1983.

Huttman, Barbara. **The Patient's Advocate.** New York: Penguin, 1981.

Inlander, Charles, and Levin, Lowell, and Weiner, Ed. **Medicine on Trial.** New York: Prentice-Hall Press, 1988.

Inlander, Charles, and Mackay, Charles. **Medicare Made Easy.** Reading, Mass.: Addison-Wesley, 1989.

Isenberg, Seymour, and Elting, L. M. **The Consumer's Guide to Successful Surgery.** New York: St. Martin's, 1976.

Kotelchuck, David, ed. **Prognosis Negative: Crisis in the Health Care System.** New York: Vintage, 1976.

Levin, Arthur. **Talk Back to Your Doctor.** Garden City, N.Y.: Doubleday, 1975.

Miller, Lewis. **The Life You Save.** New York: Morrow, 1979.

Mullan, Fitzhugh. **Vital Signs.** New York: Farrar, Straus & Giroux, 1983.

Nierenberg, Judith, and Janovic, Florence. **The Hospital Experience.** New York: Bobbs-Merrill, 1978.

Preston, Thomas. **The Clay Pedestal.** Seattle: Madrona Publishers, 1981.

Robin, Eugene D. **Matters of Life and Death.** New York: W. H. Freeman, 1984.

Schneider, Robert G. **When to Say No to Surgery.** Englewood Cliffs, N.J.: Prentice-Hall, 1982.

Starr, Paul. **The Social Transformation of American Medicine.** New York: Basic Books, 1982.

Stinson, Robert, and Stinson, Peggy. **The Long Dying of Baby Andrew.** Boston: Atlantic Monthly Press, 1983.

Thomas, Lewis. **The Youngest Science: Notes of a Medicine-Watcher.** New York: Viking, 1983.

Wohl, Stanley. **The Medical Industrial Complex.** New York: Harmony Books, 1984.

INDEX

239

About the Authors

CHARLES B. INLANDER is president of the People's Medical Society and has been its executive officer since its founding in early 1983. He is the co-author of six books on health care, with four more to be published in 1991. Mr. Inlander is a faculty lecturer at the Yale University School of Medicine, and his articles have appeared in scores of publications. Prior to joining the People's Medical Society, he was an advocate for the rights of handicapped citizens and the mentally retarded. A native of Chicago, he is a graduate of American University in Washington, D.C.

ED WEINER is former senior editor of the People's Medical Society's publications, and is currently a writer living in Philadelphia, Pennsylvania.